The French Heritage
of North Carolina

The French Heritage of North Carolina

DUDLEY M. MARCHI

McFarland & Company, Inc., Publishers
Jefferson, North Carolina

Portions of this book appeared in *FraNCe: The French Heritage of North Carolina (In Living Color)* (Lulu, 2017).

LIBRARY OF CONGRESS CATALOGUING-IN-PUBLICATION DATA

Names: Marchi, Dudley M., author.
Title: The French heritage of North Carolina / Dudley M. Marchi.
Description: Jefferson, North Carolina : McFarland & Company, Inc., Publishers, 2021 | Includes bibliographical references and index.
Identifiers: LCCN 2021047255 | ISBN 9781476685434 (paperback : acid free paper) ∞
 ISBN 9781476643847 (ebook)
Subjects: LCSH: French—North Carolina—History. | French Americans—North Carolina—History. | United States—Civilization—French influences.
 | BISAC: HISTORY / United States / State & Local / South
 (AL, AR, FL, GA, KY, LA, MS, NC, SC, TN, VA, WV)
Classification: LCC F265.F8 M37 2021 | DDC 975.6/00441—dc23
LC record available at https://lccn.loc.gov/2021047255

BRITISH LIBRARY CATALOGUING DATA ARE AVAILABLE

ISBN (print) 978-1-4766-8543-4
ISBN (ebook) 978-1-4766-4384-7

© 2021 Dudley M. Marchi. All rights reserved

No part of this book may be reproduced or transmitted in any form or by any means, electronic or mechanical, including photocopying or recording, or by any information storage and retrieval system, without permission in writing from the publisher.

Front cover image: The design of Biltmore Estate in Asheville, North Carolina, is inspired by French royal residences of the Loire Valley (© 2021 Milovzorova Elena/Shutterstock)

Printed in the United States of America

McFarland & Company, Inc., Publishers
Box 611, Jefferson, North Carolina 28640
www.mcfarlandpub.com

Table of Contents

Preface   1
Prologue   7
Introduction   11

CHAPTER 1. First Discoveries   21
CHAPTER 2. Huguenot Migrations   27
CHAPTER 3. Bath   47
CHAPTER 4. La Colonie Perdue   53
CHAPTER 5. New Bern   70
CHAPTER 6. French and Indian War   83
CHAPTER 7. Beaufort   85
CHAPTER 8. French North Carolina   102
CHAPTER 9. Entr'acte   122
CHAPTER 10. Revolutionary Allies   124
CHAPTER 11. Crusoe Island   154
CHAPTER 12. Notable Names   163
CHAPTER 13. Le Pied du Mont   176
CHAPTER 14. Go West, Monsieur   194
CHAPTER 15. Biltmore   212
CHAPTER 16. Vive le Sud!   217
CHAPTER 17. French North Carolina Today   237

Epilogue   259
Appendix 1: Family Names   261
Appendix 2: Names in Phone Directories   263

Appendix 3: French North Carolina Place Names	265
Appendix 4: Names of French Origin: The N.C. Gazetteer	268
Appendix 5: Cemetery Records	268
Bibliography	271
Index	275

Preface

I am not French and have no French ancestry to my knowledge. I began studying French in the seventh grade, I had inspiring teachers, and it became my second language. I have lived and traveled in France and have always been inspired by its history, culture, writers, and artists. It is also a topographically beautiful country, and some of my best friends are French.

I am not a native of North Carolina. I was raised in the Boston, Massachusetts, area and developed a love of American history at an early age. I visited historical sites as a child, such as Concord Bridge, Paul Revere's home, Bunker Hill, and Thoreau's hut on Walden Pond. I was an avid fan of young readers' versions of American history.

These two interests became the dual sides of my education. I have been on the faculty at North Carolina State University since 1989. My current focus is on French American cultural history in North Carolina. I have traveled throughout the state for the past ten years, gathering information and meeting people. I have taught hundreds of North Carolina students and directed study abroad programs in France during my time at State. In 2010, my previous book appeared: *Contrary Affinities, Baudelaire, Emerson, and the French-American Connection*, a study with a historical, literary, and political focus. These experiences have informed the research and writing of *The French Heritage of North Carolina*, a study that traces cultural connections between various people, times, places, languages, and historical events.

Some years ago, it dawned on me to bring together the relevance of France and French culture to the state of North Carolina. To many, the North Carolina "French Connection" is not an obvious one. To bring the connection from obscurity, *The French Heritage of North Carolina* traces the French presence in the state since its beginnings. The spirit of the project has been to fulfill an outreach mission: educating the community at large. *The French Heritage of North Carolina* is essentially a public history project.

My graduate school training in comparative literature taught me to draw relationships between what at first may seem disparate topics, in this case, how the histories of France and North Carolina are surprisingly intertwined. The comparative approach puts each subject in a new light and enriches our understanding of both.

As a professor at N.C. State, I have had the pleasure of teaching many exceptional students who hail from every county in North Carolina. I strive as a teacher to open their eyes and minds to a broader world. I work to instill in my students an appreciation of their state and national history, and how it relates to a global context. This approach is also the goal of this book. *The French Heritage of North Carolina* is an extension of my role as an educator. My previous books and articles are academically oriented, necessary publications in my profession. They are worthy but not of much interest to a general readership, my current intended audience. The reader will notice the hybrid quality, not only of the topic but also of the writing itself. The chapters also vary in length, tone, and purpose.

The French Heritage of North Carolina has a rich vocabulary and makes many historical references. However, with a dictionary, and an occasional Google search, just about any reader, from high school on, can read and enjoy this book. I have intended that *The French Heritage of North Carolina* be accessible to the general reader, outside of the strictures of pure academic writing. To develop an even more in-depth understanding of French North Carolina, the reader may access images of the many places, people, and events I have referenced at the following site: https://go.ncsu.edu/af290fq.

This book is for the people of North Carolina, and especially for those of French heritage. Although a "transplant Yankee," I have lived in this great state longer than anywhere else in my life. I joke with my North Carolina friends that I was born in Florida, and my mom's side of the family is from Memphis, Tennessee, making me part southern. North Carolina is my home, and we will learn about the fascinating story of its French history. In French, *histoire* means "history" and "story"; *The French Heritage of North Carolina* is some of both.

Similar to the topic of this book, the process to complete it has been multilayered and complex, involving many people whose diligence and generosity I would like to acknowledge. Darby Orcutt and Cindy Levine of N.C. State's D.H. Hill Library were the first persons to assist me. They put me on the path to research materials and directed me to relevant archivists and other librarians.

Mr. Victor Jones and Mr. John Green of the Kellenberger Room at the New Bern Public Library helped me dig deep into the Craven area's past. Sherri Richard of the New Bern Office of Deeds was gracious with her time and provided the opportunity to sift through hundreds of land deeds and patents. Kyna Herzinger of the Tryon Palace Carraway Library kindly gathered priceless materials from its archives for me to study. Lindy Cummings provided me images of some of the critical items in the collection relevant to our topic. The staff members at the State Archives of North Carolina in Raleigh provided guidance and materials with expertise and efficiency.

Mamré Wilson of Beaufort is a unique and special person. She has delved into the history and family genealogy of Beaufort in her *Beaufort, North Carolina*. It is the definitive book on the town's history. The research she conducted for her article "The French Connection" is a valuable document in the history of the state's French heritage. She helped this book along immensely. The attendants of the Beaufort Historical Society are helpful and knowledgeable.

Lisa Pelletier-Harman of the Carteret County Historical Society in Morehead City opened a new vista for me. She is a descendant of the Frenchman Jerome Pelletier, who landed in Beaufort in 1780, so her French ancestry reaches back to the Middle Ages. Her knowledge of the Pelletier heritage is second to none. She has been generous with her time and assistance to help me gather materials and point me to particular locations related to the project. The members of the library staff at the historical society are informed and passionate about preserving the history of eastern North Carolina. Ms. Pat Edwards, in particular, was of great help in guiding me to relevant research materials.

Colleague Dr. Brent Pitts of Meredith College once told me that this topic had always interested him. He shared with me original materials such as French mercantile records and letters of eastern North Carolina from the 1700s. He and his students have cataloged and translated many of these records into English. They give us a firsthand glimpse into the import-export trade in colonial North Carolina. Brent also provided me an informative essay on French migration to the state during the late 1700s, "A Whole Cargo of French Folks" by Barbara Cain.

N.C. State colleagues Drs. Michael Garval and Yvonne Rollins were of great support. Mike was always on the lookout for materials related to the topic. He guided me to pertinent books such as *French Cooking in Early America* by Patricia Mitchell and articles on the French in America. Over the years, he has taught me much about French culture. Yvonne and I had numerous conversations about the project. She took the time to read and advise me on the manuscript in progress. She has been a mentor since I came to State, for which I am grateful.

Professor of linguistics Dr. Walt Wolfram of the N.C. State English Department added his expertise in historical linguistics as I looked into French aspects of English spoken Down East. The following undergraduate students served diligently as research assistants: Lana Ray, Emma Craven,

Emily Reichard, Emma Frank, Christine Canale, Madeleine Guyant, Jessica Hamm, and Patrick Rowe. Ray and Craven undertook the nitty-gritty work of tracking down sometimes-obscure material such as the origins of N.C. French place names. They also sifted through county phone directories and compiled lists of French family names. Ray and Craven also read and commented on portions of the manuscript giving me insightful feedback. Frank proofread the entire manuscript and provided valuable editorial commentary. Canale and Guyant collected material for the Vive le Sud! chapter. Hamm undertook the painstaking task of compiling the cemetery records. Rowe helped research the French North Carolina Today chapter. He was diligent in the collection of information and provided insightful feedback on the final chapter. Many other students, in the classroom, or informally, also helped me along the way with their questions, insights, and valuable snippets of relevant information.

Dr. Roger Kammerer has carried out extensive research on French migration and genealogy in North Carolina. His book, *A History of the Huguenot Society of North Carolina*, is trailblazing. Some of his work was referenced in this book. I have tried to trace the North Carolina and French Huguenot connections he made back to England and France when possible. Mr. Dennis Jones of Richlands, North Carolina, has also conducted significant research on the topic. Both he and Ms. Lisa Whitman-Grice, director of the Museum of Onslow County, were generous with their time in discussing various parts of the book. Mr. Leonard Lanier of the Museum of the Albemarle in Elizabeth City provided me with crucial information, especially a hard-to-find historical map of the Albemarle region in the 1800s. He coincidentally is also a descendant of French Huguenots. To connect the dots of this vast topic is a collective enterprise.

There are anonymous folks I met during my research travels Down East. I thank the elderly local man for giving me directions to Crusoe Island at a rural mini-mart. The many tour guides, park rangers, attendants of museums and historic homes, librarians, and archivists are people dedicated to the preservation of the state's history. I could not have written this book without their assistance. Mr. David Knight, Mr. Mike Wicker, and Ms. Grace Lawrence are close friends from Raleigh, who grew up in North Carolina. Their knowledge of the state's river system, topography, geography, and history has been invaluable. Jason Evans Groth, digital media librarian at N.C. State, provided invaluable assistance with image formatting. Finally, special acknowledgment goes to Layla Milholen of McFarland, who helped me see through the intricacies of the publishing process. She is attentive, patient, and kind; it was a pleasure to work with her.

My friend Mr. Anthony Dingman proofread and edited portions of the manuscript. He helped me develop the scope of the project. He always offered insightful guidance and is a top-notch copy editor. My wife Beverly steals the show, however. *The French Heritage of North Carolina* arose from this moment of epiphany in our living room when I first explained my idea about the project. Finally, many thanks to my dear departed friend Mr. Walter Jones of Emerald Isle, who shared with me his wealth of knowledge on the history of the American South. Walt and I had many a discussion about *The French Heritage of North Carolina*, fishing on the beach, not far from where the first European ship (a French one) anchored off Pine Knoll Shores in 1524.

Pine Knoll Shores (photograph by the author).

Prologue

In the archives of Tryon Palace, the governor's residence during the colonial period of New Bern, there is a short note written in French by Governor Tryon's seventeen-year-old daughter Margaret. The note is written in ink on paper, and the document is fragile, so it is stored in special collections. The cursive handwriting is clear but not overly elegant. The note is dated Saturday, February 19, 1771, and is written to a Frenchman, "Monsieur de Lobbinièene."

The note apologizes for having missed the gentleman's visit the previous day and invites him to come the next Monday at an hour that suits him so she can have the pleasure of his visit. The use of French grammar is competent but contains some grammatical blemishes and spelling errors. The note ends, and so does any further trace of whatever became of the acquaintance between Margaret Tryon and the unknown Monsieur de Lobbinièene.

The year of 1771 was the only year the Tryon family lived in the palace. The original structure of Tryon Palace burned to the ground in 1798, and with it, historical documents and cultural artifacts perished. Some were testimonies to the French presence in North Carolina during the eighteenth century.

Miss Tryon's note is a symbolic document of the challenge of studying the French presence in North Carolina. There are few primary documents, and these, along with existing secondary materials, are scattered in archives, libraries, and private homes throughout the state. Miss Tryon's letter is just as mysterious as the French presence in North Carolina. In both, there are bits of information that offer a glimpse into the past. I delved into, pieced together, and extrapolated from these materials to provide a clearer understanding of their very existence and significance.

Tracing the history of the France–North Carolina connection and putting it into a coherent narrative is investigative work. Sound scholarship works to provide evidence to support assertions and uses logic to make arguments. At times when evidence is scant or incomplete, informed speculation and creative interpretation are also needed. I have gathered and

Carraway Library, Tryon Palace (photograph by the author).

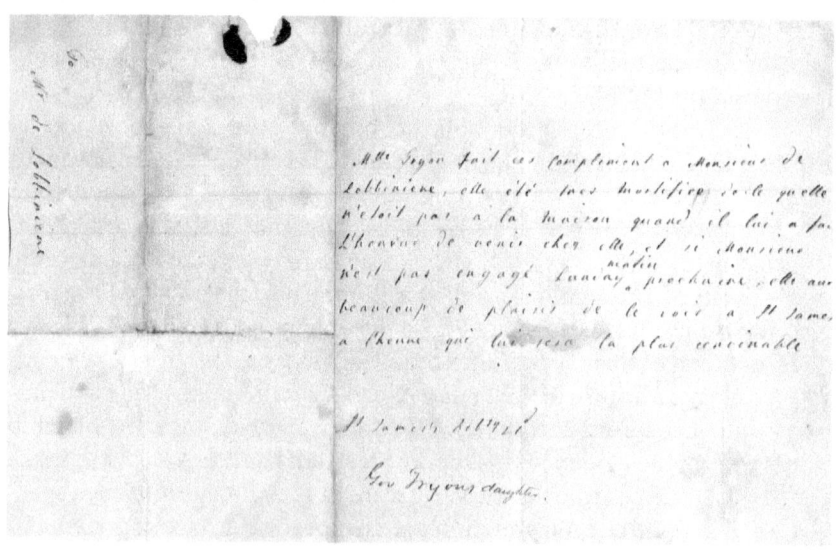

Letter of Margaret Tryon (courtesy Tryon Palace, New Bern, NC).

analyzed a diverse array of information, some factual and some incomplete and vague, and attempted to arrange it into a cohesive narrative. The result is a variegated historical patchwork that tells the story of the French heritage of North Carolina. Similar to our incomplete understanding of Miss Tryon's letter and the missed visit with Monsieur de Lobbinière, our comprehension will be imperfect. Nevertheless, such striving for clarity can open new perspectives on a forgotten dimension of North Carolina's past.

Introduction

Much research has been carried out on the French colonization of North America. The French played a significant role in settling parts of Canada and the United States. They also played a part in the development of these regions into nations. Many books have been written about the French in Québec, the U.S. midwestern states, New England, Louisiana, Virginia, Tennessee, and South Carolina. Sandwiched between the three latter states is North Carolina. For some reason, the history of the French in North Carolina has hardly been discussed, although there is relevant information available. This study traces the history of the French presence in North Carolina from its origins to the present as a remedy for this shortcoming.

The French existence in North Carolina reaches back to the origins of the state. French-named towns such as Beaufort, Faison, and La Grange are a testimony to the settlements of French Huguenots and their descendants in the seventeenth and eighteenth centuries. The city of Fayetteville is named after the Marquis de Lafayette, a French ally during the American Revolution. French officers fought in North Carolina during the Revolutionary and Civil wars. Some remained after the wars and settled here.

The first European explorers to the North Carolina region in 1524 were, as we will see, French. The Piedmont ("foothills" in French) is an area first named by French explorers and trappers. Many North Carolinians have last names of French origin. There are linguistic features of the local dialect spoken Down East today. It was influenced in part by French sailors and immigrants in the Carteret region during the 1700s (witness: "I caught me *beaucoup* fish"). North Carolina is peppered with many place names and historical remnants of the French.

There is, however, a paradox in the historical Frenchness of North Carolina. Some North Carolinians have not been very fond of France and the French over the centuries. They have even maintained a certain level of Francophobia. This attitude reaches back to the fact that the French and English have often been enemies for over a thousand years. Add to this the suffering and turmoil caused in North Carolina at the hands of the French and their Indian allies during the French and Indian War. Moreover, many Carolinians (not all) adopt the typical American stereotyping of the French. There is thus a touch of natural antipathy for the French in North Carolina.

Many North Carolinians felt rebuffed by the French (as did many Americans) when France chose not to support the U.S. invasion of Iraq in 2002. There were immediate symbolic reactions in the state: country clubs in High Point and Winston-Salem stopped serving French wine, and Cubbie's restaurant in Beaufort changed its menu to read "Freedom Fries" instead of "French Fries." Walter B. Jones, a member of the U.S. House of Representatives from North Carolina, declared that all references to "French Fries" and "French Toast" be removed from the snack bar menu of the U.S. House of Representatives. Finally, the mother of a potential student for an N.C. State study abroad program to France said that her daughter would not be permitted to go to France "until the French apologize to us."

So, let us begin our *histoire* of FraNCe. North Carolina and France are close in latitude. When looking at a map of the world, one can see how the geographical areas occupied by France and North Carolina were one before the separation of Pangaea. This supercontinent began separating slowly into different landmasses three hundred million years ago into the continental configurations we know today. The latitudes of southern France and North Carolina are not far apart (North Carolina 35 degrees and France 44 degrees, respectively). Today, both areas are in the choicest belt of the North Temperate Zone, which is amenable to excellent agricultural conditions, the raising of livestock, and wine production. The topography, soil, climate, and flora and fauna of southwestern France and southeastern North Carolina are very similar.

One can visit the Outer Banks of North Carolina and the southwestern coastal plains of France and understand the similarities in the climates and topography of the two regions. Both areas have white sandy beaches, pounding Atlantic surf, sounds, and estuaries teeming with marine life. They also share similar species of white pine trees, sea oats, pampas grass, and types of shellfish, birds, waterfowl, and especially black sandy loam perfect for agriculture. Even the origin of the cockleshell so prevalent on the N.C. Outer Banks is the same shell found on the beaches of southwestern France; "cockle" derives from the French word for shell, *la coquille*.

Looking at a map of the Atlantic Ocean and the coastlines of France and North Carolina, one can see how they were once attached. One can imagine southwestern France tucked into the Albemarle Sound. This conjuncture of latitudinal, topographical, and natural characteristics will play a role in the French migration to North Carolina. Pangaea is, therefore, a metaphor for the French–North Carolina connection.

Introduction

Although the French were in North Carolina during the early stages of European colonization, the English quickly supplanted them, and the state's populace most often descended through generations of English men and women. Most of the French immigrants, like the Irish, Welsh, German, and Scottish who settled in North Carolina, eventually assimilated over several generations into the English majority. In the U.S. census of 1800, for example, the French comprised only 1.7 percent of the state's population. This is a comparatively small number of people. Nevertheless, as we will see, the French played a significant role in the state's history. Subtle traces of French presence are all over North Carolina, and we will peer into this hidden dimension of the state's multicultural heritage.

In 1524, King François I of France commissioned Italian explorer Giovanni da Verrazzano to procure a sea route to the New World. Verrazzano sailed the ship, *La Dauphine*, with a French captain and crew across the Atlantic to the Cape Fear River basin. He continued his route along the Outer Banks and ordered his mapmaker to designate the coastal area he had sailed along as *Tera Francesca* ("French Land") and Nova Gallia ("New France"). This map was the first European designation of the land that was to become North Carolina.

The English undertook most of the subsequent efforts to explore and colonize North Carolina. The French eventually turned their attention north and south to the areas that became Québec and islands of the Caribbean, such as Haiti, Guadeloupe, and Martinique. Nonetheless, many French colonists settled in eastern North Carolina during the colonial period. They helped establish some of the first towns in the state and were an integral part of its burgeoning frontier communities.

In the 1560s, Gaspard de Coligny, an admiral of France and leader of the Huguenots, procured two sailing vessels and placed them under the command of Captain Jean Ribault and his Lieutenant René de Laudonnière. Ribault's charge was to explore the southern Atlantic coast of America and secure a suitable location for a planned colony of French Protestants. The latter were undergoing severe persecution at the time in France. In 1564, ships transported one hundred and fifty French Protestants (mostly soldiers, workers, and artisans) to a spot about twelve miles south of St. Augustine, Florida, at the mouth of the St. John's River.

Ribault left behind a contingent there to establish "Fort Caroline," under the direction of Laudonnière. Ribault then proceeded north to establish another colony on one of the Sea Islands off the South Carolina coast, today's Parris Island. He named the settlement "Charlesfort" after Charles IX of France. Among the settlers was an artist, Jacques Le Moyne de Morgues, whose task was to sketch and paint images of the people, flora, fauna, and geography of the island. His work was the basis for many sketches and drawings of the New World for a century to come. The "Arx Carolina" by the Dutchman Arnoldus Montanus is a prime example. Much of what we can imagine visually of the early colonial period has been dramatically enhanced by the work of Le Moyne de Morgues.

Upon making a return trip to England to restock his ship with supplies and recruit a crew, Ribault named the land of today's North and South Carolina "Carolana," Latin for Charles, again after French King Charles IX. It is a curious coincidence that the State Archives of North Carolina house original documents written on parchment in 1567 of French Charles IX. They do not concern the founding of North Carolina but bring us into the spirit of the time. In 1629, when the English colonized the area, King Charles I of England liked the coincidence of names and kept it for himself and his new English colony. Thus, South and North Carolina were initially named after a king of France. Ribault's attempts to establish permanent colonies ultimately failed because of tension with local Indian tribes. The Spanish eventually attacked and overwhelmed his settlements and executed Ribault and most of his companions.

Before his end, Ribault traveled back to England, where he wrote an account of the land of "Caroline." Along with Le Moyne de Morgues's sketches and paintings, he fired the imagination of Europeans to travel to America. Sir Walter Raleigh would have read Ribault's account when he was in his early teens, guiding him to his future success in establishing a colony on today's North Carolina coast. The French thus helped to pave the way for the European migration to North Carolina.

After the revocation of the Edict of Nantes by Louis XIV in 1685, French Huguenots came to settle in North Carolina along the Pamlico and Trent rivers. The Lords Proprietors were eager to induce the Huguenots to settle in the area. The latter were educated, intelligent, industrious, and more loyal to the English Crown than to the French. The Lords Proprietors even had a clause of the Fundamental Constitution, which guaranteed religious freedom, translated into the language of their French colonists.

In 1705, on a low bluff overlooking the Pamlico River, the French were part of the establishment of Bath, the first town in North Carolina. More Huguenots settled in the area, migrating from Virginia under the leadership of Charles de Sailly and Philippe de Richebourg. Some migrated from southern Virginia through the Great Dismal Swamp to settle in the Albemarle region. The temperate climate, fertile agricultural land, and favorable reports of the first Huguenot settlers stimulated an influx of hundreds of French to the area in the late 1600s and early 1700s. Many of them continued their trades as artisans and merchants as they had done in France. Some of the settlers, out of necessity, became skilled in agriculture and animal husbandry.

Introduction

The Craven County Register of Deeds in New Bern houses land deeds of French settlers from the early 1700s. One was recently discovered that was written in French. There is even evidence of a "lost colony" of French Huguenots along the Trent River between the years 1707 and 1710. The information we have is scant, but there is enough to reconstruct its existence.

The State Archives contain numerous historical documents related to the French: ship logs of Huguenot immigrants, mercantile records of French ships and businesses, official letters, maps, etc. The Beaufort Historical Association, the Carteret County Historical Society, and Tryon Palace archives contain primary and secondary documents on the French presence in colonial North Carolina. Many North Carolina counties' registers of deeds house land deeds, wills, and marriage and birth certificates of the first French settlers and their descendants. The historical French presence in North Carolina is a real one.

Even with the acceptance of French Protestants in North Carolina during a good part of the colonial period, many North Carolinians had a reason to dislike the French. Settlers and militia had fought against them during the French and Indian War. Moreover, France was still England's and her American colonies' worst enemy. Nevertheless, French immigrants, not the French soldiers who fought in the war, were, in some way, trusted allies because they also despised the Catholic monarchy and political intrigues of France. Some descendants of French Huguenots served in the North Carolina militia, fighting against their fellow compatriots. During the American Revolution, an intercultural turn-around occurred when North Carolina accepted France more fully as an ally in its struggle against the English Crown. As we will see, the French–North Carolina connection is complex.

Throughout the 1700s, French merchants made frequent visits to the ports of Beaufort, Edenton, New Bern, and Wilmington to trade luxury goods such as porcelain, fabrics, wine, and brandy. They also supplied military products such as gunpowder, muskets, and sailcloth in exchange for rice, flaxseed, tar, turpentine, timber, and tobacco. Such trade with France was extremely beneficial for North Carolina. The luxury goods served to refine the quality of life and provide citizens a touch of European sophistication in the rough and hardy North Carolina coastal frontier. The military goods helped North Carolina gain its independence as one of the original thirteen American colonies.

Beyond increased French–American commerce during the Revolutionary period, some French also served in the Continental Army. Many of the French volunteers had fought in European battles and were awarded high ranks in the army. They were seasoned veterans and understood

English military tactics. One of the French colonels, James Cole Mountflorence, who served in North Carolina, distinguished himself at the Battle of Guilford Courthouse and led several successful battles during the war. He taught classical studies afterward at New Bern Academy, drawing on his educational training at the Sorbonne in Paris. One of the French warship captains, Louis-Antoine Jean-Baptiste, Le Chevalier de Cambray, built a fort on what is now Cape Lookout to protect that portion of the coastline from the English navy.

After the Revolution, French–North Carolinian relations diminished somewhat. Nevertheless, the French, who remained in North Carolina, and their descendants, were well established in the eastern part of the state. They are the ancestors of North Carolina families of French heritage such as Piver, Paquinet, and Pelletier, as witnessed by the names of their former homesteads in Beaufort. There were enough French in the New Bern area, for example, to warrant an available subscription to a French-language newspaper from Philadelphia. Many French soldiers and sailors, like the other immigrant groups, intermarried with the descendants of English families. They assimilated into the everyday social fabric of North Carolina but took their French names with them as they migrated throughout the state.

French General Le Marquis de Lafayette visited his French troops in North Carolina in the summer of 1777. Lafayette's role in the American Revolution was essential to the war's success. He rose quickly to the rank of major general and led the troops of the Continental Army to final victory in 1781 at the Battle of Yorktown. He spent the rest of his life promoting the principles of liberty and equality as inspired by the principles of the American secession from England. On a return tour to North Carolina in 1825, he was the guest of Governor Hutchins Burton and attended balls and receptions in his honor in Raleigh. He was invited to the small town of Cross Creek in Cumberland County. To his surprise and delight, the town's citizens had changed its name to "Fayetteville." They welcomed him to a round of banquets, balls, and visits with local militia and state troops.

Lafayette's legacy has been carefully preserved in the "Lafayette Collection" of the Davis Memorial Library of Methodist College in Fayetteville. The collection contains books, commemorative medals and plates, maps of the Cape Fear region during the Revolutionary period, and nineteen letters written by Lafayette. Fayetteville's French legacy has a more humorous and fanciful embodiment beyond the valuable Lafayette Collection, such as the nearby Bordeaux Shopping Center with its miniature replica of the Eiffel Tower.

Numerous other locations in North Carolina have French connections, sundry but significant. Some have serious historical value; others are more whimsical. Many historical homes in North Carolina have French furniture, engravings, tapestries, china, crystal, and more. The Chanteloup Estate in Asheville was built by a French count and his wife, Gabriel and Sarah de Choiseul. The county subdivision Hugo in Lenoir County is named after the great French author Victor Hugo. French-inspired names such as "Benvenue Road" in Rocky Mount and the "French Broad River" in the Blue Ridge Mountains proliferate throughout the state. Fuquay-Varina was founded by a retired French officer, Guillaume Fuqua, who served in the North Carolina Continental Army under Lafayette during the American Revolution. The list goes on.

Napoléon's cavalry leader Maréchal Ney, purportedly, became a school teacher in Cleveland, North Carolina, after the Napoleonic Wars. There is a gravestone commemorating him at the Third Creek Presbyterian Church in northwestern Rowan County. Churches in Valdese and Southport still sing a French hymn or two at Sunday service, a remnant of the time when there were French among the brethren.

The tiny and little-known Crusoe Island in the Green Swamp of Columbus County was once the residence of political refugees who fled Haiti during the 1806 slave revolt and settled near Lake Waccamaw. Other inhabitants of the island were escaped French prisoners and pirates from the post–Revolutionary period. In Beaufort, Blackbeard took a French common-law wife and lived with her in the Hammock House. When he was tired of the relationship, he hung her by the neck from an oak tree in the backyard and buried her there. The young woman's screeching can still be heard on some nights according to local accounts.

Numerous other small towns and place names in North Carolina are of French origin. Some of them are as follows: Angier, Beauchamp Lake, Beauregard Ridge, Beaux, Bellair, Bellefont, Belmont, Bellevue, Blantyre, Cape Carteret, Clairmont, Cognac, Faison, Frenchman's Creek, Frenchman's Point, French Mountain, Lenoir, Olivette, Peletier, Rougemont, and Sans Souci, among many others. More well-known people and places also reflect the French heritage of North Carolina. Sir Thomas Amy, the first Lord Proprietor of North Carolina, descended from a family of French Huguenots. One of the founding trustees of the University of North Carolina system and a speaker of the North Carolina House of Commons, Stephen Cabarrus, was born in Bayonne, France. He eventually settled in Edenton, North Carolina, and became one of North Carolina's premier leaders of the nineteenth century.

Renowned French botanist André Michaux traveled through North Carolina and discovered or described over three hundred plants native to thirty counties in the state. Michaux was sent by the French government in the 1780s to travel throughout America to collect seeds, plants, trees, and shrubs that would thrive in France. He sent back to France dozens of crates of seeds and plants indigenous to North Carolina, mostly to the town of Versailles near his birthplace in Satory. Vestiges of North Carolina greenery still grow in France in a unique botanical, transatlantic migration.

Medoc Mountain State Park in Halifax County is another significant North Carolina location with French heritage. Starting in the 1830s, the land was used for the cultivation of grapes by Dr. Sidney Weller, a noted farmer, scientist, and educator of the nineteenth century. Dr. Weller is credited with developing the American system of viticulture and winemaking. He based his techniques on French winemaking traditions and practices.

Dr. Weller named his land Medoc after the Médoc region in the Bordeaux province of France, which is famous for its fine wines. Weller produced high-quality wines. His "Weller's Halifax" was widely acclaimed at the time. North Carolina's wine industry is thriving today, with over one hundred and thirty-two wineries that produce a wide variety of vintages. Some North Carolina vineyards grow imported French vines that thrive in the local soil and climate that are similar to those of southern France.

One of the most scenic places in North Carolina is the town of Badin, which is listed in the National Register of Historic Places. The town's motto is "A French-flavored town at the foot of the Uwharries." In 1913, a French company, L'Aluminium Français, began work at a narrow portion of the Yadkin River. A dam was constructed to power the aluminum plant town built for the company's workforce. The town was named after the company's president, Adrien Badin, who designed it with the well-being of its employees in mind. Alongside the work buildings, for instance, were a clubhouse, hospital, school, theater, commercial buildings, and individual residences.

Many of the employees of Badin's company were Black. Having such quality housing and cultural facilities provided for them was an innovation. Monsieur Badin was ahead of his time and helped to humanize this small niche of North Carolina rural life across racial and cultural lines. Today the town offers a glimpse into its French roots with its small, stylish wooden homes designed in the French colonial style, white picket fences, and well-tended gardens.

The crown jewel of French heritage in North Carolina is the eight-thousand-acre Biltmore Estate in Asheville. George Vanderbilt transported France into the North Carolina mountains in the late nineteenth century. Richard Morris modeled the Renaissance-style castle after the most elegant royal residences of the Loire Valley in France, such as Chambord, Chenonceau, and Blois. Along with its woodlands and meticulously arranged fields and gardens, the work of Frederick Law Olmsted, Biltmore provides a sophisticated, pastoral European setting; yet, it is also a fully operational working estate.

Replete with priceless French art, furnishings, tapestries, books, and sculptures, the Biltmore Estate is a prominent example of the American Gilded Age. Biltmore relies on the magnificence of French high culture to display its wealth and splendor. Biltmore's popularity is due, in part, to the economic benefits it brings to the state's economy. It is also because much of North Carolina's populace is educated and culturally informed, and appreciates the beauty and sophistication of French culture. Everywhere one travels in the state of North Carolina, there are vestiges of French history and pockets of French culture to explore.

Today, many long-standing and successful academic French programs flourish in the North Carolina university system. N.C. State alone teaches French to over twelve hundred students annually. It has successful French academic majors and minors and sends dozens of students to study abroad in France and Francophone countries each year. A French business program, SKEMA, was established at N.C. State in 2010. All of the principal colleges and universities in North Carolina have French academic programs.

The Triangle area has an active chapter of the French cultural organization, the Alliance Française, as does Charlotte. Significant French holdings are on view at the North Carolina Museum of Art and other museums at the University of North Carolina at Chapel Hill and Duke University. French bakeries, wine shops, shopping venues, restaurants, and film festivals can be found throughout the state. Many public and private schools teach French and sponsor study abroad programs to France. There is even a French immersion school in Raleigh, L'Ecole, as well as a French cooking school, C'est si Bon!, in Chapel Hill.

An active North Carolina chapter of the American Association of Teachers of French and a French-American Chamber of Commerce of North Carolina have been in existence for many years. The North Carolina French Huguenot Society is active and hosts an annual luncheon. The capital city Raleigh has an exchange program with its French sister city, Compiègne. Many other cities and towns in the state have French sister cities. There is a French "Friendship Train" that was given to the state by France after World War II in 1949. It is housed today in the North Carolina Transportation Museum in Spencer.

There are French and Francophone companies in North Carolina that are part of the state's global economy. Nevertheless, even with all of this "Frenchness" in North Carolina, most of its citizens are unaware of the historical life of France in the state. Increased awareness of it could stimulate educational opportunities while preserving and promoting an essential part of North Carolina's multicultural heritage. Such recognition could provide economic opportunities for the state by making North Carolina a travel and study destination for French students, teachers, and tourists. This would benefit the state culturally and economically.

Introduction

The French Heritage of North Carolina works within the paradox of the French–North Carolina connection and traces the history of the French North Carolina phenomenon from its origins to the present. We will explore the topics outlined in this introduction and others. The project is broad in scope; the first part covers the period from the state's origins until the mid-1700s, at which time the French had been fully integrated into the social fabric of colonial North Carolina. The second begins with the Revolutionary War, moves through the western migration of the French in North Carolina in the 1800s, and ends with an analysis of the French North Carolina landscape during the twentieth century up to the present time.

My goal has not been to glorify French culture at the expense of North Carolina's history. I have worked to provide a more thorough understanding than we have had of a subtle but essential historical layer of North Carolina's past. Significant numbers of French immigrants came to North Carolina in the seventeenth and eighteenth centuries and beyond. As we will see, they played an integral role in the state's history.

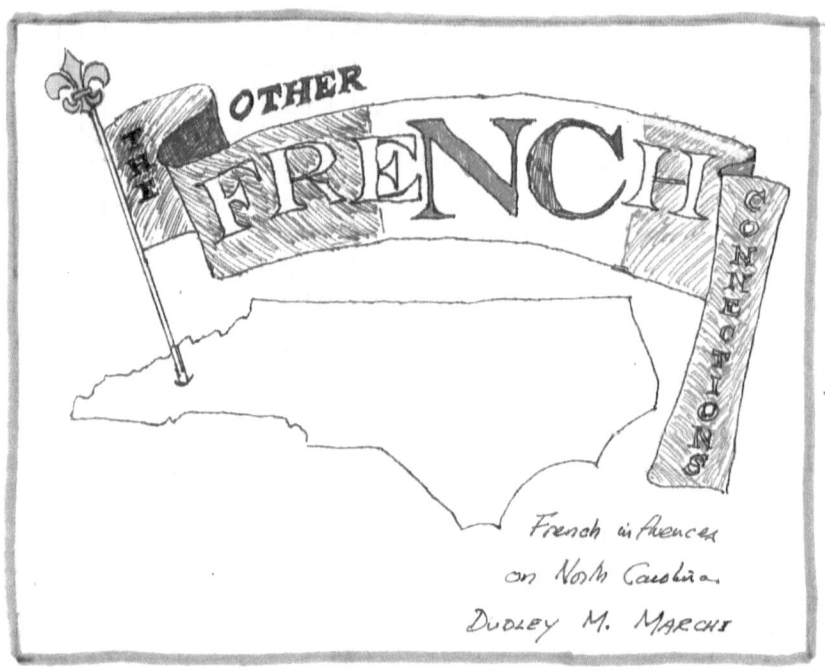

The Other French Connections (sketch by Anthony Dingman).

Chapter 1

First Discoveries

Native Americans first settled North Carolina thousands of years ago. Several tribes would encounter the French at different times during the colonial period. The most significant among them were the Tuscarora and Cherokee. The former battled colonists for territory during the Tuscarora War. The latter sided with the French during the French and Indian War. When Europeans first landed along the North Carolina coast, they encountered, however, peaceful Woodland and Mississippi Indians. These tribes were open and friendly, and cultural exchanges ensued between them and the first European explorers they had ever met.

Italian explorer Giovanni da Verrazzano accomplished the first European discovery of the area covered by today's North Carolina coast. François I, visionary king of the French Renaissance, commissioned him to explore the region between Newfoundland and Florida. The goal was to find a passage to the Pacific Ocean. French and Italian merchants and financiers were also eager to open up sea trade routes to Asia. Verrazzano, funded by the Italians and the French Crown, was their man.

Verrazzano was born in Florence, Italy, but spent much of his life in France. In his will, housed in the archives of Rouen, France, he even signed his name with French spelling, "Jehan de Verrazane." Verrazzano was an ambitious gentleman explorer. He traveled to Lyon in his early twenties, where he befriended a group of Italian merchants and investors. Verrazzano convinced them to fund François I for his planned voyage to America. He then went to Dieppe to study maritime navigation and readied himself to set sail.

François I had recently married Claude, daughter of the Duchess of Brittany, and had her province at his disposal. Brittany is situated in the northwestern corner of France. It is a region of ships, sailors, and seafaring. François I also loved all things Italian. He had seen Italy firsthand as a young man, and noted how culturally advanced Italy was in comparison to France. Italy also had a more robust financial system. François I thus invited into the French court Italian merchants, artists, artisans, chefs, and investment counselors. In doing so, he brought the Italian Renaissance into France and boosted the country into the modern era. Verrazzano was a part of this Italian migration. François I was open-minded yet crafty. He patronized the Italians to enrich France. Leonardo da Vinci even came to live in France and died in the arms of François I. This is symbolic of how intertwined the French and Italians were during the Renaissance.

In 1524, Verrazzano traveled on a three-mast sailing ship, *La Dauphine*, commissioned by François I. The French captain Antoine de Conflans piloted the ship and commanded his predominantly French crew of fifty men. Verrazzano's brother, Girolamo, served as navigator and mapmaker for the voyage. *La Dauphine* sailed out of Le Havre and arrived at the American continent on February 24, 1524, after a stormy winter voyage across the Atlantic Ocean. It anchored offshore at the current location of Pine Knoll Shores, on a chilly, cloudy day, as seen in our first image that was taken in February 2015.

Conflans and Verrazzano named the waterway and stretch of land south of today's town of Beaufort "Bogue." It is a word derived from Old Norman French, meaning a "narrow channel." This area is today's Bogue Banks. Today, the town of Bogue in Carteret County harks back to Verrazzano's landing. Flying under the banner of the French flag, Verrazzano, quite by chance, begins the French–North Carolina connection. North Carolina's first place name is a French one. Today, at the location where one of Verrazzano's crew members swam ashore, there is a housing community named "Genesis." It is a coincidental name, but a fitting one, since this location marks the beginning of French North Carolina.

Antoine de Conflans was a skilled sea captain with a well-trained and toughened crew. As he and the Verrazzano brothers explored the North Carolina coastline, Giovanni gave the name *Tera Francesca* ("French Land") to all of the areas he discovered. He did so during the rest of *La Dauphine*'s voyage in honor of François I. The name *Nova Gallia* (Latin, "New France") is sketched on his brother's groundbreaking map of 1529. The first names of the area occupied today by North Carolina were thus French ones. Finally, the Verrazzanos may have navigated the way, but it was the French captain Conflans and his crew who made sure *La Dauphine* arrived at "New France" and returned home safely.

The first European to set foot on North Carolina soil was a young French sailor of hardy stock from a Norman family of seafarers. Conflans anchored near the beach at Pine Knoll Shores. Verrazzano sent this young crewmember to swim ashore to offer the natives a gift of small bells, mirrors, whistles, and other such novelties. The sailor intended to throw the trinkets on the beach from the surf, but the powerful winter waves washed him ashore. The natives gathered up the young man, dried his clothes, and

Verrazzano's landing at Pine Knoll Shores (photograph by the author).

warmed him by the fire. They then brought him back to the shore so he could swim back to the ship, embraced him, and bid him farewell. This event must have been an extraordinary event for the crew to watch and a terrifying experience for the young French sailor. The crew thought that the natives were going to roast and eat him, but their hospitality proved the opposite.

Upon his return to the ship, the young sailor described the physical appearance and personality of the natives. The first eyewitness account we thus have of North Carolina's Native American population is that of this Frenchman. Verrazzano wrote down these observations about the natives in his journal. It would eventually be published as an official report of the voyage. He described the natives as friendly, generous, cheerful, "sharp-witted," and "with well-formed bodies" (Morison, 189). The name and identity of the young Frenchman will most likely never be known. This

French–North Carolina transatlantic adventure is the first of many to come. Many of the ships that sailed to North Carolina for trade and the transport of French Huguenots in the next century embarked from Le Havre and other ports in northern France.

La Dauphine eventually reached Pamlico Sound, and Verrazzano's exaggerated description of its size gave birth to the notion of "Verrazzano's Sea." Verrazzano mistakenly thought that he had discovered the opening of a water passage to the other side of the American continent that led to Asia. Girolamo drew the first map of the North Carolina coastline and indicated on it the *Mare Occidentale* (Latin, "Western Sea"). This area is Pamlico Sound. The rest of today's North Carolina land area was thus mistakenly mapped as the Pacific Ocean. Girolamo's map also displays the *Antille Insula* (Latin, "Caribbean Sea,"), what the French would eventually name the *Antilles*. Girolamo also sketched in some of the Caribbean islands, among them Santo Domingo. It is an island, along with the Antilles, that will play a role in the history of French North Carolina, as we will learn in future chapters.

La Dauphine continued to explore the Outer Banks. Verrazzano described in his journal, in abundant and accurate detail, the pristine

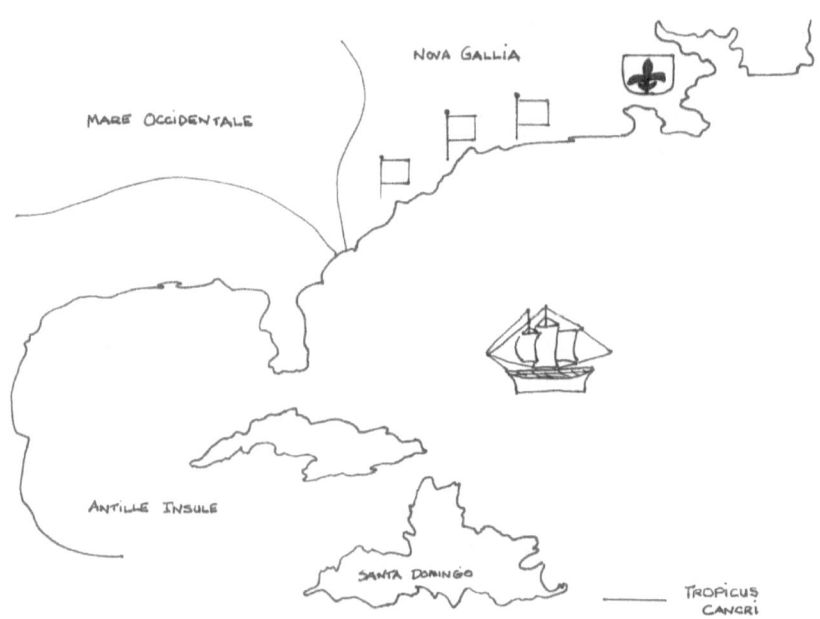

An adaptation of Giovanni da Verrazzano's 1529 map (sketch by Beverly J. Marchi from a facsimile, Washington State Library).

natural beauty of the region and its hardy and resourceful inhabitants. Verrazzano even named one beautiful place he described "Arcadia," at the approximate location of today's Kitty Hawk. In Verrazzano's words, the land was "salubrious and pure" (Morison, 194). In his poetic and eloquent description, he invokes the ancient Greco-Roman theme of "Arcadia." It was a fantastical land of exquisite beauty, deep forest groves, verdant meadows, wild animals, and abundant fruits. Verrazzano's North Carolina Arcadia was an Edenic paradise on Earth.

While in the Kitty Hawk area, Verrazzano sent a boat ashore to trade with the natives. He betrayed them, though, and kidnapped a young boy who accompanied the crew on the return voyage. The first Carolinian to go to Europe went to France, and it was by treacherous means. We can barely imagine the boy's experience and fate. This event begins the dark side of colonization. Many Native Americans in North Carolina were later forced into slavery by English landowners during the colonial period. The plight of North Carolina's Native Americans has been chronicled in Alan Gallay's *The Indian Slave Trade: The Rise of the English Empire in the American South*. The native boy taken back to France is the symbolic first step of the enslavement of North Carolina Native Americans. As we will see, there are pleasant and unpleasant sides in the French–North Carolina connection.

La Dauphine arrived back in France on July 8, 1524. Verrazzano's belief that he had discovered the Pacific Ocean was erroneous. Nevertheless, he had brought attention to the region that became North Carolina, captured the European imagination, and helped spark the development of early American history itself. The maritime gateway to Asia foretold of enormous profits to be made, and this imperfect map was used for almost a century by European explorers.

Girolamo's map and Verrazzano's report were included in the widely read travel book, Richard Hakluyt's *Divers Voyages* (1582). Sir Walter Raleigh referenced Verrazzano's report when he was formulating his plans to establish a colony at Roanoke. *Nova Gallia* was strategically located on the Pamlico Sound. Raleigh presumed it would be the main route to Asia ("Cathay," in his terms) once the sea passage was discovered, navigated, and mapped. As we will see in the next chapter, French Huguenots followed the English migration to settle in North Carolina, but it was Verrazzano and the French who paved the way for the English.

Verrazzano and Conflan's discovery sparked French interest in further exploring "New France." François I was looking to establish a French colony in America. The North Carolina area that Verrazzano had navigated for him was a possibility, but it did not happen.

François I sent Jacques Cartier on his famous voyage in 1534. France would subsequently colonize what became Québec, Canada. Moreover, as we know, North Carolina did not become a French colony. That accomplishment would belong to the English. North Carolina consequently became a state of predominantly Anglo-Saxon heritage. However, the first discovery of North Carolina was funded by the French monarchy and achieved by the French crew of *La Dauphine*. North Carolina was now on the French radar. It became an area of interest for French explorers. In the next two centuries, hundreds of French Huguenot families and other French immigrants would come to settle in North Carolina.

Verrazzano's 1529 map changed European exploration for the decades that followed. It opened a new space in the European cultural psyche. Verrazzano's French ship prepared the way for the European colonization of North Carolina. The three flags imprinted on it along the Atlantic coast are French. The approximate location of today's Carteret County is located in between the left and center flags. They are destination markers to which future generations of French would travel and establish centuries of French North Carolina heritage. Girolamo's map is housed at the Vatican Library in Rome, the origins of French North Carolina enshrined in its prestigious setting.

CHAPTER 2

Huguenot Migrations

The French Huguenots were Protestants. The European Reformation reached France in the early 1500s and was quickly embraced by many members of the aristocracy, the intellectual elite, and professionals in artisanal trades, commerce, law, and medicine. They were some of the most accomplished people in France at the time. The Huguenot Church proliferated. Early in his reign, François, I favored the Huguenots because of their abilities and valuable contributions to France's burgeoning economy during the Renaissance. However, 90 percent of France was Roman Catholic, and eventually, the Church and the Crown, after the death of François I, severely persecuted the Huguenots. Bloody civil wars took place from the 1560s to the 1590s. It was not until 1598 that the first French Protestant king, Henri IV, issued the Edict of Nantes, which granted religious freedom to the Huguenots.

When King Louis XIV came to power in the 1640s, he and his finance minister Jean-Baptiste Colbert respected and depended on the Huguenots for their hard work, dedication, and thrift. However, Louis also maintained Catholicism as the official state religion and sought to contain Huguenot expansion. Later in his life, Louis became more conservative, religiously devout, and annulled freedom of worship for the Huguenots. In 1685, he revoked the Edict of Nantes with his Edict of Fontainebleau. This ended seventy-eight years of religious tolerance of French Protestants. There was an ensuing resurgence of persecution.

The result was a mass migration of nearly half a million French Protestants to England, Germany, Switzerland, the Netherlands, and America. Many of these Huguenots were resourceful and successful middle-class citizens. Some ended up in Verrazzano's "New France" and eventually settled in North Carolina. France suffered a significant loss with the departure of many intelligent and capable citizens, but France's loss was the American colonies' gain. The Huguenot colonists carried on their professions when possible as ministers, merchants, artisans, and physicians. Yet, some turned to farming and animal husbandry out of the necessity of providing for themselves and their families. Whatever their occupation, the French Huguenots were successful in the New World.

As the French fled France to seek asylum in England, the English Crown and the early Lords Proprietors of North Carolina were eager to help them settle in America. Most English were virulent anti-Catholic and upset at the atrocities committed against the Protestants in France. The Huguenots generally received a warm welcome and a significant level of charitable support in England. They were an industrious people and grateful to the English for providing them a haven from persecution in France. They would, in turn, become loyal colonists.

The first French Huguenots to settle in North Carolina began to do so in the early 1690s. As early as 1630, the British had regulations for French immigrants. In the document (written in French), "Regulations for French Protestants wishing to settle in Carolana" (March 12, 1630), the French colonists were required to be sponsored by their pastors ("attestation de leurs pasteurs de France"). They were then given a certificate ("un certificat"), granting them the freedom to settle in the Carolina region (State Archives of North Carolina, 21.19.2.11).

In general, Huguenot migration in the late 1600s to North Carolina occurred so early in the history of the state that many documents that could help us trace the French presence have not survived. They were burned in courthouse fires, destroyed in wartime, or lost over the centuries. The empirical information we have about the French migration to early colonial North Carolina is minimal. Fragments of particulars are scattered here and there throughout the state in books, articles, letters, land deeds, wills, marriage and birth certificates, graveyards, and family genealogies.

However, with some archival digging, details of the French Huguenot presence can be resurrected from libraries, archives, and personal collections. The existing information is an amalgam of spotty, disconnected, yet essential data that can be connected into a meaningful whole. Empirical historical information does exist, but it requires constructive assembly, using informed speculation to analyze the rare gems of information we do have.

The 1683 *Fundamental Constitution of the Province of Carolina*, one clause of which guaranteed religious freedom, was translated into French for the newly arrived Huguenots. It may be no coincidence that one of the first of the Lords Proprietors was Sir Thomas Amy. He was related to Sir Hugh L'Amy, a wealthy French Huguenot, who promoted colonization of Carolina for his French followers in the late 1600s.

"Amy" is the Old French spelling of the word *ami* ("friend"), and Sir Thomas was certainly amicable in aiding the Huguenots to settle in Carolina. A French descendant played a vital role in the early settlement of

Chapter 2. Huguenot Migrations

North Carolina by the French. Subsequently, over the next twenty years, thousands of Huguenots migrated to "Carolina" (before it was divided into two states). The majority of them would settle in today's South Carolina along the Santee River, but hundreds of families would make today's North Carolina their home.

The French were part of the first waves of immigration into the Albemarle region. English King William III of Orange had awarded lands to some of these settlers. During the "Glorious Revolution" in 1688, among William's eleven-thousand-man army were seven hundred and fifty French Huguenots. In gratitude for their support, he offered them parcels of land in the Nansemond region of southern Virginia. Part of the Nansemond region is in today's Gates County, North Carolina. Many of the settlers who first came to Virginia, both English and French, balked at the idea of the Lords Proprietors' goal of setting up a feudal-like system of indentured servitude. Some set out southward from Nansemond through the Great Dismal Swamp. Among them were escaped servants, enterprising farmers, and migrant Huguenots. They all sought freedom from the Virginia plantation hegemony.

The Great Dismal Swamp is a twenty-two-hundred-square-mile morass. Mosquitos and biting flies were waiting in the stagnant water. Rotting vegetation, poisonous snakes, bobcats, wolves, shrub hogs, and briars made the journey a dangerous and miserable one. Other migrants from Virginia took the longer, less direct, but easier route via the Nansemond and Elizabeth rivers to the Chowan River and then headed south to the Albemarle Sound. Those traveling through the Great Dismal Swamp eventually came to the Perquimans River and began to settle along its banks from today's town of Hertford south.

The first land patent in North Carolina dates back to 1660 and belonged to the speculating partners Nathaniel Batts and George Durant. They bought land from the Yeopim tribe and lived peacefully with them for decades. The name Durant is of French origin and was introduced into England after the Norman Conquest. The name derives from the Old French "Durand" stemming from the Latin "durus" (hard, or firm). It seems a fitting name for a man who must have been as tough as nails as he trail blazed and settled the untamed wilderness. His wife, Elizabeth Durant, was a resourceful and resilient colonist in her own right. She became the first woman attorney in the state in 1673.

Groups of Quakers were among the first settlers in the Albemarle region. The Quakers had been under scrutiny and persecuted by the Puritans and the General Assembly in Virginia. The English Quakers had beliefs similar to those of the French Huguenots. They shared the values of self-reliance, love of liberty, and freedom of worship. With the Quakers established in an area where there was no religious authority to constrain them, they were free to worship as they wished. Around 1685, French Huguenots began to find their way to the area and were welcomed to this quiet retreat by the Quakers. There was a general spirit of tolerance that permeated the Albemarle region. The area thus became "a shelter for dissidents," both political and religious (McLivenna, 12).

The Albemarle region, with its many rivers and tributaries, coastal breezes, and soil enriched by floodwaters, made the land perfect for agriculture. The forests provided an abundance of game, deer, and turkey. The rivers teemed with trout, bass, and bluefish. The coastal plain area was isolated and provided a haven with the buffer zones of the Great Dismal Swamp to the north and the sand shoals to the east that made sea navigation treacherous. The first settlers had an abundance of natural resources on which to live and began clearing the land for growing corn, vegetables, and a cash crop: tobacco. They quickly became self-sufficient and prospered.

Other groups of French Huguenots came by ship to the region via the Atlantic Ocean. To do so, it took a skilled sea captain and crew to navigate the treacherous barrier islands, today's Outer Banks. If the ship made it through the Currituck Inlet, it would land at the location of today's Elizabeth City on the Pasquotank River. Some ships did not make it. Other Huguenots made the journey to the Albemarle region from the James River in Virginia. It was a slow and hazardous trip requiring travel on small boats and rafts from the James to the Blackwater River. They had to travel through some of the most desolate and inhospitable terrains. The Blackwater River eventually becomes the Chowan River, which flows into Albemarle Sound.

The French were part of the more extensive migration of English, German, and Swiss to northeastern North Carolina. All of these groups came for either economic or religious reasons. Many of the landholders in Virginia saw themselves as feudal barons and the farmers that worked on their land little more than medieval serfs. The Church of England was also inflexible on the question of freedom of conscience. Finally, prime property in southeastern Virginia was becoming increasingly scarce. The Huguenots, along with the other groups of settlers, were slowly squeezed out and forced into migration. They eventually found their new homeland after many painful years of persecution, poverty, and harrowing travels. They could now live off the plentiful land and worship as they wished without fear of retribution.

Unlike the Puritans of New England, the Huguenots had a Gallic cheerfulness of spirit and the French appreciation of beauty, as seen in their architectural and horticultural artistry. In 1864, Beverly Tucker of Williamsburg, Virginia, wrote in her diary, "They are sprightly and full of fire, but serious and earnest in all essentials, seeming something like a cross

Chapter 2. Huguenot Migrations 31

between the Frenchman and the Scotchman" (Davies, 70). This description applies to our Carolina Huguenots of the early colonial period. They were determined, principled, and believed that to serve God gave meaning to their lives. They also understood that suffering is essential to the matter of a soul. This belief guided them through countless hardships over many years. A good number of the Huguenots who fled France were trained ministers and doctors. They were essential to the success of the Huguenot colonists. These hardy, resourceful people had what it took to survive and settle in the harsh colonial frontier.

There were other English Lords Proprietors of North Carolina of French descent, namely Peter Colleton and John Carteret. They were instrumental in the Huguenot migration to Carolina and were supportive of the small but thriving groups of French settlers. Carteret's French ancestry runs deep. His grandfather George was the son of a French couple Helier de Carteret and Elizabeth Dumaresq of St. Ouen on the Isle of Jersey, which is just off the northern coast of France.

George Carteret married Lady Grace Grenville, whose family name harks back to the town of Granville in Normandy, France, not far from the

Land deed issued under the rule of Lord John Carteret (courtesy State Archives of North Carolina).

Isle of Jersey. Today Carteret and Granville counties are named after these descendants of the French nobility of the Middle Ages. Peter Colleton also had French ancestral roots. His father, John Colleton, was a second cousin of George Monck, the Duke of Albemarle, and married Katherine Amy of French descent. The French ancestral origins of several of the first Lords Proprietors are inscribed in the early history of the state.

The transatlantic voyage of the Huguenots was an uncomfortable and unsafe one. Passage of three to four months was not uncommon in crowded and unsanitary conditions. Some ships foundered on treacherous reefs, and the passengers drowned. There was the possibility of attack by marauding pirates, and contagious disease was prevalent. If the journey took longer than planned due to stormy conditions, food and water sometimes ran out, and the voyagers died of privation. However, braving the journey was preferable to the torture and cruel executions of Protestants that were commonplace in France.

A contract of the passenger ship *Nassau*, which regularly transported Huguenots to the mouth of the James River in Virginia, gives us insight into the travelers' experience. The price for passage was five pounds sterling per person, not an insignificant sum at the time. The Huguenot passengers' diet consisted of bread, cheese, beef, pork, and peas. The children were allowed oatmeal, fruit, sugar, and butter. A small store of brandy, sugar, figs, and sweet biscuits was set aside for those that became ill. The Huguenots brought with them whatever items and supplies they could carry to help them start a new life: farming tools, cooking utensils, firearms, seeds, and other articles to help establish their new settlements.

Some Huguenot passengers brought vine plants in small chests covered with fertile French soil from their country farms in France. Others who were less well off came with a few bundles of clothing, food, and blankets. These travelers were basically homeless. Some were sick and would not survive the arduous journey. Others persevered and would establish new homes. Many of the Huguenot families were not well prepared for the harsh realities of frontier life and subsistence agriculture, but they prevailed. The Huguenots also brought with them less tangible, but invaluable human commodities such as industry, intelligence, devoutness, and an intense desire to see their families survive and grow.

One small group helped establish a settlement on Pamlico Sound at the point where the Tar River widens into the sound, just west of today's town of Bath. Thus, "a great many French Protestants" began to migrate to the Albemarle region under the governance of England that guaranteed "exercise of the Protestant Religion" (Hawks, 76). Subsequently, in 1704, on a low bluff overlooking the Pamlico River, Bath, the first town in North Carolina, was incorporated. Some of the town's early citizens were French or of French descent. We will revisit Bath in the next chapter.

Chapter 2. Huguenot Migrations

The name Albemarle is the Latinized form of the French farming commune Aumale in Normandy, France (Latin, *Alba Marla*, meaning "White Marl"; marl is a type of fertile soil). The English monarchy frequently created peers as counts and dukes of Aumale. One of them, George Monck, Duc d'Aumale, was named one of the original eight Lords Proprietors of the Carolina region. This appointment was out of King Charles II's gratitude for Monck's many years of loyal service to the Crown. The Albemarle region thus took the name of Monck's French dukeship. There is a 1669 French map of North Carolina displaying the *Comté d'Albemarle*; the French were very interested in the area and were preparing the way to colonize it.

There is another map drawn by Samuel A. Ashe and Stephen B. Weeks, a uniquely informative one, designed for Ashe's classic work *History of North Carolina* (1908). The map depicts the chronological expansion of European settlement by various ethnic groups in North Carolina. The two main French colonies are small compared to the other groups. One cluster

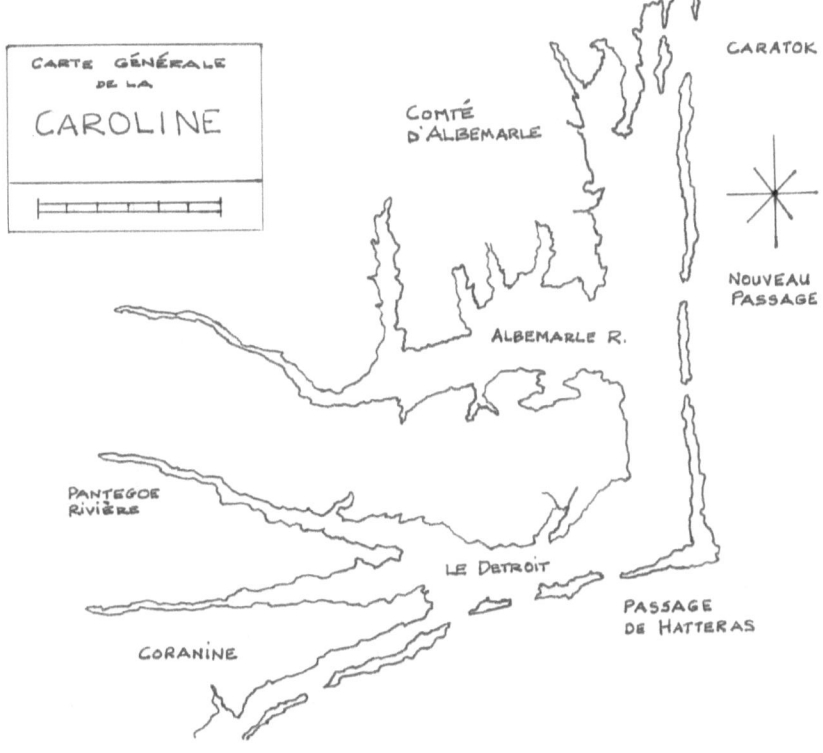

French map of the *Comté d'Albemarle* (1669) (sketch by Beverly J. Marchi from the original, courtesy State Archives of North Carolina).

is in the Bath region and a larger one in the Craven County area (State Archives of North Carolina, 33MAP-04–00). They were small but thriving French communities.

In 1704, a new migratory wave of Huguenots came to join their brethren, whose numbers had started to spread through the Albemarle region. They traveled for the most part from Manakin Town, a French settlement in Virginia near today's Richmond that was established in 1700. In a few years, harsh economic conditions and less religious tolerance than had been expected under colonial rule in Virginia caused a group of disgruntled Huguenots to leave Manakin Town. They had heard favorable reports from the Huguenots in the Pamlico region of a milder climate. The latter were prospering and spreading to other areas along the Neuse and Trent rivers. The warmer climate, abundance of land, and religious freedom attracted these several hundred Huguenots from Manakin Town. They had an even lengthier and tougher journey than Huguenot colonists in the 1690s. Once they arrived, this new group, just as skillful, industrious, and thrifty as their predecessors, settled in and made a go of it.

Some of the Manakin Town settlers had family names that are now

Manakin Town settlement (photograph by the author).

found widely in the state. Most, but not all, were Anglicized after a generation or two (Kammerer, *passim*). Among them are Ammonnette (Amyette), Chaumette (Shumate), Chastain, Dieppe (Depp), Dupré (Dupree), Duval, Guerrin (Gerrans), Lanier, Lefevre, LeJeune (Young), Maupin, Michaux, Moulin (Mullen), Muce (Muse), Salle, and Tailler (Taylor). The Huguenots had endured such hardship and suffering in their native country that many left behind their national identity and were absorbed over the years into the English majority.

In 1705, another group of Huguenots arrived from Virginia led by Pastor Claude Phillipe de Richebourg. They settled in the Albemarle Sound and Craven County regions and joined the existing communities. They also began to settle in the area occupied by today's town of Beaufort. Among this new group were families of wealth and standing. They had commercial interests and planned to create a maritime entry at Ocracoke Inlet that would foster trade. Descendants of some of these early French colonists still live in Beaufort and Carteret counties. Among them are the names Delamare, Pasteur, Longveille, Rieveset, and Pacquenet (Fisher, *Early Records of North Carolina*, 22). We will revisit these French North Carolina colonists in later chapters.

The growing of hemp and flax and the making of cloth helped the Huguenots succeed as they established their agricultural communities. They also knew how to cultivate grapes and make wine and brandy, so cherished by their neighboring English colonists. The Huguenots also grew corn and wheat, set up gristmills, planted orchards, and bred cattle. They raised sheep to provide wool for their looms, for among them were skillful weavers. The Huguenots obtained a reputation for producing excellent wine, fruit, woolen goods, and textiles. They were important contributors to the cultural fabric and economic growth of their settlements.

Let us keep in mind too that Huguenots were skilled in the following trades: the making of textiles, jewelry, glass, and silversmithing. Some were expert gunsmiths, tanners, and winemakers. They also introduced new agricultural products to America, such as Brussels sprouts, carrots, cauliflower, beets, tulips, lilacs, and roses. They even knew how to design fields divided by hedges, stone walls, and fences (Davies, *passim*). The Huguenots enriched North Carolina's commerce, culture, and landscape.

John Lawson, English explorer, naturalist, and author of *A New Voyage to Carolina* (1709), visited the French settlers on the Trent River, near today's city of New Bern. He wrote of them: "They are much taken with the pleasantness of that country, and indeed, are a very industrious people. The French are good neighbors amongst us, and give good examples of industry, which is much wanted in this country" (Lawson, 34). Let us keep in mind that Lawson's praise for the French was motivated in part by the fact that he was being compensated as a publicist and recruiter by the Lords Proprietors. He wanted to attract more French settlers and so wrote favorably about them. In 1710, the Swiss Baron von Graffenried and his Swiss colonists met the French Huguenots and got along well with them. The baron set up his own settlement nearby, which would eventually become the town of New Bern, where the Swiss and French coexisted together. There most likely were some French speakers among the Swiss, and the French from eastern France might have known some German and Romansh (a Gallo-Romance language).

In 1709, there was the first documented landing of French Huguenots in the town of Beaufort. They were not the only French people to come to Beaufort. Privateers, pirates, and political refugees also began to frequent the surrounding coastal area of today's Beaufort and Carteret counties. Beaufort soon turned into a thriving fishing, maritime, and merchant town. It was helped along by a group of influential French families whose names and ancestry can be traced to medieval France. We will meet these families in the Beaufort chapter. The name of Carteret County also has French origins: Sir John Carteret was the grandson of Sir George Carteret, one of the grantees of the Carolina region under King Charles II. The ancestry of the Carteret family reaches back to the Carteret commune in Normandy, France. Some family members migrated to England during the years that followed the Norman Conquest of England in 1066.

Other Huguenots came to North Carolina in varying scenarios. In the 1690s, some came directly from French towns during the Protestant diaspora. Former Huguenot strongholds such as Dieppe, Le Havre, La Rochelle, and Bordeaux were the departure points for hundreds of Huguenots traveling to America. Some of these groups first went to Massachusetts, New York, New Jersey, and other northern states before migrating southward to North and South Carolina. One reason they migrated southward was that the climate in the south was similar to the one in which they were raised in France. Let us remember the Pangaea effect. There was also a tolerant attitude shown to them by the Carolina Lords Proprietors concerning religion. It is estimated that six hundred Huguenots migrated to North Carolina after reaching the Virginia port of Norfolk during the late 1600s and early 1700s (Kammerer, 17).

Some Huguenots who were to be sent to Manakin Town refused to go when they arrived in Virginia. After landing in Norfolk, this group moved directly to join the French, who had already settled in the Albemarle Sound region in the 1690s. In 1700, Virginia governor Francis Nicholson wrote in a communication, "Regarding Huguenot Refugees on Board Ship *Mary and Ann*," that he was not settling the Huguenots in Norfolk or "thereabouts." There was no vacant land except some that was "in dispute betwixt us and

No. Carolina" (Bugg, 371). The Huguenots thus moved southward to this land and onward to the Albemarle region, where the Carolina Lords Proprietors welcomed them.

The English had greatly aided the Huguenot refugees in settling Manakin Town. On the other hand, the underside of their Christian charity shows a scheming attitude toward them. The Lords Proprietors did not want to depopulate England and enticed, and even funded, people from other countries to settle in Virginia and Carolina. Some English also did not wish the French Huguenots to be in their homeland forever, and the authorities helped them move on to the New World. In London, the French had provided competition in the workplace with their artisan skills in metalworking and glass making, along with their strong work ethic, as Lawson reminds us. Many Londoners wanted the French gone.

The Manakin Town group had been promised before leaving England that they would be allowed to settle near Norfolk. It was a thriving shipping port since it had a natural harbor. This promise appealed to the Huguenots, who had planned commercial enterprises to export the textiles and wine they intended to produce. Upon arrival, Governor Francis Nicholson and his colleague Colonel William Boyd told the French settlers that they were being sent to the land of the Monacan Indians. The land was more plentiful there than it was in the burgeoning Norfolk area. In reality, Nicholson and Byrd were using the French settlers as a buffer colony between their extensive landholdings and the Monacan Indians. The Manakin Town group had been deceived, and life proved to be challenging the first few years. Many of the settlers died of illness, famine, or exposure to the elements.

The exact numbers are not known, but of the seven hundred French refugees who arrived in Norfolk, no more than half settled at Manakin Town. Those that had the means decided to set out as a group on their own. They migrated south to the northeastern region of North Carolina and joined the French settlers who had arrived there in the 1690s. These original settlers were prospering in the favorable agricultural climate. Among them were Jean Palin, Nicolas Chevin, and François Delamar, whose descendants reside in the state to this day.

As the Huguenots migrated down the Chowan River on the way to the Albemarle Precinct, some stopped and settled in the Chowan, Pasquotank, and Perquimans precincts. Other Huguenot refugees paid for ocean transport to the Virginia Tidewater and came directly to these precincts to join their brethren. Some in this group would have made that miserable journey starting at Nansemond and through the Great Dismal Swamp. As young men, many Huguenots raised in seaports were trained in seamanship. Some were expert sailors. This skill certainly helped the trip from Virginia to Carolina since most of the travel was by water, sometimes through tricky currents.

Some of the families traveled together, often with small children. Many of the families were related by marriage and had known each other for generations. They were a community. They could talk and worship openly, share fellowship, and support each other in their daily lives. The Huguenot refugees had suffered much trauma in their diaspora. Some of their relatives had been tortured, burned alive, or massacred. The survivors fled France for their lives, lived as refugees in London, made the perilous journey across the Atlantic, and braved the hardships of making their way to French North Carolina. They then toiled diligently to clear the land and settle into a new life. The English authorities encouraged families to immigrate together. This helped the French population multiply, and they established roots.

The Huguenots were grateful for their newly established lives, and at first, remained close-knit. Speaking French together helped them maintain memories of their homeland and family ancestry. Still, there were only so many French families, and they began to intermarry with their English neighbors. Some also did so to blend in and not suffer any prejudice for being too French. They were caught in the immigrant paradox. They wanted to integrate with the majority populace while maintaining their ties to history, culture, and heritage.

Yes, although their government had persecuted these French religious refugees, they still loved the regions from whence they came. Anyone who has traveled to France and visited Normandy, the Loire Valley, Languedoc, or Provence understands that French hearts belong to their town or village where they grew up. The homesickness of these French immigrants must have been a heavy burden. The French North Carolina Huguenots thus worked to recreate their homesteads in the pastoral and fertile setting that Carolina offered.

For several generations, the Huguenots held together essential parts of their cultural identity: language, food, and handing down family stories and keepsakes. Some of their wills give us a glimpse into the other small ways they tried to preserve their heritage. Some bequeathed family belongings were from the old country and would remind their descendants of their French ancestry: a gold button, an embroidered shawl, a lace tablecloth, a silver cloak clip.

The wills of various Frenchmen witness the presence of the French settlers in the Pasquotank and Perquimans precincts: John Arderne (1707), John Moncrief (1712), Nathaniel Cheven (1715), Gregoire Garfort (1703—a name of French-Norman origin), Stephen Delamare (1732), and John Ballard (1736—from the French-Breton *Abelard*, "of the high town"), and others. Ballard, of English and French ancestry, is one of the few whose profession is noted in his will; he was a cooper. Settlers, French, and those of

French descent were not only landowners and planters; they were working members of the community. A cooper made casks and barrels for the storage and transport of everything from tar and turpentine to cloth, corn, and pork. Ballard was a vital member of the region's economy, and he was successful enough to have left a registered will. The Ballard family spread eastward to Halifax and Granville counties, where many Ballards reside today.

There are land deeds of the Perquimans Precinct in the Hertford Courthouse from the early 1700s that document land transactions of settlers who are either French or of French ancestry: Peter Baudry, Jean Chesson, Vallentine Barton, John Valluay, and Benjamin Moulin. The French names Aydlett, Midgette, and Millard appear in other land deeds. Documents in the Pasquotank Register of Deeds in Elizabeth City testify to descendants of the French Huguenots living in the area through the centuries: Brosier, Caron, Chesson, Delon, Foulon, Jennette, Laboyteaux, Laverty, Marriette, Minsoir, Picard, and Seguine are some of the French family names frequently listed.

Albemarle County court records from 1678 to 1737 document land transactions of Edward Batchelder, Henry Montfort, Robert Molynes, Roger Montesquieu, Simon Fosque, and Benjamin Blanchard. John Bethea, who migrated from the James River colony in Virginia, owned a plantation of one hundred and fifty acres in the Nansemond area located in today's Gates County. Names of French origin also appear in birth, marriage, and death certificates in the Perquimans County Court Minutes from 1688 to 1730: Isaac Arthaud, Peter Avelin, Benjamin Balance, Jean Bayard, Jean Brosier, Nathaniel Chevins, William Delaney, Benjamin Dumas, Sarah Delon, Anne Duboise, William Fellure, Peter Fourre, William Larance, Jean Moncrief, Chrestien Palin, Francis Petit, and Anne Prousse.

In the Albemarle County colonial records, there are registered wills with names of French origin: Peter Fourre (1697), Isaac Fourre (1726), John Chesson (1727), and Nathaniel Rosier (1703), the latter a ship's carpenter. Peter Fourre was from the Chilly-Mazarin suburb of Paris. His French countryman Francis De La Mare witnessed his will. Isaac Fourre leaves "1/2 of a plantation I bought from Francis Delamar" to his son Isaac Jr. (Bradley, 43). This transaction shows that the French stayed together and pursued common commercial interests. They held onto their roots the best they could forty-five hundred miles from their homeland. In the case of Rosier, the French have a long tradition of being excellent shipbuilders, witness *La Dauphine*. A ship's carpenter was a valuable member of a maritime community.

The French were fortunate to have such a worker as Rosier among them; he was a valuable asset to their survival on the frontier. The Huguenots had made the journey from Virginia in small boats, perhaps built by Rosier and his fellow workers. Rosier's father was the French Huguenot Jean Rosier of Forez, France, in the Loire Valley. He escaped France in 1688 and took the dangerous boat ride across the English Channel to London. He made his way to the Albemarle region in the 1690s. The Rosier blazon is a blue shield with a gold chevron between three silver roses. It is an icon of the medieval French chivalric age. French ancestry runs deep in North Carolina.

Other French colonists migrated to northeastern North Carolina; they were from all walks of life. They were bonded together by the persecution they had faced in their homeland and their arduous journeys together. They settled in their new home in a setting not too different from what they had known in France. They became successful farmers, tradesmen, and merchants, as their ancestors had done in the old country.

Land deeds document business transactions of the French. In some cases, their lands bordered one another's. This shows that they tried to remain in physical proximity to their compatriots. In 1681 John Chesson sold one hundred acres, Georges Durant bought land on Lilley's Creek in 1687, Peter Fourre purchased a plantation in 1688 on Alligator Creek from James Caron, which included "all housing, fencing, orchards, etc." (Haun, 18). Francis Delamare witnessed the deed.

The lands of Jean Byer, Thomas Philippe, and William Bogue were joined at the "narrows of the Perquimans River" (Haun, 22). One can visit this spot today; it has not changed much since the 1680s and is still a pastoral paradise cooled by river breezes. Perquimans County records list several land transactions of Pierre Baudry. He would eventually acquire a patent of five hundred acres in the Craven Precinct. In 1701, Nicolas Chevin served as clerk of court. In 1722, John Pettiver sold two hundred and sixty-three acres to Henry Bonner on Rockyhock Creek. The location is several miles north of today's Edenton on the Chowan River. James Palin witnessed the transaction. Bonner, like Ballard, is a name of English and French ancestry; we will revisit it in the Bath chapter.

In another transaction, Pettiver purchased one hundred and fifty acres on "Ballard's Swamp." There are also land deeds of James Fuget, Cornelius Gilles, and others. The family name of Corneille Giles reaches back through medieval French to the Latin "Aegelius," a renowned Gallo-Roman warrior of Northern Gaul. These French were active and successful members of the region. Most would go on to achieve English citizenship and Anglicize their names and those of their children. Other French names appearing in the Perquimans County land deeds are as follows: Thomas Ayres, Richard Bachelier, William Bogue, Jean Byer, Jacques Caron, Richard Fontaine (Fountain), Ezekiel Mauldin, William Parieter, François Richard, and Jean Valois (John Vollway).

Francis Delamare was born in 1665 near Calais in the northern

Land deed of Peter (Pierre) Baudry (Onslow County Register of Deeds).

Pas-de-Calais region of France. He fled to England soon after Louis's Edict of Fontainebleau and became an important French North Carolina citizen in the Albemarle region. He came to the Pasquotank Precinct around 1691. When he applied for citizenship in 1702, Francis stated that he had been involved in local government for over eleven years. He served as an attorney, justice, and churchwarden.

Francis and his brother Isaac settled in Pasquotank in 1692 and recorded a joint grant for one hundred and twenty-five acres of land in 1694. Francis's name appears on the 1697 tax list. He was prominent and wealthy, and paid his taxes. The brothers were so close that Francis named one of his sons after his brother Isaac. The Delamare family multiplied in the Pasquotank region, and some migrated to Craven and Carteret counties. Today, many Delamars are alive and well in North Carolina.

There is evidence of an even earlier French–North Carolina migration. In 1679, the English Admiralty Office ordered the captain of the sailing ship *HMS Richmond* to transport to "Carolina, twenty-three families of 'Foreigne Protestants,'" who were mostly French (State Archives, 74.1127.1-2). The order contains a passenger roster of "Names of French Protestants going to Carolina in the Richmond." The list includes the names of eighteen men, the heads of the families, the number in each family, and the area of France from where they came. On the roster are Thomas de Lamare of Normandy with his "family of three Persons" and "Piere (*sic*) Foure of Paris with his family of Eight Persons." The other families come from a broad range of French towns and regions such as Bordeaux, Orleans, Picardie, Rouen, and Brie, among others. This voyage marks another beginning of French–North Carolina migration.

The case of the Moulin family is an interesting one since we have a fair amount of information about it. Abraham Moulin was born in Paris

French passenger roster, names, and hometowns (courtesy State Archives of North Carolina)

in 1630. He married Madeleine Churpre, and his first son, Abraham Jr., was born in London in 1675. Abraham Jr. married Rachel Broret in 1700, and they sailed on the *Mary and Ann* to James City, Virginia, in the same year. They lived in Manakin Town for a few years but left with one of the unhappy groups to settle in the Perquimans Precinct.

Abraham Jr. and Rachel purchased their first property at Beaver Cove on April 8, 1707, for ten pounds. They were assigned by Samuel Cretchington "right to within deed unto Abraham Moulin of same" (Perquimans County Register of Deeds). Beaver Cove is about fifteen miles south of Hertford. It is a tributary of Yeopim Creek. The place name no longer exists; it last appeared on a map of Perquimans County in 1929. The closest modern road is Snug Harbor Road. One can visit the place indicated in Moulin's land deed on the banks of the lower Perquimans River; it is an area of fertile fields and tall trees nourished by the river. The spot has not changed much since the early 1700s. It is as peaceful and remote as it would have been in Moulin's time.

Abraham Moulin, Jr., is listed in a Perquimans census of the time as a "faiseur de savon" (soap maker). His son, Abraham III, married a French woman, Eléonore Minge, in 1762. Another son, Jean, was listed as an "avocat" (lawyer). Another son, Jacob, registered his last will and testament in 1757. The name Moulin eventually was anglicized to Mullen, then to Mullens. Many live in the state today and are direct descendants of Abraham Moulin, Sr.

The Moulin family became successful and oversaw a profitable plantation enterprise. In 1716, Abraham purchased another two hundred and ten acres as he expanded his property holdings. In 1734, Richard Whedbee sold Abraham one hundred and fifty-three acres in exchange for thirty barrels of pork. In 1743, he made a deed for the "love I bear my son Abraham, have given 105 acres, on the northeast side of Perq River, near the head of Beaver Cove Swamp" (Perquimans County Deed Book). Abraham Jr. died soon after. His children had many offspring who one by one married into English families; nevertheless, some French ties remained. In the 1770s, for example, Abraham's great-granddaughter married the Frenchman Gideon Maudlin.

There are other wills of Frenchmen from the Perquimans Precinct (Francis Gilbert—1734), Bodie Island (Matthew Midyette—1734), and the Berte District (Richard Turbavell, planter—1726). In all of the wills, the family patriarchs bequeathed their land resources to their immediate and extended families, leaving their modest estates to the next generation. Their children and grandchildren would go on, thrive, and have families of their own. They tried to preserve their French heritage the best they could. After several generations, though, they blended in with the English majority. But their French ancestry has survived to this day in North Carolina. This is witnessed by the many French family names in the state, more of which we will see in future chapters. One final item of note is that over three hundred years after the French settled in the area, on the land of the original George Durant land patent, is the grave of a woman of French descent, Amie Farrar.

Amie Farrar (photograph by the author).

After establishing settlements in Bath, New Bern, and Beaufort, the French began to expand their presence to the Albemarle Sound and Carteret regions. During the Tuscarora War in the early 1700s, however, many of the Huguenots were either massacred or frightened off. Some of the survivors sought a safer haven. They decided to migrate to South Carolina with the missionary Philippe de Richebourg, although some chose to remain put. In 1712, Richebourg moved a French colony from Virginia to Saint Santee in today's South Carolina. Some Huguenots from the Albemarle Sound region went with him. Some of these migrants settled in South Carolina. Along the way, however, some decided to stop at the mouth of the Cape Fear River, not far from today's Wilmington. A group of Scots was establishing the Cape Fear Colony. Among these Scottish settlers were French Huguenots. They had fled from France to Scotland before coming to America. Some in Richebourg's group decided to remain at Cape Fear with their brethren. They were weary from their trials and travels of the last few years.

One of Richebourg's young associate missionaries in South Carolina,

John LaPierre, would eventually settle in North Carolina with another group of French Huguenots. He established a church and religious community in the Cape Fear area around 1729. State historical marker D-73 in Winnabow, Brunswick County, commemorates LaPierre's mission. Some of the town names in Brunswick County, such as Clairmont and Belville, are a testimony to the French presence in the area. We will return to LaPierre and the Cape Fear region in the New Bern chapter.

During the Royal Period (1729–75), there was less French–North Carolina immigration than during the 1690s and early 1700s. There was nevertheless a steady stream of French colonists who continued to migrate, settle, and assimilate into the English cultural fabric of early North Carolina. Colonial records show Governor Dobbs in 1755 allocating funding and a small plantation for the production of silk by an enterprising group of French settlers. In 1757, the state legislature allotted twenty-five sterling pounds for subsistence to some of the poorer of the French colonists in Chowan County who were struggling to get by.

As a religious denomination, the Huguenots eventually became absorbed into the Presbyterian and Anglican churches. As the French spread throughout North Carolina, they often did not do so as a coherent group, but rather as individual families. There were, nevertheless, small French colonies in the Albemarle, Craven, and Carteret regions. Added to the French North Carolina mix, some descendants of the South Carolina Huguenots migrated northward to the Wilmington area around 1740. Pierre, "Peter" Du Bois, and Dr. Armand De Rossett were some of the most prominent members of this group of immigrants of French descent. Four generations of De Rossetts would work as physicians and merchants in the greater Wilmington area. We will return to these families in the French North Carolina chapter.

In the first U.S. census of 1790, North Carolina's population included just 1.7 percent of its citizens with French heritage. Small in number, perhaps, but it is a group that had a substantial impact. The French Huguenots helped establish agriculture, crafts, commerce, cuisine, and architecture in early North Carolina. After Louis XIV's Edict of Fontainebleau, France experienced a considerable loss of some of its most skilled and intelligent citizens. Those that settled in North Carolina acted as a catalyst for the establishment of the state and its economic development. As Esther Forbes wrote in *Paul Revere and the World He Lived In*: "France had opened her own veins and spilled her best blood when she drained herself of the Huguenots, and in every country that would receive them, this amazing strain acted like a yeast" (Forbes, 3).

The Huguenot migration to North Carolina was too small to sustain a cohesive community. The French thus became integrated into the English genealogical fabric. By process of acculturation, the Huguenots adapted to English ways and assimilated, most often keeping only their trades, skills, and derivations of their French names. This was also the case for the Germans, Swiss, Scottish, Irish, and Welsh, who, along with the French, became part of the eastern North Carolina melting pot.

Even though they were a minority, the French kept a group identity within their host English culture, at least for a few generations. The linguistic change was inevitable. Second generation Huguenots were bilingual. By the third and fourth generations, most Huguenot descendants no longer spoke French, though there were exceptions. Kinship and family ties kept the Huguenots together more than shared linguistic, religious, and national heritage.

French Huguenots resided in ten of the original thirteen colonies. Although small in number, their influence was considerable in shaping the new nation and the state. Huguenot ideals are at the heart of American values. Descendants of the French Huguenots promoted the core principles of the emerging American identity: religious freedom, individual rights, personal liberty, scholarship, education, and representative government. These were the very reasons the Huguenots were a threat to the French monarchy during the seventeenth and eighteenth centuries. In the New World, the Huguenots would thrive.

As we will see, North Carolina, one of the thirteen original colonies, benefited from the French presence in the state during its formative years. The Huguenot immigration experience is at the center of the American character. Like the English Puritans and Quakers, the French Huguenots sought the opportunity to worship openly and without fear of persecution. The small clusters of French settlers added a vibrant human resource to their communities. They played a role in the establishment of the towns of Bath (1705), New Bern (1710), Edenton (1712), Wilmington (1740), and others. As we will see in future chapters, during the 1700s, the French would continue to spread and settle throughout the eastern part of the state.

CHAPTER 3

Bath

European settlement near the Pamlico River in the 1690s led to the founding of Bath in 1705, North Carolina's first town. By 1708, Bath had twelve houses and fifty inhabitants. Political rivalries, Indian wars, and piracy marked its early years. In 1746, Bath was considered for the colony's capital. However, the county government relocated to Edenton in the late 1700s. Bath became less important, and trade declined; nevertheless, it remained a diverse and close-knit community. Bath's original town limits encompass the historic district today. It has a current population of two hundred and fifty, not much larger than that of the early 1700s. Walk in the early morning through the peaceful historic neighborhoods toward Bonner's Point, and one is transported back to early colonial times.

The name Bath is imbued with French and Roman history. The town was named in honor of Englishman John Granville, Earl of Bath. The name Granville reaches back to its Norman origins of the twelfth century. The town of Bath, England, is renowned for its two-thousand-year-old Roman baths. Bath, North Carolina, has impressive ancestral pedigrees in England, France, and France's Roman ancestors.

The first settlers consisted of a few wealthy sponsors and the poorer classes who were their indentured servants. They migrated slowly southward from Tidewater, Virginia, in the middle 1600s, to farm the fertile soil of the Pamlico River region. Among these early settlers (mostly English), were French Huguenot families. I have identified the approximate location of the French settlement near the town with the help of Herbert Paschal's *A History of Colonial Bath*. It is just to the west of Bath Street Bridge.

The Huguenot and English colonists found the Bath location an ideal one. It had easy access to the river and the Atlantic Ocean at Ocracoke Inlet. It was a perfect location for agriculture and commerce. The commerce in naval stores such as rope, tar, furs, and tobacco grew. Bath became the first port in the state. In 1707, entrepreneurs built a gristmill and shipyard. The town was thriving. The Huguenot settlers were among the founding members of Bath. Educated and open-minded, they helped establish

Bath, location of a French Huguenot settlement (photograph by the author).

the first public library in the colony. They were also involved in opening a free school, St. Thomas Parish.

The Huguenot immigrants worked with their fellow English settlers to lay out the town, sell lots, and establish agriculture and commerce. The thrifty and industrious Huguenots were backbones of the community. Some of the Bath Huguenots eventually owned plantations and became involved in the town's governance. The Huguenots were an essential part of the growing community's success. They had found their promised land.

A Bath precinct deed of 1712 mentions, "the house French people live in" (Beaufort County Deeds, 312). The *Beaufort County Deed Book*

Chapter 3. Bath

(1696–1729) includes the names of some of the early French settlers: Bodett, Brossard, Chabanas, Coutanch, Davanne, Delamar, DuVall, Dupuis, Faucheraud, Fontaine, Fonvielle, Guillard, Jadrian, Lassiere, Luellyn, Maule, Mellyue, Noé, Perdree, Rieusselt, Simon, and Venters. Messieurs Luellyn, Perdree, and Jadrian were among Bath's leading citizens. They all had numerous landholdings. Many families with these French surnames live in eastern North Carolina today.

Things were not always so pleasant for the Bath Huguenots. They toiled endlessly to survive and establish roots in a harsh and dangerous colonial frontier. In September 1711, the first main event of the Tuscarora War occurred. The Tuscarora tribe attacked the unsuspecting colonists in Bath on the south side of the Pamlico River. The settlers were overwhelmed. The Huguenots, in particular, suffered heavy casualties. Their settlement was located on the western outskirts of town and the first to be attacked.

Some of the colonists escaped to the nearest point of refuge. It was a crude but capable fort that had been built on the land of Joseph Bonner; today, the location is known as Bonner's Point. The name Bonner is of Norman-French origin. It has numerous spellings, all of which derive from *du bon air*. It indicates a person "of good bearing and appearance" or one with "good manners." The English word debonair originates from this phrase. The French name Bonair migrated to England in the 1100s after the Norman Conquest. They eventually assimilated with the English, and the name was Anglicized to Bonner. Many Bonners in North Carolina descend from this lineage.

Bonner's fortification would have been rough hewn, made of picketed trees and hemp rope. It was sturdy and practical, modeled after Roman military design. Bonner followed this medieval French model of wooden fortress construction. It is the same style and method used in the creation of French colonial strongholds throughout North America. Once the war was over, the surviving Huguenots resumed their lives, grew their families, and fanned out into the region. The Bonner family remained a prominent one in the area. Throughout the 1800s and 1900s, they worked as merchants, shippers, and plantation owners. They were also active in town and county governance. In the early 1800s, some Bonners were turpentine distillers. In 1820, Joseph Bonner participated in the creation of an innovative steam sawmill, one of the first in the area.

The current Bonner House was built in 1830 and is on the original partition of family land from the 1690s. This is a testimony to the importance of one of the founding fathers of Bath, one whose ancestry reaches back to medieval France. The house was built as a summer home. It was a place for the family to get away from the plantation and its stifling heat. They could enjoy the waterfront breezes and participate in the town's social activities. Today the Bonner House is on North Carolina's historical register.

Captain Michel Coutanch (Anglicized from the French Coutances) was a descendant of French Huguenots. In the 1750s, he became a leading merchant, legislator, and commissioner in Bath. He built the town's oldest existing house; it was the largest residence in North Carolina during the colonial period. It is today's Palmer-Marsh House. The house is in part named after the owner who purchased the home from Coutanch, Colonel Robert Palmer (also a descendant of French Huguenots). The home's design is a mixture of solid English colonial homebuilding with a chimney system in the French-Norman style. Excavations of the Coutanch house have uncovered pieces of window glass with the letters "Michael Cout..." engraved on them. It is a small but valuable piece of French North Carolina history.

The ground floor and basement of the Palmer-Marsh House were used to store and ship naval goods such as tar, turpentine, and resin. Traces of these items have been found on the basement floor as proof of this. Some of these supplies traveled by ship to France; they were part of a thriving mercantile exchange. In turn, French ships would arrive at the port with luxury items, such as cocoa, tea, sugar, clothing, fabrics, rum, wine, and brandy. Such goods helped provide a splash of refinement and culture to the Coutanch home and early Bath. Other items found over the years in archeological digs at the Palmer-Marsh House include broken wine bottles, clay tobacco pipes, and a black earthenware teapot with delicate gold gilt. This home was that of a successful and cultured man.

Coutanch contributed significantly to the success and reputation of the town. He was wealthy and known to be a generous, warm-hearted person who helped others. His warm Gallic voice spoke for Bath's citizens for many years in the General Assembly. A close friend of Coutanch was another citizen of French descent, John Rieussett. He was also involved in the town's governance and economic success. He served as one of the town's commissioners along with Coutanch in the 1750s.

During the colonial period, the Coutances family made significant contributions to culture, art, sciences, and religion in New France (today's Québec). Michael Coutanch of Bath was a descendant of this lineage. The name originated during the Middle Ages from the town of Coutances in Normandy. The etymology of the surname derives from the Latin, "Constans," meaning steadfast and faithful. Michal Coutanch was the epitome of these qualities. Coutanch infused his intelligence and industry into the social fabric of early North Carolina.

Due to the French presence, in the early 1700s, Bath was a locale that had a trace of cultural diversity. It was a small but bustling international port with inns, shops, and taverns. French wine and brandy were regular offerings in the town's eating and drinking establishments. Some of the food

Blackbeard's house (photograph by the author).

and drink of early Bath were permeated with exotic spices, fruits, vegetables, and spirits such as rum and curaçao. French ships brought these items from their colonial islands in the Caribbean, such as Haiti, Martinique, and St. Martin. This Francophone alimentary influence would spread from Bath and enrich the culinary offerings of colonial cooking in eastern North Carolina. We will return to French frontier cooking in the La Colonie Perdue chapter.

In the early 1700s, Bath also became a temporary refuge for the pirate Blackbeard. He and his crew lodged, conducted business, and reveled at will in the town's taverns. Anchored in the bay was Blackbeard's ship, the famous *Queen Anne's Revenge*. It was a stolen slave ship whose original name was French: *La Concorde de Nantes*. Blackbeard captured her off the coast of the French colonial island Martinique. It became his flagship. There were undoubtedly some French among his crew and also French-speaking slaves when he came to Bath. Some of these slaves were sold to landowners in the area to work on the plantations and turpentine forests. Their presence would have diversified the cultural and linguistic fabric of the area.

In early October 1718, Blackbeard and his crew hosted a feast for the town. Among the items on the menu were wild roast pig seasoned with spices from the French West Indies, grilled shrimp and mangoes, skewered pigeons with pepper sauce, sweet potatoes, and sugar cake. The sumptuous meal was washed down with copious quantities of wine, rum punch, and

French brandy (Le Bris). Blackbeard and the French among his crew left their culinary tracks in the area. They introduced recipes, spices, beverages, and other culinary products of the French-speaking Caribbean islands to the Bath community. We will revisit Blackbeard in the Beaufort chapter.

The King's Highway came to Bath in the 1760s. The highway connected the community to towns from Virginia to South Carolina. Bath experienced an economic revival. In 1769, the renowned mapmaker Claude Sauthier, a Frenchman, drew the first official map of the town. Bath's French heritage, little known to most people, is a meaningful part of the town's history.

CHAPTER 4

La Colonie Perdue

When I began researching *The French Heritage of North Carolina*, one of the first people I contacted was Mr. Victor Jones of the Kellenberger Collection of the New Bern Public Library. In Mr. Jones's reply to my inquiry about the French presence in North Carolina, he mentioned that there had been French settlers in the Craven area during the colonial period. Victor had recently come across a 1793 land deed from Craven County written in French. He also informed me that there was a local legend about a French "lost colony" (in French, *une colonie perdue*) of French Huguenots along the Trent River during the early 1700s.

The term French "lost colony" is Alonzo Dill's, author of the history of New Bern. The North Carolina historian Alan Watson has supported Dill's claim that the French had a minimal presence in the state during the colonial period. My curiosity piqued, I began to research the French migration to the area of today's Craven County to find the French "lost colony." Was the French colony truly "lost?" Alternatively, has its existence been overlooked in a desire to write the narrative of the English origins of North Carolina's history? Dill's claim that the "lost colony 'consisted of only a few families at the most'" (Dill, 61) might not be correct. There is evidence of a more significant French presence in the Craven area that eventually spread into eastern North Carolina, one that has never been given its due.

The French were aware of the Craven area as early as 1629 when Charles I granted the land called "Carolana" to Sir Robert Heath, who transferred the patent to a French Huguenot, Henry Howard, Lord Maltravers. French Huguenots contemplated a settlement between the Pamlico and Neuse rivers. Such a colony never materialized, but the region was on the radar of the Huguenots. The Carolina proprietors were very interested in populating the area and welcomed French and, eventually, Swiss immigrants into the Craven Precinct.

Charitable contributions from England helped the struggling French refugees settle in Virginia and Carolina. In the "Proceedings of the Board of the Lords Proprietors" of August 1719, there is a testimony of the French desire to establish themselves in the mid–Atlantic area, "particularly the province of *Carolana* of which they seem very fond having already made some settlements and are preparing to make more and greater" (Weeks, Vol. II, 764).

The English authorities and Carolina Lords Proprietors welcomed the French Huguenots since the latter were grateful for having been given asylum from persecution in France and were loyal to the Crown. They were also very industrious and resourceful people. The English hoped that they would become productive citizens of the early colony, and they did. However, some of the English colonists did not care much for the French.

The English and French had been archenemies at least since the time of the Battle of Hastings in 1066 and during the Hundred Years War in the fifteenth century. There was a natural animosity harbored by some English colonists toward the French. Some English landholders had challenged French rights to own land and settle in the area. In 1695, this antipathy prompted a group of early Huguenot settlers in the region to write a letter to the governor of North Carolina, John Archdale. They pleaded for fair and equal treatment under the law.

There were also defenders of the French right to settle equally among the English. In a letter of September 1695 to Archdale, Joseph Boyd makes a plea for the Huguenots: "since the death of Peter Colleton, the state of affairs are here much altered, concerning the French inhabitants" (State Archives of North Carolina, CGP 1, 308.1.3). Boyd goes on to say that the French had been peaceable and responsible colonists who had volunteered to serve in the "offices of the militia." Colleton was an Englishman of French Huguenot descent. He sympathized with the French and oversaw their interests in the Craven area. Boyd's letter goes on to remind Governor Archdale that "many inhabitants of Craven County are French" (State Archives of North Carolina, CGP 1, 308.1.3). He asks him to naturalize the French as citizens of the Crown. It was only fair that they enjoy the same rights as their fellow English colonists.

In November 1695, Governor Archdale sent a letter to three Frenchmen, Peter Brutell, Jacques Le Seurier, and Peter LaSalle. It stated that they did not yet have the right to vote, but they would in the future once the formalities of acquiring citizenship had been completed (State Archives of North Carolina, CGP 1, 308.1.5). Governor Archdale was a Quaker and had known his share of religious persecution in England. He was a wise and tolerant man who sympathized with the plight of the French Huguenots. He ultimately ruled in favor of fair treatment for them (State Archives of North Carolina, Z.5.106).

A curious aside is that the state acquired Governor Archdale's letters in 1732. They were purchased from the library of a French estate, the

"Bibliotheque de la Chevalière Deon." One can only speculate how the letters of an English Lord came into the possession of a female French aristocrat, whose identity remains unknown. The missing accent on the word "Bibliotheque" (*bibliothèque*, "library") is a small orthographic imperfection. It is indicative of the missing information in the history of French North Carolina. The enigma of Madame Deon adds to our mysterious French North Carolina story.

The Craven area became a destination for other French Huguenots. Many of the settlers did not make it through the first years and died of famine and disease. Those who survived settled in as farmers, artisans, and merchants. They were reliable members of the frontier community. They grew their families and were content with their new habitat. They could live a decent life and worship freely. Men like Boyd, Archdale, and others are to be commended for their open-mindedness and fair treatment of the French immigrants in North Carolina.

Along with Charles de Sailly, Pastor Claude Philippe de Richebourg was one of the leaders of the French Huguenot frontier settlement at Manakin Town. Richebourg was a catalyst in the French colonization of the Craven area. He was born in the town of St. Sevier in the province of Berry, France, around 1670. He fled France in 1699 to avoid persecution and went to London. In 1699, he married Anne Chastain, and they sailed for Virginia on the passenger ship *Mary and Ann* in October 1700. They arrived safely at Manakin Town a few months afterward. The passenger roster lists: "Claude Philippe et sa femme" (Simpson, 19). Richebourg helped settle Manakin Town and eventually became one of the spiritual leaders of the French colony. In 1704, he became the primary minister of the Episcopal Church the French Huguenots had established there.

In 1702, Charles de Sailly left the Manakin Town settlement with several dozen of his followers. They settled on the Trent River in the Craven Precinct. The location is just to the southwest of today's city of New Bern. In 1705, Richebourg, his young family, and a larger group of his followers (several hundred) also migrated south to this warmer climate. It was one that had better agricultural and economic possibilities. Richebourg joined up with Sailly and his group.

There were also political reasons that caused the Manakin Town settlers to leave. The Virginia Lords Proprietors refused to allow the Huguenots to call themselves a colony and required them to use the English language in all communications with the colonial authorities. The French resisted such prejudice and the suppression of their language. There were also religious reasons. There was disagreement between various factions of the settlement on how the colony should be governed and ministered. Manakin Town was not the haven Sailly, Richebourg, and their followers had dreamt of when immigrating to America. They thus made the journey to a destination where they could be free and prosper and established the Trent River colony.

Richebourg was in correspondence with the Baron von Graffenried and knew of the latter's plans to settle a Swiss colony in the Craven area. Richebourg had already traveled to Bath to establish a small French congregation. There he met John Lawson, English explorer and speculator, who suggested settling in the Craven Precinct. It took Richebourg several years of negotiations with the Lords Proprietors for permission to settle a colony in the area. When the migration occurred, several hundred of the Manakin Town French settlers followed Richebourg to Bath. Lawson then guided them to the confluence of the Neuse and Trent rivers.

Sailly and Richebourg had their followers' trust as they broke away from the Manakin Town group and braved the wilderness to reach Lawson's destination. Richebourg was a well-mannered man of high moral character, and one of devoted piety. He also had the forceful personality of a strong leader. He helped establish and became the leader of the first Presbyterian Church in North Carolina. The congregation was initially comprised of the Manakin Town group of French settlers; other French immigrants later joined.

When the French began to settle along the Trent, they were unaware that the Tuscarora were planning to destroy the English settlers who had been kidnapping and enslaving their people. The French Huguenots were unfortunately caught up in something with which they had nothing to do. They also did not believe in slavery. On September 22, 1711, the Tuscarora attacked the colony and massacred one hundred and eleven of Richebourg's followers. As a reaction to this horror, Richebourg decided to relocate to the Santee River in South Carolina. It was a safer area, and there was a well-established colony of French Huguenots who welcomed them. In 1712, some of his group went with him, taking the coastal route through the Cape Fear Valley, near Wilmington, and down to South Carolina. Some of his followers remained on the Trent, however, and made the best of it.

By 1707, farms and plantations, some owned by French Huguenots, began to spread on both sides of the Neuse and Trent rivers. In his *New Voyage to Carolina*, Lawson tells us that the French were very good at making quality linen thread and cloth and that they were well versed in cultivating hemp and flax. They also made wine and brandy from local wild grapes and fruit. They exchanged their material and beverages with their neighboring English settlers for livestock and other goods. Lawson also tells us that "[t]he French give Examples of Industry, which is much wanted in this Country. They make good Flax, Hemp, Linnen-Cloth, and Thread; which they exchange amongst the Neighborhood for other Commodities, for which they have occasion" (Lawson, 120).

Chapter 4. La Colonie Perdue

The French also took advantage of the fertile land along the Trent. They planted corn and wheat, set out orchards, bred cattle, cultivated the vine, and raised sheep to provide wool for their looms. They prospered and got along well with their English neighbors. In the words of one of the Lords Proprietors, "They were sober, frugal, industrious planters and in a short time became independent citizens" (Vass, 49–50). Lawson consulted with the French settlers on how to propagate and tend to grapevines "the French way" (Lawson, 99). He tells us that a "very ingenious French Gentleman" advised him on how to trim his apple and fruit trees (Lawson, 99). The French settlers were instrumental in establishing productive vineyards and orchards for the colony.

The location of the Trent River French colony is two miles southwest of New Bern. It is at the narrowest point on the river where the colonial toll bridge used to stand (Martin, 232). There is scant evidence today of the presence of a French colony along the Trent. However, there is enough to determine the location and identity of a French colony three hundred years ago. This was the area settled by the French from Manakin Town, and it became their American haven.

The area where John Lawson lived is indicated today on the map of New Bern as Lawson's Landing. Lawson tells us that the location of the French colony was two miles west of the land and cabin he occupied. Although in the shadows of various road and highway bypasses, Lawson's Landing today is still a pleasant spot. The wagon road from the west to New Bern passed close to Lawson's front yard. He knew his French neighbors well and admired them.

Other historical accounts mention the location of the settlement. The most detailed was written by Frenchman François Xavier-Martin in 1829 in New Bern and is the most reliable. He spent many years in the town gathering local historical information. He also wrote the first history of North Carolina. We will meet him again in the Beaufort and Notable Names chapters. Here is Xavier-Martin's account of the French: "a number of them began a settlement on Trent River, near the spot, on which a toll bridge was afterward built on that stream" (Martin, 232). Another account corroborates Martin's, citing the location as being two miles from New Bern "where the old county bridge stood" (Vass, 49).

Today, there is a "Bridge Creek," which runs into the Trent two miles from Lawson's Landing at the narrowest point on the river. This is the most likely location for a bridge. The bridge no longer exists, and no map of colonial New Bern has it listed. However, remnants of the wagon road that led to it and the wooden bulwarks remain. It is here that the French settlement was located: near today's Trent Woods and Pembroke Ferry residential areas. Graffenried's 1710 map of the Craven area indicates the farms

Lawson's Landing (photograph by the author).

and homes of his Swiss settlers. There is a blank spot on the map that is at the same location where the French colony had settled a few years before Graffenried's arrival. Graffenried's map is housed in the public library of Bern, Switzerland, although one may view a 1914 copy of it at Tryon Palace.

Nearby, across the Trent, is a location called "Brice's Creek." John Fonville II (the French name Fonvielle had been Anglicized) married the

Chapter 4. La Colonie Perdue 59

Location of the French Lost Colony (photograph by the author).

daughter of William Brice, Elizabeth (*aka*, "Brousse"). The name Brice is an Anglicized version of a French surname, which harks back to "Bries," a fifth-century saint and disciple of St. Martin of Tours in northwestern France. There are many French variations of the name Brice, and one of them is Brousse. This family migrated to England after the Norman Conquest and represented the French lineage of the Brice family's ancestry. Brice Fonville built a residence at Brice's Creek and fortified it during the Tuscarora War to protect the settlers. The French, who remained in the area, gathered there and fought for their lives alongside the English colonists against the Tuscarora.

A Craven County land deed of 1764 indicates the latitude and longitude of a hundred-acre plot that is located near today's Brice's Creek. The deed indicates that the land is on the "south side of the Trent at a place called 'French Town'" (State Archives of North Carolina, S.108.638). This spot is near the location of the French colony, as Lawson indicated. By the middle of the 1700s, the French settlement had grown and occupied both sides of the river. It is a fertile area, and much of the land is still cultivated as it was three hundred years ago.

Much of the Trent riverfront near the old bridge crossing is occupied

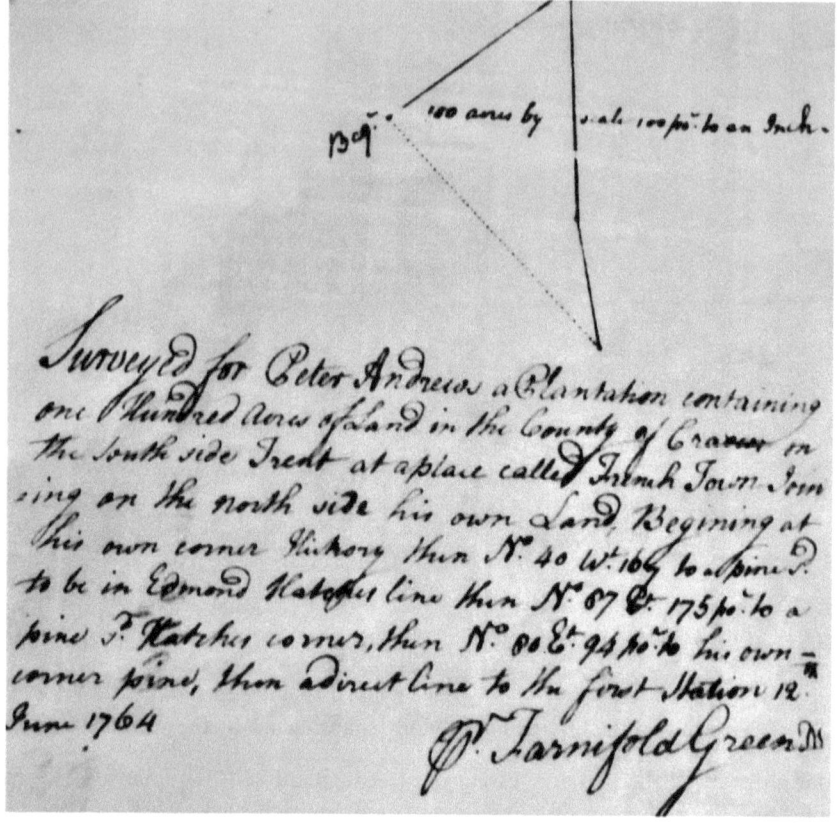

Land deed citing French Town (courtesy of Craven County Register of Deeds).

today by an upscale housing development. One can still admire the area's natural beauty and understand why the French colonists were attracted to this pastoral setting. Nearby, the French-named Lake Clermont and Madame Moore Road provide further evidence of French presence in the area. William Maury settled in French Town in 1723. His name was eventually Anglicized to Moore. Before that time, the French would have called the road Rue Madame Maury in honor of his wife. Down the road is Walt Bellamy Drive (in French, *bel ami*, "dear friend").

The French population was small in comparison to the English settlers who eventually became the majority population of Craven County. However, as we will see, French presence in North Carolina is witnessed by land deeds, wills, and cemetery records. French Town was a thriving colony, and its members were among Craven Precinct's early settlers.

As the threat of Indian wars ended, the Huguenot families began to increase and spread westward in search of new land in Jones, Onslow,

Carteret, Duplin, and Lenoir counties. The last three of these counties have names of French origin. The French made significant contributions to the economy and culture during the early days of these counties. Mr. Dennis Jones of Richlands, North Carolina, has conducted extensive research on the French presence in eastern North Carolina. His knowledge of historical geography, genealogy, and migration patterns is impressive. He has documented hundreds of names of French origin in eastern North Carolina; many of them stem from French Town. Appendix 1 contains Mr. Jones's roster of French North Carolina names. We will return to his research in the French North Carolina chapter.

In the Craven County Register of Deeds, there is a land patent for a Monsieur Pierre Baudry, who received a grant in 1707 of five hundred and fifty acres on the Trent. Baudry was one of the Manakin Town settlers. This was a significant landholding, and Monsieur Baudry would undoubtedly have had French brethren working and living on his land. There are other names on the Manakin Town register that appear on church rosters in the Craven area, such as Delamar, Dupuy, Duval, Faison, Fonvielle, Fouquet, Magny, and Paquinet. They testify to French–North Carolina migration and settlement.

The land deed of a Monsieur Barry is the one referenced by Victor Jones. It is a unique document that tells of a more subtle French presence in the area. Monsieur Barry himself writes it. His full name is the dignified "Adrian-Marie Magdelaine Barry." However, Adrian Barry was a common man who could not write in English and wrote in imperfect French. The document shows the rough handwriting and flawed grammar of a semieducated farmer. The document concerns Barry's receipt of two-thirds of the estate of "Monsieur St. Leger" and bequeathing it to "Madame Marie St. Leger" so she can "en jouis commerce d'usage," poor grammar roughly translated as "to use as she pleases." That is the end of the document. One of the witnesses was a "Peter Henrion" of Huguenot descent who spoke both French and English and served as an interpreter between the notary and Monsieur Barry.

There is no other known mention in any state archive of Monsieur Barry. He becomes as obscure as the Monsieur de Lobbinière of Miss Tryon's letter, lost in time. The document testifies, however, to a more ingrained level of a French presence in the area—that of the common man. Surely, there would have been more of such French transactions in the area. Some took place off the record with a handshake and exchange of cash. Let us keep in mind too that many French land deeds as well as birth, marriage, and death certificates burned when the New Bern courthouse was set ablaze by the Tuscarora during the war. The French citizenry comprised no more than 5 percent of the area's population at the time, but it was an integral part of the community.

French land deed of Monsieur Adrian Barry (1793, courtesy of Craven County Register of Deeds).

One French settler about whom we do have a fair amount of knowledge is Jean Dieppe, whose name was Anglicized to John Depp. He was naturalized as an English citizen in Manakin Town in 1704, along with Sailly, Richebourg, and one hundred and forty-eight other men. Unfortunately, no ship roster listing his name on it has been found, nor do we know precisely where he hailed from in France. His name is a modification of the French city, "Dieppe," located in the Seine-Maritime region in northeastern France on the English Channel. One presumes that he was from this region since it is a common name there. There were Huguenots in the area with the name Dieppe, and they sailed out of the port town Boulogne-sur-Mer to escape France.

The next trace of John Depp that we have is when his name appears on the 1712 "tithable list" of the Trent settlement. Depp was in the Craven area during the Tuscarora War with his wife and family. They were among the fortunate survivors of the massacres. His name appears in the minutes of a 1713 local council meeting in Chowan. The document explains that Depp was to be paid five shillings to replace a handsaw that had been taken to help fell trees to make fortifications by the militia during the war. Yes, this is the same lineage of the contemporary actor Johnny Depp, who is of French Huguenot ancestry. Pierre Deppe (Peter Depp), John's brother, also settled in Manakin Town but remained in Virginia. He is Johnny Depp's direct ancestor.

Chapter 4. La Colonie Perdue

A Craven County land deed of January 1714 documents the first land purchased by Depp as follows: "William Brice of Bath County Province, for twenty pounds sterling, sold to John Depp planter of the county aforesaid 200 acres lying on the west side of Brice's Creek beginning at a corner old oak tree next to Robert Coleman." It is no coincidence that this land is in the area that became French Town. John Depp's 1724 will shows that he had other significant landholdings. He allotted them to his wife Penelope, sons John and Peter, and his daughter Anne. Cameron Allen has carried out extensive work on many generations of Depp's descendants, some of whom live today in the area. John Depp was an integral part of the French "lost colony." However, is the colony truly lost? Just north of today's city of Jacksonville, the town of Depp commemorates the name of Jean Dieppe of France.

We have no eyewitness accounts of the customs and culture of the Trent River settlement. Still, there is ample documentation on the Manakin Town colonists of Virginia and those of the Santee River colony in South Carolina, especially concerning agriculture. The Trent River French colony planted corn and wheat for their basic sustenance needs, vegetable gardens, and various fruit trees. Wild fruits, chiefly raspberries, blueberries, and grapes grew in the area and were gathered during the summer. There was not much orchard fruit, although some seedling trees were brought from France, planted, and thrived in the fertile soil of North Carolina. The Huguenots also raised cows to make milk, butter, and cheese. An abundance of game and fish was at their disposal.

The French were adept at making cider, wine, and brandy. The English have always been keen on good French wine, and the Huguenots traded it for their livestock needs. The fact that there are land deeds with French landowners and French names on church registers throughout the 1700s attests to the fact that what began as frontier subsistence farming became successful plantation enterprises. The French Huguenots were also allowed to worship freely and were content with their new lives. For decades, the French colony preserved its individuality, spoke its own language, and enjoyed its Old World customs. Gradually, the French intermarried with the more numerous English and became Anglicized. This became the French North Carolina ancestry of so many folks Down East.

The French Town settlers lived in simple log cabins covered with pine or cypress shingles. In the humid climate of eastern North Carolina, open porches were added, which reflected the influence of the French West Indies. As more settlers came, the French colonial cabin style became more prevalent. This method of construction used a heavy timber frame of logs installed vertically on a sill (*poteaux-sur-solle*) or into the earth (*poteaux-en-terre*). An infill of lime mortar or clay mixed with small stones (*pierrotage*) or a mixture of mud, moss, and animal hair (*bousillage*) was used to pack between the logs. It was a rustic, practical, but ingenious method of frontier construction. The homes consisted of one or two rooms with floors of dirt covered with animal skins. The homemade furniture consisted of beds, a few chairs, some wooden chests, and a table. It was a rough but natural life. The settlers ate organically and seasonally, hunted and salted their own game and fish, and lived wholesomely.

Tallow made from various types of fat and grease were made into candles. A spinning wheel and handloom would have been familiar to most French families. Many were expert spinners and weavers, making clothes out of the hemp and flax they grew. Most of the footwear was made at home, usually from deer hide. In the winter, the settlers wore *bottes sauvages* (oiled moccasin boots) with thick socks made from coarse homespun yarn. In the summer, the women and children usually went barefoot, and the men wore clogs made of cowhide to work in the fields or forests. The young Huguenots learned the survival skills of weaving and farming at an early age. Most importantly, for the French Town settlers, they could worship together with no fear of retribution. They worked hard to maintain their native language and culture and to keep together their immediate and extended families.

Regarding culinary practices, the settlers consumed the essential frontier diet of what they hunted, caught, and cultivated, but with a flair based on regional French cooking. French colonial cuisine was characterized by the skillful use of sauces, the liberal use of wine and herbs, and expertise in confectionery items. The French colonists prepared soups and stews such as "Rendezvous Stew," made with water, dried peas, onion, and any sort of fowl (Mitchell, 4). They made jerky from deer or turkey, and they were experts at making one of their favorite items, *boudin* (seasoned blood sausage).

The French women were skillful bakers and made a variety of corn and flour bread as well as biscuits. They baked corn cakes in the Indian fashion from ground maize. Salt pork was a staple during the winter, and the settlers put up a supply of smoked eels each autumn from the Trent River. The Huguenot children were often served *pain perdu* ("lost bread"), the ancestor of French Toast (slices of stale bread dipped in beaten eggs and sweetened milk then cooked in butter or animal fat). Dessert items consisted of macaroons, custards, and fruit compotes. Frontier life was a hard one. The French propensity to cook well-prepared food helped make day-to-day existence a bit more bearable. The French knew how to civilize the wilderness in this small way.

The 1850 census of Craven County lists fourteen families with French names, some of whom were descendants of the original Trent River colony.

Chapter 4. La Colonie Perdue

The names Fonville, Gilbert, Foy, and Delamar appear repeatedly. This is a testament to the small but vivid presence of the French over one hundred and fifty years after their arrival. Remnants of the Fonville plantation north of New Bern are still in existence. We will learn more about the Fonville family in the next chapter. Today the phone directories of Craven County list dozens of families with names of French origin. Some of these names appeared on the Manakin Town roster and were members of the French Town settlement, such as Duval, Foy, Du Pré, and Fonvielle. The French names in the phone directories of Craven County and surrounding counties are summarized in appendix 2.

We know that some of the settlers of the French Town colony left for South Carolina with Richebourg. Nevertheless, some remained, and we can appreciate their legacy. Then, there is another group of Huguenots: those that followed Richebourg to South Carolina. They would have known John LaPierre. LaPierre came to South Carolina in 1708 and was a young colleague of Richebourg. He served in South Carolina until 1728. He was a French Huguenot, born in LaSalle, France. John's father was Charles LaPierre, who married Jeanne Roque. Charles was a prosperous bourgeois and emerged as a Huguenot leader and Protestant minister in the late 1600s. He eventually served as minister for the "Chapel of Spring Garden" in London.

Charles's first wife, Jeanne, died in France as a Huguenot martyr. He then married Madeline Le Noir, who became young Jean's stepmother. Charles left France in 1700 and sent Jean as a pensioner to Trinity College in Dublin. His name is now Anglicized. John received a classical education and could read, speak, and write English and French fluently. He later married an English woman, Susanna, who was blind and whose last name is not known; the couple had five children. John LaPierre dedicated his life to the service of others. Having known emotional trauma at a young age due to his mother's violent death, LaPierre was a resilient man. He worked tirelessly to alleviate the suffering of his followers on the harsh colonial frontier. The fact that he married a blind woman shows genuine love and dedication.

John was one of the earliest clergymen of the Church of England in the colony. The Society sponsored him for the "Propagation of the Gospel in Foreign Parts." LaPierre braved the hardships of the colonial experience, as had his mentor Richebourg. They were educated men, but also hardy ones. In 1728, LaPierre was sent to North Carolina to found St. Philip's Church on the Cape Fear River in Brunswick and the St. James Church in Wilmington. Some of his congregation went with him. Among them were descendants of the Trent River colony who had followed Richebourg to South Carolina. Some will end up back in New Bern a few years later in a strange circular migration pattern. They will be reunited with extended family members from the early days along the Trent.

John LaPierre (photograph by the author).

LaPierre and his followers imprint another French North Carolina presence Down East. Let us also remember that the French letter of Margaret Tryon was written in the 1770s when Governor Tryon was temporarily residing in Wilmington during the final stages of the construction of Tryon Palace. She asks Mr. Lobbinière to meet her at the St. James Church. Some forty years after LaPierre established the church, the French were still frequenting it. This attests to their presence in the Wilmington region, one to which we will return.

In 1734, LaPierre took his ministry to Craven County and helped establish the Christ Church Parish in New Bern in 1741. LaPierre became the church leader and conducted services, ministered to the congregation, and provided educational instruction for children. He also frequently traveled throughout the area. He offered sermons in English and French. There were still enough French-speaking colonists to warrant sermons in their language. He purchased acreage ten miles west of New Bern and a home in town on Jones Street. LaPierre endured poverty both in New Bern and Brunswick Town and had to grow his own crops at times when he was not paid enough by the congregations. He would work in the fields on blazing hot summer days to support his family. This benevolent man, so educated and intelligent, was not above hard labor.

The people knew LaPierre as a sage and generous person, especially in the autumn of his life. He ministered to an extensive territory that extended into Onslow and Jones counties. He was instrumental in the organization of more than twenty churches. Among them are the Grace Episcopal Church in Trenton, St. Paul's Church in Vanceboro, and St. Mary's Church in Kinston. He would be away from home for several weeks at a time as he visited the regional churches to preach and conduct marriage services, baptisms, and last rites. As an educator, he taught hundreds of children over the years.

He was a model human being, a backbone of frontier communities who so needed his comforting words and kind deeds. In the words of W. Keats Sparrow: "His grandfatherly figure must have been a familiar and welcome sight to the many—young and old—who were touched by his ministry, instruction, and example" (Sparrow, 3). The last mention of LaPierre in the New Bern Assembly minutes is January 1755. He was buried either in the Christ Church or Fordham-Bryan cemetery. In 1968, descendants placed markers in the latter to commemorate John and Martha LaPierre. In 1976, a plaque was placed in the Christ Church Parish House to memorialize his ministry.

There are numerous descendants of Jean LaPierre living today in North Carolina. In the late 1730s, one daughter, Susanna, married John Riggs and another, Martha, married Benjamin Fordham, Sr., of Craven County. Benjamin was a planter, colonial soldier, and officer in the North Carolina Assembly. Many North Carolinians descend from LaPierre through the Fordhams. In a 1740 land deal with John Fonvielle Jr., John LaPierre exchanged his Cape Fear properties for three hundred and sixty acres on the Neuse Road at Batchelder Creek. The land exchange shows former countrymen sticking together in the New World after nearly two generations. When Martha LaPierre married John Riggs, her dowry was a land deed for sixteen acres at Batchelder Creek. The French roots are deep in Craven County, and many Riggs descend from LaPierre through John and Martha.

The Brunswick Town Historic Site is a bucolic site on a bluff overlooking the Cape Fear River; located on a commercial waterway, it was a thriving town in the 1700s. Ruins of St. Philip's Church still stand. N.C. marker number D-73, near Winnabow, reminds us of LaPierre and his followers from French Town. LaPierre's mission was to help civilize the rough colonial social environment, using religion to do so. His brand of religion, formed by his Huguenot background, was one tempered with an enlightened, philosophical view, the heart of the Huguenot mindset. In a letter to the bishop of London, LaPierre called the Carolina region "a lawless place … with scattered people" that needed a "parsonage to receive them" (Weeks, Vol. III, 342). LaPierre was a man of vision and a strong leader. The

Huguenots that followed him became members of the thriving community of Brunswick Town.

Brunswick Town today recalls of a missing chapter in North Carolina history. Ruins of the town in the shadows of the church's brick framework remind us of the story of French North Carolina. Near the LaPierre marker, there are two gravesites with the names John and Elizabeth Guerard. They were French Huguenot members of LaPierre's church and among the original settlers of Brunswick Town. Mr. Guerard is praised for his "Industry and Temperance" and "Social and Domestic Virtues." The French Huguenots left France for a better life, and some of them found it under LaPierre's guidance. After the trials and tribulations of two generations of migration from France, to England, to Manakin Town, to French Town, and finally to the area of today's Brunswick County, many of them found their home.

As the French spread out, some settled just to the east of today's Wilmington, and some moved northward. The French presence in the area has traces of the trail from the Trent River to Brunswick County with French-named towns such as Belville, Clairmont, Leland, Lanval, and Navassa. Navassa was named after La Navasse, a small island near the former French colony Haiti. It was one rich with guano phosphate, an element essential in the making of organic fertilizer. French transport ships were a frequent occurrence in the importing of phosphate to the Navassa Guano Factory. In the 1800s, the area had significant success, and the French played a role in it as workers, merchants, and shippers. The phosphate industry was central to the success of agriculture in the state.

These French of "lost colony" ancestry were among the founding citizens of these towns. The French Huguenots, who settled in Brunswick County, extended the growth of the French Huguenot presence in the colonial period. We will soon explore the possibility that descendants of some of the Brunswick area French families played a role in another intriguing instance of French–North Carolina migration. These descendants of the French Town settlement may have helped a desperate group of French refugees from Haiti find refuge inland at Crusoe Island during the early 1800s.

The Huguenots found a way to work in harmony under the Crown of England and the shadow of a dominant English culture. Their religious beliefs of tolerance and hard work allowed them to integrate themselves successfully with the English. The history of the French North Carolinians in Craven County has been subsumed under the dominant narrative of the English colonization of North Carolina. I do not mean to detract from the critical work of Dill and Watson. Their research is authoritative. This project could not have been undertaken without it. Their work was my starting point. I simply pieced together another layer of the state's history, one that was not their primary focus.

Chapter 4. La Colonie Perdue

It was never easy for the Huguenots who migrated to Carolina. At times, they faced unfair treatment by the English majority. Nevertheless, they managed to thrive and are a worthy topic of study. Remnants of the "lost colony" are alive and well in the Craven and Brunswick areas. The full story of the Trent River settlement is still shrouded in mystery. Without the discovery of more primary documents, which are few and far between, it will remain so. Nevertheless, we have seen that the French colony is not "lost" at all but rather embedded in the ancestral fabric of the state's history.

Brice's Creek, location of French Town (photograph by the author).

Chapter 5

New Bern

The city of New Bern in Craven County is located at the confluence of the Trent and Neuse rivers. It was settled by German-speaking Swiss immigrants in 1710 under the guidance of Baron Christoph von Graffenried of the town of Worb, Switzerland, in the canton of Bern. John Lawson had surveyed the area and proposed the site to the baron. Also involved in Graffenried's enterprise was his French-speaking fellow Swiss man, Franz Michel. Graffenried knew of the French Trent River colony and met some of its members. He was able to converse in French with them, a language that he spoke along with German and English.

The French–North Carolina connection also had some negative aspects. During the journey across the Atlantic, one of Graffenried's ships was attacked by French privateers who stole most of the Swiss travelers' belongings. In his account of establishing the settlement, Graffenried writes: "one of the vessels, loaded with the best goods and the most well-to-do colonists, had the misfortune to be assailed and plundered by a French captain at the very mouth of the James River" (Weeks, Vol. I, 909). This occurred with a British ship in sight, but one whose masts had been removed for repair. The French marauders robbed the vessel right under the nose of their archrivals.

Graffenried and his settlement learned how to survive in their new habitat. They saw what the French were doing, especially concerning agricultural techniques. The French gladly shared the information and were happy to have Swiss neighbors as they had in France. We can only imagine the conversations they had. They were impromptu and informal, and there is no record of them.

Graffenried's colony struggled to survive. It was finally dispersed as a result of the Tuscarora War. Graffenried fled his failed colony and returned to Switzerland. The Swiss stayed together and intermarried for several generations. Then, many were eventually subsumed by the English majority. Nevertheless, the Swiss ancestry of the Craven area remains alive today. Along with the French, Swiss culture and heritage added to the area's multicultural social fabric.

Chapter 5. New Bern

As we saw in the previous chapter, the French had a presence in the Craven area. One of the most prominent among them, after Monsieur Baudry, was Jean Fonvielle. He was born in the eastern French province of Lorraine in 1679 and died in Craven County in 1741. His father, Jean, became a successful merchant in the town of Mazères in the southwest region of Ariège. He died when Jean was in his early teens as a result of the French Huguenot persecution. Jean fled to England along with his brother Pierre and sisters Magdelaine and Marie. He married another Huguenot refugee, Françoise l'Amy, in London in 1699. In 1701, Jean and Françoise took the passenger ship *Nassau* with a group of Huguenot colonists bound for Manakin Town.

Pierre would come at a later time and eventually join his brother in North Carolina. There is no record that Jean's sisters traveled to America. A Manakin Town church registry lists Jean as a vestryman from 1701 to 1705. He and his wife had three sons, Jean the Younger, Thomas, and Cornelius. Jean the Elder moved to the Craven area around 1705 with the Richebourg group. He would have been a man of resources. He was the first-born son and most likely the sole recipient of his father's estate. A map of New Bern from 1744 shows a plot of six hundred and forty acres that Jean purchased in 1713. This land would become the Fonvielle plantation that was overseen by generations of Jean the Elder's descendants.

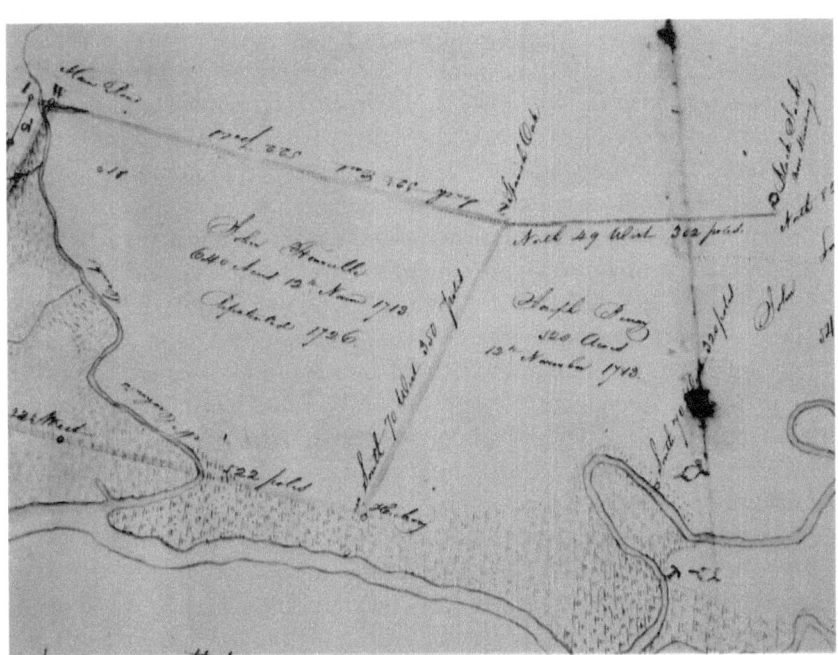

Jean Fonvielle's plantation (courtesy State Archives of North Carolina).

Françoise died in 1709, and Jean remarried in 1714 to an Englishwoman, Sarah Anne Graves. The couple had two more children, Anne and Priscilla. Thus begins the lineage of the Carolina Fonville ancestry, which has been carefully documented by family genealogists. Today the name Fonville is a common one that appears all over North Carolina. In written documents, we can see the gradual Anglicizing of the Fonvielle family name, although Jean preserved his heritage and taught French to his children and grandchildren. A French immigrant, Jean learned enough English to function in a predominantly English-speaking colony. He also was proud of his ancestry and passed the language down to his children, who would, in turn, do the same to their children and so forth. This is typical of many minority immigrant families who remain bilingual for a few generations before the dominant culture linguistically subsumes them.

Evidence that the Fonville family maintained its native tongue can be seen in the accomplishments of Jean's descendants. In 1751, Jean's grandson, Francis Marion Fonville, enlisted in the state militia during the French and Indian War. He later served as an interpreter for the Marquis de Lafayette during the Revolutionary War. We will see more of Francis, and other Fonvilles who served in the war, in the Revolutionary Allies chapter. The Anglicizing of the name "Fonvielle," like those of many of the first French settlers, was inevitable. Jean and Françoise's first son would come to be known as John Fonville. He was a successful plantation owner, churchwarden, and prominent citizen in the Craven area for decades until his death in 1773.

John was born in 1701 in Manakin Town and traveled with his family as a child to the Craven area. In 1733, he married Elizabeth Brousse, daughter of Jacques Brousse and Sara Le Cornu. They, too, were Manakin Town settlers. Their families originally came from the southwest region of Languedoc, France. Another origin of the Brousse family name can be traced to the *castle Brousse-le-Château* as far back as 975. One of Jacques Brousse's sons, Peter, eventually migrated to and settled in Halifax County. Jacques and Sara traveled on the ship the *Mary and Ann* to reach Manakin Town in 1700. They came to the Craven area around the same time as the Fonvielle family. One of the sons of John and Elizabeth Brousse was named the Anglicized Brice Fonville, whom we saw in the La Colonie Perdue chapter. He also became a prominent citizen and the patriarch of the extended family until his death on the plantation in 1780.

Fonville cemeteries were discovered in 1993 by the current landowners of what was the original plantation. There were purported to have been three small graveyards, but only two have been found. This discovery has been documented by Mr. John Green of the Kellenberger Library in New Bern. The gravesites, dating from the 1830s and 1840s, mark the lives of descendants, seven or eight generations removed, of Jean Fonvielle of Mazères: Elizabeth (1843), Richard (1838), and Price (1830), among them.

There are other family gravestones, but the names have faded with time and are illegible. The two gravesites are near each other, at a tranquil, verdant spot on the edge of a field under a grove of oak trees, a stone's throw from the nearby creek. Today, the path to the graveyard is overgrown, and the graves are challenging to access: a metaphor for how hidden the story of French North Carolina has been until now. In the evening, the eastern Carolina wind whispers over the distant grandchildren of Jean and Françoise Fonvielle.

Today, the location of the Fonville plantation has not changed much. It is still a peaceful agricultural area twelve miles to the northwest of New Bern on a country road. The creek that runs through the plantation is Batchelder's Creek, the Anglicized version of *Bachelier*, its original French name. It is just to the south of the Neuse River. A trail named Alonza French winds through the nearby cotton fields, and the road Quartre Circle borders the creek. Remnants of French North Carolina are inscribed in the area's very place names: evidence of our original French settlers in the 1700s.

Another instance of French North Carolina presence in this locale is the plantation with a French name, *Bellair*. The breeze from the nearby Neuse River inspired the plantation's name, translated into English as "pleasant air." Bellair is located just south of the former Fonville land. The mansion (French, *maison*, "house") was built in 1719; it is the largest brick plantation in the state and a stellar example of the Georgian style of the pre–Revolutionary period. The Georgian style, chiefly characterized by symmetry and proportion, was, in part, influenced by the French neoclassical style; the Palace of Versailles is the most well-known example. The Georgian style used artistic flourishes such as cornices embellished with decorative molding, characteristic of the French rococo.

An Englishman, John Lovick, was the original owner of the plantation and had the house built in 1719. There were various owners over the years. The Richardson family purchased the Bellair Plantation in 1838, and it has remained in the family since that time. Today the home stands in its original splendor, approached by two small roads lined by old cedar trees. The imposing eight-paneled front door is handcrafted woodwork. Bellair is reminiscent of a French country home. In 1859, survey maps were made of Bellair for John Richard Lewish *French*, Esq. (emphasis added). The French North Carolina phenomenon appears time and again in so many surprising ways.

The Bellair Plantation collection, housed at East Carolina University, contains historical materials from 1719 to 1910, including newspapers, periodicals, legal records, letters, livestock magazines, and more. The legal papers contain hundreds of land deeds and legal briefs. They document the transfer of property to various individuals and disputes of ownership over the centuries. There are boundary disputes and land transactions of Jean Fonvielle in the collection. The Bellair Plantation borders the southern extremity of the Fonville plantation. The name Bellair was most likely named by the French living in the vicinity, or maybe by Fonvielle himself.

On the land of Bellair was a cemetery that was destroyed when marl pits (a calcium carbonate used as a soil conditioner) were created during the 1940s. Some of the names on the gravestones were as follows: Jeremiah Fonvielle (1782–1852), Mary Brock Fonvielle (1790–1853), and Mary Fonvielle French (1807–45). This shows the long lineage of Fonvilles living on and around the Bellair Plantation well into the nineteenth century.

John Fonville had his own bucolic estate, one that was economically successful. John Fonville's will of 1773 offers us insight into the standing of the family at the time of John's passing. John bequeathed to his wife and sons hundreds of acres of land, slaves, household items, china, furniture, pewter ingots, livestock, horses, plantation tools, and his rifle. The will is several pages long and shows the extensive holdings and properties of the Fonville family. Today, most of the area of the old Fonville plantation is still productive farmland. The only traces of the Fonville family are the gravesites and a dilapidated house dating from the 1800s that has been left to stand. The old home provides a haunting reminder of the decay that time inflicts upon the past and how so much history has been lost to us.

Jean Fonvielle was a courageous and resourceful man. He fled persecution in France for his religious beliefs and made his way to London. He then braved the dangerous sea voyage across the Atlantic. He and his wife survived the difficult years at Manakin Town. Having preserved his father's inheritance carefully, he was able to establish himself successfully. He settled in and watched his family grow and thrive. Jean Fonvielle is an icon of French North Carolina.

There are other instances of French presence in New Bern and the vicinity. In 1765, a French traveler found New Bern "a lively place" (Watson, *A History of New Bern and Craven County* 60). As the colonial capital, the town was a regular destination for French tourists, merchant ships, and speculators. Let us remember that the first regular minister in New Bern was a Frenchman, John LaPierre, "quite in keeping with the multi-ethnic character of the area" (Dill, 484). There is evidence that LaPierre's first services, before the building of New Bern's first church, were held in Jean Fonvielle's home located at today's Union Point Park. The park is at the southeastern part of today's New Bern on the Neuse waterfront. It has as magnificent a view today as it did when LaPierre preached there to his

The Fonvielle plantation today (photograph by the author).

French congregation. One can imagine how inspiring it must have been to worship at this location.

Other documents attest to the fact that there were more than, as Dill claims, only a few French families in the area. There is a legal brief of John and Suzanna LaPierre bequeathing parcels of land near Batchelder's Creek to their grandchildren. There are land deeds on file with the French names Chareron, Pettiver, Buset, Dupuis, Barbez, and Falleau among them. There is also a 1714 "Craven Precinct Tuscarora War Claims" that lists compensation claims for losses suffered during the war to be paid by the local legislature. On the list are the French names of Dupuye, Marten, Barden, Depries, and Fonville. At the onset of the Revolutionary War, New Bern swarmed with Frenchmen: patriotic volunteers, deserters from French ships, and fortune hunters. In 1777, the French came to New Bern in significant numbers. We will return to this wave of French influx into New Bern and the Craven area in the Revolutionary Allies chapter.

The crown jewel of colonial New Bern's French legacy is the Tryon Palace's collection of French art, books, household items, and written

Inventory of the Fonvielle estate (courtesy Craven County Register of Deeds).

documents. William Tryon was a British officer and colonial administrator. He became governor of North Carolina in 1764. He commissioned an elegant palace to be built with the ten thousand pounds allotted him by the precinct's legislature. It was a considerable sum at the time. Englishman John Hawks designed the Georgian-style mansion. Claude Sauthier, who had come to North Carolina with Governor Tryon on a commission to survey and map the town, was involved in designing the palace gardens.

Tryon was a wealthy, educated, and cultured English gentleman, the son of a Surrey aristocratic family. He served in the military and spent several years in northern France during the Seven Years War. Tryon spoke and wrote fluent French and knew firsthand the refinement of French culture. His wife, Margaret Weeks, was a landed heiress who brought a substantial dowry of thirty thousand pounds to the marriage. She was a woman of discerning taste, thoroughly versed in English as well as French aristocratic culture. William and Margaret oversaw the construction and furnishing of the palace.

Chapter 5. New Bern

Business transaction of William Brice Fonvielle (courtesy Craven County Register of Deeds).

Tryon brought in specialized workers from Philadelphia. There were French among them. They had the knowledge and skills, lacking in North Carolina at the time, to build such a high-quality building. They had learned their crafts as apprentices in their homeland. The palace, with its European-style brick masonry, hand-carved woodwork, and interior plastering and finishing, was an exceptional structure. When completed, the Tryon Palace was a "monument of opulence and elegance extraordinary in the American colonies" (Bisher, 55–56). Atop the palace's door was a gilded sculpture symbolic of the English monarchy, one that displayed the French inscription: *Dieu Et Mon Droit* ("God And My Right"). The words hark back to the centuries during which the English court and nobility spoke Norman French.

Palace furnishings were imported from England and France. At the time, French decorative items, books, household implements, paintings, and engravings were at the peak of their beauty and luxury. They display the elegance of what were to be final decades of the French aristocracy, the *Ancien Régime*, before the French Revolution. The household furnishings of French provenance were typical of those of an English aristocratic family such as that of William and Margaret Tryon. The Tryons also brought with them a French chef, Pierre LeBlanc. The dinner table, as the palace's replica shows today, displays a blend of English and French colonial cuisine. Highlights include sautéed doves, braised rabbit, a cabbage beef torte, a meringue cake, and a tart made of small pancakes with fruit compote. Beverages included French cordials, wines, and brandies.

Tryon lived in the palace for only a year before moving to New York to become governor of that state. Many of the palace furnishings were personal belongings of the Tryon family and were transported with them to their new residence. The palace was consumed by fire in 1798 and reconstructed during the 1950s. Today, nothing remains of the original palace except the stable offices. Few of the original furnishings have been found. Today's Tryon Palace Historic Site was rebuilt and furnished to replicate the original mansion. It contains a significant collection of French items that would have been typical of the palace's furnishings during the Tryon family's residence there.

The Tryon Palace Collection contains over one hundred and twenty-five items of French provenance: maps of Europe, rare books, engravings, andirons, curtains, quilts, paintings, china, candlesticks, written documents, and more. Some highlights of the collection are as follows: a gracefully designed 1737 edition of the complete theatrical works of the renowned seventeenth-century actor and playwright Molière; delicate enamel wine labels with silver chains; an engraving of George Washington by the French artist Noel Le Mire; a graceful oval shaving bowl with French proverbs stamped in gilded lettering; the private memoirs of the Countess Adelaide de Sancerre; several books on the customs of Native Americans (*Moeurs des Sauvages Amériquains*); and letters written in elegant French and the marvelous penmanship of William Tryon. One of Tryon's letters is to a Frenchman, Monsieur Joseph de Montfort, a wealthy acquaintance, asking him for a donation of five hundred pounds for the erecting of public schools and the purchasing of glebes. This is an instance of the English and French working together to improve life in colonial society.

One sampling of the richness of the collection can be found in the

Chapter 5. New Bern

The Theatrical Works of Molière (courtesy Tryon Palace, New Bern, NC).

description of an eighteenth-century quilt from the collection's inventory list: "large quilt used as a bedspread, of antique quilted blue and white check of flame (*flamme*) pattern. The reverse side is brocaded in wool with detached woven flowers in red and green on a soft yellow linen ground" (Tryon Palace Archives). Also of note are framed colored engravings of birds from the Comte de Buffon's *Histoire des Oiseaux*. They are detailed and elegant depictions of birds from around the world. Finally, there is the Miss Tryon note on delicate faded beige stationery that always brings a smile when read with its charming, yet imperfect French, of an English teenager.

Perhaps the most noteworthy item in the Tryon Palace Collection relevant to our topic is a seventeenth-century French engraving depicting the renewal of the alliance between King Louis XIV of France and the Swiss Cantons. Governor Antoine von Graffenried, one of the Swiss ambassadors, attended the ceremony. The engraving reworked a well-known painting by Louis XIV's royal painter Charles le Brun. The scene takes place at Versailles and is a lavish one. The engraving's gold-leaf wooden frame displays elegant decorations that include angels, birds, and mythological symbols.

Antoine von Graffenried was an attendee at the ceremony. Antoine was born in Bern, Switzerland, in 1631; his grandson is the very Christoph von Graffenried, who founded New Bern. In a strange transatlantic circular pattern, Graffenried has come to live in this French engraving housed at Tryon Palace in the town founded by his grandson. The French–North Carolina connection never ceases to surprise. Let us also remember that it was Louis XIV's Edict of Fontainebleau outlawing freedom of religion that prompted hundreds of thousands of Huguenots to leave France. Ironically, without Louis's cruel decree, they most likely would not have immigrated to America and settled in North Carolina. Louis XIV's image is now nestled in French North Carolina that was, in part, his unintended creation.

There are two landscape design maps on file at Tryon drawn by Sauthier in 1769 that show two different garden plans for the palace. It is not known if the gardens were planted at the time of Tryon's residence there. Sauthier was not only a skilled cartographer but also well versed in garden design. His teachers were Dezallier d'Argenville and Jean Baptiste le Blond. The latter studied with the master garden designer of Versailles, André le Nôtre. Horticultural and landscape specialists have since made educated guesses about the design of the gardens in their re-creations of them.

In 1991, palace researchers discovered another plan—one also attributed to Sauthier. Sauthier's design was that of the French neoclassical rectilinear style. It is one of geometric shrub and floral patterns, formal tree plantations, a concentric arrangement of Greco-Roman sculptures, and graceful walking paths. The garden displays symmetry, balance, grace, and harmony, qualities dear to the French aesthetic eye. The design also has a plan for a lane and an open lawn running from Pollock Street to the palace courtyard. There are formal parterres that extend behind the palace to the Trent River. The design is reminiscent of the Jardin des Tuileries in Paris. There is no evidence that this plan, which had been lost for over two centuries, was ever implemented. Today, the exquisite garden designed by Sauthier has been restored for us to marvel at and enjoy.

Other gardens at Tryon Palace were assembled in the French fashion, following some of the details of the Sauthier design. Maude Moore Latham of New Bern and, after her passing in 1951, May Gordon Kellenberger of Greensboro were both instrumental in the building reconstruction and garden restoration of Tryon Palace during the 1940s and 1950s. They were educated women of discerning taste who knew much about English and French culture. Kellenberger attended Barnard College, where she studied music, art history, and European languages, French among them. She was instrumental in the gathering of the palace furnishings, especially those of French provenance. She had traveled extensively in France and was well versed in French history and culture.

The path to the Trent that Sauthier designed is symbolic of French North Carolina. It leads southward from the New Bern area toward Route 17, the North Carolina Coastal Highway. The French–North Carolina migration pattern followed this route. Route 17 winds through

Maude Moore Latham Memorial Garden (photograph by the author, Tryon Palace).

Pollocksville and Maysville, passes near Swansboro and Peletier, and eventually reaches Jacksonville and beyond. We will visit these areas in the French North Carolina chapter. Today's phone directories of these towns are sprinkled with French names. Some reach back to the families we met in the La Colonie Perdue chapter, such as Foy, Dupuy, and Delamar, and, of course, Fonville. These current residents are direct descendants of the Manakin Town and French Town settlers.

Just north of Pollocksville is the meticulously preserved Foscue Plantation Home, built in 1824 by Simon Foscue. The home has remained in the same family for eight generations. The English family name Foscue harks back to its original French ancestor, Richard le Fort. He saved William, Duke of Normandy, at the Battle of Hastings in 1066 by protecting him with his shield against a volley of arrows. Richard was thus given the name *Fort Escu* ("strong shield"). Richard Fortescu returned to France, but his son Adam settled in South Devon, England. Generations of English Fortescues descended from this French bloodline. Some migrated to America, and some of those ended up in North Carolina. The name by then had been Anglicized and shortened to Foscue.

The Foscue family was a prominent one in the Pollocksville area during the nineteenth century. Simon's son, Henry, married Gertrude Fonville. She was a member of a successful branch of the Fonville family that had landholdings and business interests in Onslow County. In Stephen E. Bradley's *New Bern District Estate Papers: 1775–1810*, there are legal transactions of John Fonville and John Foscue. In one document, the family names are listed alphabetically next to each other. This is symbolic of the closeness at the time of these two prominent families of French descent in North Carolina.

Mariana Francenia Foscue (photograph by the author).

Gertrude is at rest in a small family graveyard in front of the Foscue historical preservation site. The plantation and home are located on the eastern side of Route 17, a few miles north of Pollocksville. The graveyard is just a few feet from the road and displays the Fonville and Foscue legacies for all to see. The home contains many of its original furnishings. On the second floor, in one of the children's bedrooms, is a small embroidered French quilt. One can only imagine if it belonged to one of the Foscue children in the graveyard, Mariana Francenia, who is buried next to her mother and near Aunt Gertrude.

CHAPTER 6

French and Indian War

The French and Indian War (1754–63) occurred in between the Huguenot migration and the American Revolution. North Carolinians had accepted French Huguenots for over half a century. During the war, however, a negative attitude toward France arose. This creates another layer in the complex history of French North Carolina.

In 1756, military construction began in the eastern part of North Carolina to protect from potential French invasion. Fort Johnston was erected at the mouth of the Cape Fear River. Gun batteries were built on Ocracoke and Topsail Inlets to ward off French naval vessels, marauding French pirates, and mercenary privateers. In 1760, one French privateer sloop from Cape François (today's Haiti) managed to slip into the Ocracoke Inlet and plunder a merchant ship from Boston. The sloop then went to Bath and seized one of the town's merchant ships and took it back to the Caribbean.

This is quite a turnaround from the peaceful Huguenots. These marauding and sometimes murderous French were most unwelcome. There were other such incidents during the middle 1700s, in which the underside of French North Carolina can be seen. It is a dark one of thievery and treachery. Ironically, descendants of French Huguenots were threatened and sometimes attacked by the very people of the country from which they hailed. These upstart French drew the ire of British and French colonists alike.

Fort Dobbs, located in today's Iredell County, was built as a defense against the French and Cherokee Indians with whom the French had allied. In one skirmish, French soldiers disguised themselves as Cherokee fighters to instigate a war with settlers. During another nearby clash, Catawba Indians allied with the English colonists killed two French and three Northward Indians. War spilled French blood that stains the historical ground of the state. It would not be the last time. The fighting between the North Carolina frontiersmen and the French–Cherokee coalition was often intense. Massacres, pillaging, scalpings, and burnings were a regular occurrence.

At one point in the war, the Cherokees were provided firearms by the

French superior to those of the North Carolina militia. This further raised the anger of the English settlers and colonial authorities against the French. It was a tense time for French–American relations in North Carolina. In a letter of February 1759, Governor Arthur Dobbs summarized the dislike that the citizens of the state had for the French during the war: "The next campaign will expel the French from the Continent, that it may be safe from an insatiable and cruel hereditary enemy" (Weeks, Vol. VI, 9).

Francis Marion Fonville was born in 1738. He was the son of John Fonville and Elizabeth Brousse. His name is listed on a 1751 colonial infantry roster for Craven County. In 1754, at the height of the war, Carolina militia regiments were reinforced, and some of the Fonvilles served in it, among them John, Francis, David, and William. John served as an ensign; the others were privates. David was Francis's uncle, and William and John were the latter's brothers.

The Fonvilles were loyal to the cause of their English colony and fought against their former French countrymen. The Fonvilles were bilingual and served not only as soldiers but also as interpreters. The Fonvilles were fighting for the survival of the Carolina colony and contributed to the cause uniquely. Some families related to the Fonvilles also served, such as Slade, Taylor, and McCoy. Most of the militia rosters are lost, and some were never recorded at all. There were other French North Carolinians who served alongside their fellow citizens, the Fonvilles. They, too, fought for their way of life for which they had worked so hard.

When the war ended, the French had been ousted as a fighting force. Most of the French troops retreated to Québec or returned to France, but some veterans chose to remain and settle in eastern North Carolina and elsewhere in the state. These were not educated Huguenots. They were former soldiers and sailors—a rough, but resourceful bunch. They settled into the lives of labor, farming, and commerce, married English colonists, and lived out their lives. They knew that they were welcome to settle in North Carolina if they were peaceful and adopted the customs of the land. The descendants of this group of French add another thread to the fabric of the state's French heritage.

CHAPTER 7

Beaufort

Since the first arrival of French Huguenots in 1709, French settlers, political refugees, pirates, and patriots alike have visited Beaufort. It is North Carolina's third oldest town after Bath and New Bern, and like them, it had a French Huguenot presence. Beaufort is located on an ocean inlet in Carteret County. In colonial times, it was a thriving port, and as we will see, one of diverse cultures. It is purported that one early French traveler referred to the first settlement of Beaufort as a *beau fort* ("handsome fort"), hence the eventual name Beaufort (Xavier-Martin, ix). François Xavier-Martin, a Frenchman from Marseille, put forth this account. Xavier-Martin migrated to North Carolina in his early twenties and became a writer, printer, and lawyer in New Bern. He was overstepping the facts in his claim, most likely out of patriotic pride; yet, there could be some truth to it. More significantly, this Frenchman, who was fluent in English, wrote the first history of the state, another interesting twist in the French–North Carolina connection.

The more commonly accepted reason for the naming of the town is that Henry Somerset, the Duke of Beaufort, settled it. He was a descendant of French Huguenots who migrated to Beaufort, South Carolina, in the 1720s. When he moved to Beaufort, North Carolina, a few years later, he likewise named the town after himself. The English House of Beaufort has descendants that can be traced back to the Royal House of Plantagenet of the English Middle Ages. Therefore, we can understand that the Duke of Beaufort was a man proud of his French–English heritage.

The Plantagenet ancestry, the name Beaufort among it, dates back to the French Counts of Anjou in the Loire Valley region from the 800s. The name is a Gallicized (early French) version of the Latin *planta genista* ("sprig of broom blossom"). It was worn as a crest by and given as a nickname to Geoffrey, Count of Anjou. He was the father of Henry II, who married the French countess Eléonore d'Aquitaine. Eléonore had been a queen of France. She was an independent and powerful woman during the 1200s, a rarity at the time. The name Beaufort was brought to England from

France in the decades that followed the Norman invasion of 1066. This is another instance of the genealogical roots of North Carolina that reach back to medieval France. Beaufort, North Carolina, has the name of ancient pedigree stemming from French nobility.

The mixture of English and French heritage in the name Beaufort is symbolically similar to the French Huguenots in North Carolina. We have seen so far in *The French Heritage of North Carolina* that the French strain is smaller and overshadowed by the dominant English narrative. However, it is there, and we can appreciate it. Beaufort became an arrival port for French refugees coming to settle in North Carolina during the 1700s and 1800s. The first French immigrants who settled there successfully, and the town's French name, made it a welcoming destination for the French who followed.

In 1708, Carteret County began to attract all manner of settlers, the French among them. A few families bought land on the North River, which became the Core Sound settlement. Among those first settlers were the Frenchmen Peter Piver and John Shackelford of English and French descent. Subsequently, other French Huguenots followed these pioneers. Their names were Paquinet, Noé, Magny, Delamar, and Midyette. These families played a prominent role in establishing the town. The unpublished work, "The French Connection," by Beaufort's Mamré Wilson, is essential reading. It traces the genealogies of these families from their first arrivals in Beaufort to the present day.

One of the most prominent of these families is that of Michel Paquinet. He was born on his family's estate near Paris, France, in 1690. Refusing to convert to Roman Catholicism, he left with his inheritance of gold in a strongbox and made his way to London. Michel made the transatlantic sea voyage and arrived in Manakin Town in 1705. He stayed there a few months and, in the same year, left with a group led by the Marquis de Muce to migrate southward. He lived for a year at the Trent River settlement and moved to Beaufort, North Carolina, with his nephew Michael in 1706.

Paquinet was a hardy sea-faring man of some wealth and education. He established a farm and a lumber business and made an excellent living in the timber trade. Paquinet was a prosperous merchant and influential figure in the town's economic growth. This is witnessed by frequent references to him in court and commercial documents of the day. Census records for 1723 in Carteret County list Paquinet as a "Freeholder." The term designates men who owned their land "free and clear" (of debt) and were eligible to be chosen for membership in the county governing body (Fisher, *One Dozen Pre-Revolutionary War Families* 22).

In 1726, he married Mary Bolling of Newport, North Carolina. In the 1730s, he built a house on Front Street in Beaufort that still stands and is lived in today. It is a French American historical and architectural jewel (in French, *un bijou*). Paquinet was a pioneer in Beaufort's maritime trade. He was actively involved in building the town into a thriving port and became a wealthy man. Paquinet's land holdings in 1740 totaled thirteen hundred acres, and his shipping business was thriving. Calico Creek, in today's Morehead City, was named after the imports of calico cloth brought by Paquinet's ships, which were frequently anchored in the creek.

Michel's ships would sail from Beaufort with lumber products to the French West Indies and return with cargoes of French glassware and cloth, calico, sugar, coffee, rum, molasses, and cocoa. Such trade brought economic success and gave Beaufort a European and Caribbean luster. These luxury goods added to the town's cultural diversity. French merchant ships were also part of the lifeline of the colony. They would sail from the French West Indies to Beaufort stocked with the goods listed above. They then returned to France laden with beef, pork, lumber, corn, turpentine, and tar.

The French merchant ships had a French captain, crew, and slaves who spoke French Creole. The officers and crew would frequent the town's inns and taverns. Some of the slaves were sold and integrated into the local slave population. The town was certainly not entirely French in its complexion, but it did have a Gallic flavor. The Frenchman Michel Paquinet was at the hub of this activity.

In 1747, Paquinet bequeathed his property to the nephew, who had traveled with him from Manakin Town. The younger Michael Paquinet continued to oversee the successful family business. He followed his uncle's example and managed the ocean shipping business. In 1740, he had married Mary Powell. The couple had nine children: four sons and five daughters. Paquinet served in the militia regiment under the command of Colonel Thomas Lovick to repel a Spanish attack on the town in 1747. In Michael's will of 1772, he left his sons James, John, and Isaiah his plantation, one hundred acres on Cane Creek, and two hundred acres on Broad Creek.

Michael's sons and daughters married into prominent local families such as the Fishers and the Fullers. His daughter Mary married Nathan Fuller; another daughter, Charity, married William Fisher. Today, there are numerous Fishers and Fullers in the Beaufort area, and many of them have French blood in their veins. Two other daughters married men of French descent. Rebecca married Isaiah Severin, and Sarah married James Noe. Paquinet's sons John and Jacob married and also had numerous children. These descendants of the elder Michael Paquinet flourished and spread throughout the region. The 1790 U.S. census lists Ann, James, Isaiah, and John Paquinet of Carteret County.

The Paquinet family burial plot is just off Route 100 on Adams Creek, a few miles northeast of Beaufort, and hard to find. It is an isolated area of scenic streams, fertile farmland, and coastal plains. The land is bathed by the salty breeze and is teeming with natural beauty and wildlife. Michel Paquinet rests here. The exact location of his gravesite is not known at this time, but the search continues. He is one of the founding fathers of French North Carolina. Descendants of Paquinet, and the families into which the Paquinets married, live in Carteret County today. Their ancestor, Papa Michel, with his coffer of gold, adventurous spirit, brave heart, and enterprising ways, was the genesis of the Paquinet French North Carolina ancestry.

Pierre Piver (1690–1758) arrived in the Beaufort area in 1708. Over several generations, he and his son and grandson, both named Peter (English for "Pierre"), acquired various plots of land, including acreage just west of today's Moore Street. Peter Jr. also served during the 1747 Spanish attack. He was a friend of Michael Paquinet. Carteret County court minutes note that Peter Piver III and his wife sold half of "Piver's Island" to Elijah Bell. The island retains its French name to this day. It is a low bluff overlooking Core Sound just to the south of town. Piver Sr. and his descendants built many houses in the Beaufort region. Some are still standing and occupied. One of the most well known is the Piver historic home on Ann Street.

The archives of the Carteret County History Museum list the genealogy of the industrious and wealthy Piver family. There are hundreds of descendants traced through the late 1800s. The 1790 U.S. census lists Peter, Johann, and Daniel Piver of Beaufort, North Carolina. A great-grandson of Peter Sr., Jesse, married Elizabeth Paquinet in 1817. Over one hundred years after the arrival of the Pivers and Paquinets, the families remained connected through French–North Carolina kinship.

The Pivers who did survive the Huguenot persecution in France created a prosperous firm in Paris, the L.T. Piver Cosmetic Company. It specialized in talcum powder and perfumes. These luxury items were sold in the Beaufort general stores for many years. The Pivers were enterprising people in both France and Beaufort. They played a central role in the early history of the town as landowners, plantation managers, and shipping merchants. There are Piver families who still call Beaufort their ancestral home today. They are the living legacy of French North Carolina.

One intriguing story of the Piver clan is that of Peter Piver's descendant, Susan Piver Longest. During the Civil War, Miss Piver Longest smuggled food, medicine, supplies, and letters to soldiers stationed at Russell Creek. She was a proud and determined southerner and walked five miles each way on her forays. She once threw a bucket of water in a Yankee general's face because he had let his horse drink from the bucket she had drawn from the town pump (Wilson, 16).

Other families of French ancestry played roles in the early history of the Carteret region. The Beaufort area was like a magnet that drew French settlers and those of French descent. Roger Shackelford (1629–1704) was a distant descendant of *Jacques le Fort* ("James the Strong"). The name was Anglicized over the centuries to Shackelford. He was a Norman nobleman and officer in the army of William the Conqueror. Shackelford sailed to Virginia in 1658 with Edward Palmer, a French Huguenot. The name Palmer derives from the Old French *palmier*, a palm branch brought from the Holy Land to France during the Crusades. Palmer had received a land grant of four hundred acres, and the two men went into business together as plantation owners.

In 1660, Roger Shackelford married Edward's sister Mary. They lived out their lives in Essex County, Virginia, and had numerous children of blended French and English ancestry. Two of their sons, John and Peter, migrated to the Carteret region in 1708. They received a land patent for a plantation on the west side of the North River in 1708. In 1713, John and a business partner, Enoch Ward, purchased seven thousand acres of land referred to at the time as "Sea Banks." The western portion of the area eventually came to be known as "Shackelford Banks." John's son, John Jr., served in the local militia from 1712 to 1743. John Sr. even quartered and fed the militia garrison on his land for many years. He was a vital member of the community.

The name Shackelford begins to disappear from Carteret County after 1792. Family members migrated southward to Onslow County as the Carteret region became more populated. In his will, John Sr. bequeathed gold rings to his daughters and livestock to his daughter Ann and son-in-law Joseph Moss. He also left Ann and Joseph pewter dishes, a cedar cupboard, a beaded blanket, and an iron skillet for their daughter Hannah. Shackelford was well off upon his death and a generous man.

John Manney's French name was Jean Magny when he left France in 1685, immediately after Louis XIV's Edict of Fontainebleau. He first settled in Rhode Island. In 1691, the Huguenots were forced to leave for reasons of religious differences. Jean moved to Oxford, Massachusetts, and then finally settled in Poughkeepsie, New York, until his death. His grandson Dr. James Manney moved to Beaufort in 1812. Dr. Manney's house was built during the same year and stands today on the corner of Craven and Ann streets. His son, Dr. James Lente Manney, was also a successful doctor.

We have seen the presence of the Delamar clan in the Craven area. In 1668, Francis De La Mare (the name before it was Anglicized) was born in Calais, France, on the English Channel. He died in Pasquotank County in 1713. His will was referenced in the Huguenot Migrations chapter. He was a successful plantation owner and had a flock of French North Carolina descendants. Some of them eventually migrated southward to Carteret

County in the 1850s. Today, the Delamar House, circa 1860, stands on the corner of Turner and Broad streets. It has been transformed into a bed and breakfast, the Delamar Inn, where one can stay and enjoy the historical ambiance of our French North Carolina ancestors.

Today, there are numerous Delamars listed in local phone directories. The De La Mare family is one of the oldest on record in Normandy, France. The ancestral castle is still called *Grande Mare* ("Great Sea") and is not far from the English Channel. The name Delamar is imbued with French history. A land deed of 1793, on file at the Craven County's Register of Deeds, displays the elegant signature of Demson Delamar. He was a descendant of the French Town colonists.

The Midyette family, originally from Normandy, France, has an intriguing story. They were early inhabitants of Bodie Island in the late 1600s. Mathew Midyette's 1734 will, like that of Francis Delamar, was

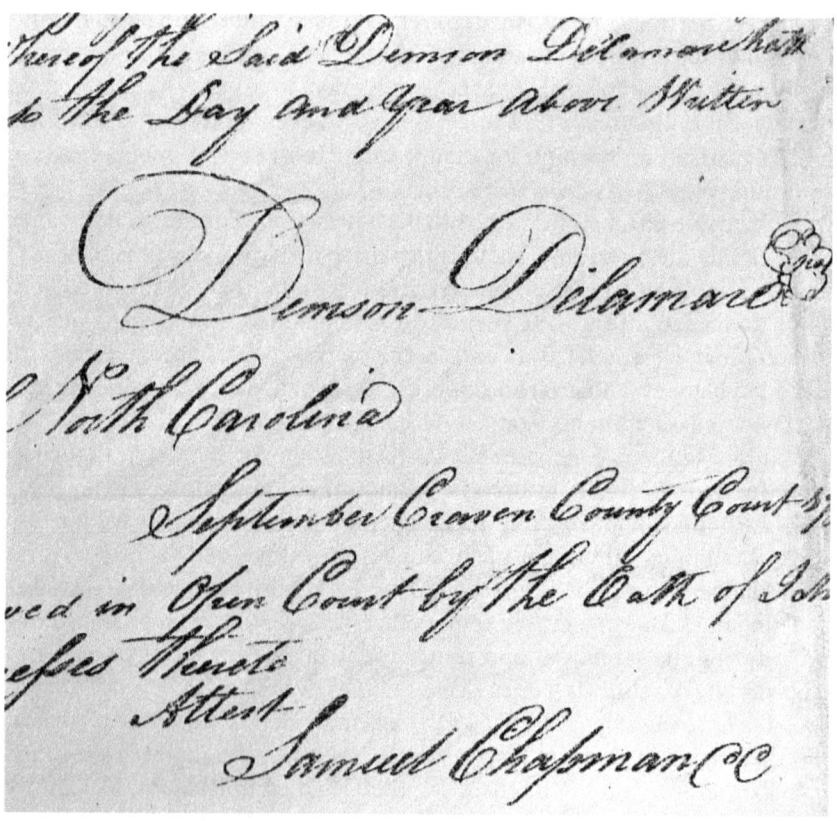

Land deed of Demson Delamar (1793) (courtesy Craven County Register of Deeds).

discussed in the Huguenot Migrations chapter. Midyette was a sea captain who was shipwrecked off the shore of the Outer Banks. Finding Bodie Island an amenable place to start a new life, he purchased and maintained a plantation there. Other Midyettes followed, and they set up a small community.

Some of the Midyette young women married sailors who had served on Blackbeard's ships. These sailors were perhaps French themselves. Some of the Midyette family settled in Beaufort in the 1850s. Their descendants live there today; others spread throughout the region. The Midyettes helped start the U.S. Coast Guard by establishing life-saving stations on the Outer Banks. Louis B. Midyette and his wife Rebecca were the first settlers of Oriental, North Carolina, and named the town. Three miles from Bath, on Opossum Road behind the old Midyette home, can be found the family grave markers of Ennie, Henry, Herman, Nancy, Rosa, and Talula. Today, there is a Midyette Avenue in Morehead City that commemorates this French North Carolina family.

As we look further into the French families in Beaufort, the information becomes spotty. Nevertheless, we can still follow a few other traces of French presence in North Carolina. The Fodrie and Noe families, for example, were prominent in the 1800s, and there has been some documentation of their family lineage. When and how the Fodrie family came from France to North Carolina is not known at this time. We do know that the Noé family was from the Pays de Vaud region in eastern France near the Swiss border.

We have some information on the Noé arrival in French North Carolina. Pierre Noé left France for the Netherlands around 1680 to escape persecution. He migrated to Elizabethtown, New Jersey, in the early 1700s. Some Noe family members (the accent was dropped to Anglicize the name) moved to Beaufort in the mid–1700s, and they have been successful members of the community for centuries. James Noe married Polly Paquinet in 1829. Michel Paquinet would have been pleased to know that his lineage was alive and well and that Polly had married into a family of French descent. One hundred years after first settling in the area, the families of French origin were still intermarrying. The James Noe house, circa 1828, stands on Moore Street and is inhabited today.

Then, there is the Geoffroy family of Beaufort. Malachi R. Geoffroy and his wife Nanine migrated from France to Canada and eventually to Beaufort in the 1880s. This branch of the Geoffroy family descended from French Huguenots. The Geoffroy house, built circa 1885, is on the third block of Ann Street. The 1790 U.S. census lists other, lesser-known French names such as William Bourdin, David Sipon, Caselton Moncrief, James Longness, and Price Penevil. We do not know, unfortunately, much about these people and their families; nevertheless, the search continues.

Finally, the story of the Pigott family is an intriguing one and worthy of attention. Carteret County heritage books tell us that Elijah Pigott, born in 1725, was one of the early settlers in the area. His grandfather François was the patriarch who came from France by way of England to Virginia, escaping persecution as a Huguenot. Lord Picot of Cambridge (1022–90) was born in Saye, Normandy, and was a wealthy Norman landowner. The Pigotts of Beaufort descend from this prestigious lineage. Elijah migrated southward from Virginia to North Carolina, like so many other French immigrants to the state, in search of cheaper land and a better opportunity to succeed as a farmer. We do not know much else about the details of the Pigott's migration to Carteret County in the first decades of the 1700s.

The Bell-Pigott house (circa 1830) witnesses the family presence today. The house is under a protective covenant held by Preservation North Carolina. It is located in Gloucester, North Carolina, to the southeast of Beaufort. Near the home, on Harker's Island, is Pigott Road, and several Pigotts are buried in Beaufort's Old Burying Ground: Jochonius, Micagah, and Nancy. The Pigott families of Carteret County were prosperous ones.

The most interesting Pigott story is that of Emeline (1836–1919), François Pigott's distant granddaughter. She, like her neighbor Susan Piver Longest, aided the Confederacy during the Civil War. Emeline began working for the army by tending to the sick and wounded soldiers of the 26th North Carolina Regiment. The regiment was garrisoned across the creek from her parents' farm at Crab Point. She gathered food, clothing, medicine, tobacco, and other personal items and would leave them in designated hollow trees for the Confederate soldiers. This kindness eased their difficult circumstances.

Emeline eventually became a spy and smuggled messages, tobacco, and food in the hoops of her billowing skirt to Confederate officers. She hosted dinner parties and entertained Union officers. She used these parties as a ruse to gather information. The local fishermen would eavesdrop on the Yankee soldiers at the fish market and channel it to Emeline. She would pass all of this information on to the local Confederate authorities. She traveled between Beaufort, New Bern, and other seaports hiding secret communiqués on rough carriage and boat rides, often in punishing weather.

Emeline had a Huguenot's strength and resourcefulness in her. She was also fiercely committed to her cause and was once arrested. While the Yankee soldiers sent for a woman to search Emeline, she ate some of the incriminating messages and tore others into tiny pieces. Toward the end of the war, she was captured again and stood trial in New Bern. She was accused of being a spy and sentenced to death. However, for reasons unknown, and never divulged by Emeline, she was released and allowed to return home. We will return to the Civil War in the Vive le Sud! chapter.

Emeline Pigott (courtesy History Museum of Carteret County).

Emeline is at rest in the Pigott family graveyard on the north shore of Calico Creek. The location is in Morehead City near 20th Street and Emeline Place. The Beaufort area is inscribed with the historical memory of its French ancestry, right down to the street signs. Emeline defended her southern land and culture that had been home to her French lineage in North Carolina for over a hundred years. Today, one can view up close

Emeline Pigott's hooped skirt, carriage, and other personal belongings on display at the History Museum of Carteret County in Morehead City.

The Beaufort courthouse contains Carteret County's Register of Deeds. Land deeds of the 1700s and 1800s testify to the continuing French presence in the area. There are hundreds of property and real estate transactions of the Delamar, Noe, Paquinet, Pigott, and Piver families dating from the 1730s. The first Piver deed was that of Peter Piver to John Shackelford in 1750.

There are also land deeds with the names of lesser-known families of French descent, such as Amyett (1830), Diamant (1890), and Ange (1902). Even the Navassa Guano Company discussed in the New Bern chapter purchased land in the 1880s as the company expanded. Some of the land deals as late as 1902 document transactions between families of French ancestry in North Carolina: Herman Ange purchased a plot from Erastus E. Piver in 1902, and Peter M. Noe bought land from Joseph Piver and Jechonius Pigott in the 1830s. Beaufort's French–North Carolina connection was alive and well.

Calico Creek, named after the most cherished fabric during the colonial period, is a small inlet port near Emeline's burial site. This is where the Paquinets and Pivers operated their shipping businesses. Other French families lived in the neighborhood, and French ships went in and out of the port regularly. The English word "calico" is an exotic name with Arabic and French roots. Calico (its Arabic name is *calicut*) was first brought from the Middle East to France during the Crusades in the 1100s. The French version, *calicot* (pronounced "calicoe"), moved northward to England. The English Anglicized the word and eventually dropped the silent French "t."

Calico Creek's etymological and cultural roots are steeped in French history. The French merchants, shippers, and their families who settled in the area during the 1700s were successful minority immigrants. Calico Creek feeds into Money Island Bay, which takes its name from the Money family. The name is a variation of the French Monnette, an ancient title of nobility from Savoie in the southeastern part of France. Some members of the family migrated to England after the Norman Conquest; others fled France after 1685 when it was no longer safe to be a Protestant. Jacob Monnett, whose name was Anglicized to Money, came to North Carolina around 1748. Some of his family and their descendants settled in the Beaufort area. Other members of the Money family migrated to Person County. One of them, Jacob, ran a small business as a barrel maker.

The Old Burying Ground in Beaufort is a special place. Its moss-covered gravestones (many not legible) are located next to the Ann Street United Methodist Church. It is in a peaceful, colonial-style neighborhood. Some homes date back to the 1800s. An iron and stone fence

Calico Creek (photograph by the author).

surrounds the orchard, its lush greenery, and hundreds of gravestones. Most of the names on the headstones are English, yet some show French descent. Many of the engravings are partly legible, others not at all. Some of the identities in the graveyard are lost to us. Local legend has it that neighborhood residents hear women's voices murmuring in the Old Burying Ground late at night, sometimes in French, haunting us to remember them.

The Old Burial Ground opens onto intriguing French North Carolina stories. Nancy Manney French (1821–86) is a legendary figure. She loved Charles French, her tutor. Nancy's father opposed the romance. Charles, discouraged, moved to the Arizona Territory to seek his fortune, yet pined for Nancy. The postmaster in Beaufort, a friend of Nancy's father, intercepted their love letters at the latter's direction. Although they never heard from each other because of this ploy, Charles and Nancy remained in love. When Charles returned to Beaufort decades later, his and Nancy's love had not faltered. The couple was married, but Nancy was sick with consumption and died a few weeks later. No one currently knows if the letters survive.

The tale is worthy of a realist short story typical of nineteenth-century French writers such as Émile Zola and Guy de Maupassant. In many of their stories, there is love, heartbreak, a strange twist, and often a sad ending.

Old Burying Ground (photograph by the author).

Nancy's story is a mixture of sweetness and tragedy in this style. She finally married the man she loved but spent most of her life unmarried, not knowing the joy of a husband and children.

There are other stories to tell. A cousin of Nancy's, Captain James Lente Manney, lies in the Old Burying Ground. He became a renowned physician in the area. Vernon Geoffroy is buried there. Finally, there is the French name of Annie Beauregard Cabriel, who died at the age of four in 1865. We know nothing of her except that she died tragically young.

One of the unique French North Carolina residents in the Old Burying Ground is Pierre Henry (1838–1902) (formerly Henri). He was an emancipated slave from the French West Indies. Unique at the time, he received a formal education in the 1850s. Pierre Henri was born in St. Croix, French West Indies. He was the descendant of African slaves who worked on sugar cane plantations and distilleries. He was one of the few children of slaves chosen each year to attend a French Catholic missionary school.

Pierre took full advantage of this opportunity and rose from a child of slaves to become an educated man. He came to Beaufort after the Civil War as a teacher. He could speak and write English and French fluently. Pierre and his wife Annie were leaders in the education of the children of

Headstone of Pierre Henry (photograph by the author).

emancipated slaves at the Washburn Academy. Pierre and Annie Henry are the only known persons of African descent buried in the graveyard.

The Henrys' contribution to establishing a school for young African Americans in the state was unique for its time. Beaufort was a multicultural town from its beginnings and always had a progressive attitude. The area's citizens were accustomed to frequent travelers, merchants, and sailors from other countries and of many colors and races. Beaufort had the heart and mind to accept a previously unheard of idea: providing a school for Black people.

Now for a comic aside to lighten things up. Professor Emeritus Roch C. Smith of the University of North Carolina at Greensboro tells of the time he took the renowned postmodern novelist and philosopher Alain Robbe-Grillet to Emerald Isle and Beaufort some twenty-five years ago. Monsieur Alain, a native of Brittany and resident of Normandy, France, was delighted to find a place called Carteret County. There is a commune in Brittany called Barneville-Carteret, not far from where he grew up. This is the very homeland of our Lord John Carteret.

Monsieur Alain was quite amused to find a "No Trespassing" sign on the gate of the Old Burial Ground. In French, *Défense de Trépasser* means "it is forbidden to die." Roch and Alain laughed at this linguistic irony. Roch took a picture of Alain next to the sign; today it is in the special collections at the UNC Greensboro Jackson Library. Unfortunately, Monsieur Alain *a trépassé* in 2008, and this humorous moment preserves a pleasant memory of him (Smith).

Other towns in North Carolina followed suit during Reconstruction and opened schools for the children of freed slaves, but Beaufort was one of the first. Henry was bilingual and would have taught his students French. The French language was becoming a part of the general education curriculum in the state at the time. Beaufort's leaders were also practical and entrepreneurial-minded and saw the value of having an educated Black workforce. Pierre Henry's legacy is a unique one in French North Carolina.

Hammock House is the oldest house in Beaufort. It has been a harbor landmark since the early 1700s. We know the story of Blackbeard's common-law French wife. When he was tired of her, he hung her from an oak tree in the backyard. Over the centuries, residents who live near the house have heard the muffled wailing of a young girl in the wee hours.

Let us delve a bit more into the story. The young French girl was a sixteen-year-old captive who became Blackbeard's concubine. She was stolen from her merchant family in one of Blackbeard's ship raids. The women on board were often brought along after Blackbeard and his crew had killed all of the men and plundered the ship. She was one of the dozens of "wives" Blackbeard had in his lifetime. Blackbeard dazzled her with his lavish collection of silks, jewels, and gold. She agreed to marry him. However, in a short time, Blackbeard's cruelty toward his "wife" made her rethink the marriage. She protested openly, and that led to her quick demise.

Before he became known as Blackbeard, Edward Teach had received a fair amount of education and spoke acceptable French. He negotiated with French merchants, seamen, and pirates. Having a French concubine was normal for him. The abuse the French girl suffered at the hands of Teach is unthinkable. If she had been picked from a group of female captives, Blackbeard surely would have chosen the most attractive one. A teenager of a well-to-do family, the young woman was most likely a virgin.

This beautiful girl resisted him when she could take no more. One evening they had quite a row. Blackbeard, drunk on rum, dragged his wife out of the house, tied a noose around her neck, threw the rope over a sturdy branch of an oak tree, and slowly raised her as she died gasping for air. Blackbeard ordered his crewmembers to bury her in the backyard.

An addendum to the legend is that Blackbeard was a jealous man and would not allow his French wife to leave the house. He, therefore, hired a local young man to bring food and goods from the town. The young man and Blackbeard's wife started an affair when Blackbeard was out parlaying with his crew about his next caper. He finally learned of the relationship and slit the young man's throat as the latter tried to flee the house. There is a staircase in Hammock House still imprinted with the indelible bloodstain of this young man. The French North Carolina legacy of the Hammock House is a cruel and sometimes macabre one.

Blackbeard's Frenchness in North Carolina is significant. His name translates into French as *Barbe Noire*. We saw in the chapter on Bath that he was quite a player on the high seas. He ruled the ports of North Carolina in which he resided from time to time. There is more to his story than legend.

Students at Meredith College in Raleigh under the direction of Dr. Brent Pitts have translated colonial North Carolina mercantile records. The records document frequent commercial transactions of French ships and merchants in eastern North Carolina in the towns of Beaufort, Edenton, and Wilmington. There were even French retail shops in these towns. One French shipping merchant, René Montaudain, regularly sent ships out from Nantes that would end up in North Carolina ports.

This commerce shows the darker side of the French shipping trade in North Carolina. It was part of the "French Atlantic Triangle" (Miller). From French ports, ships were loaded with trade goods such as cloth, bars of iron, pots, pans, alcohol, firearms, and luxury items such as crystal, jewelry, and silks. These goods were brought to the coast of French West Africa. A portion of them was traded to various tribes for slaves and gold.

The ensuing three-month voyage to the Caribbean was a miserable and inhumane one for the enslaved Africans. They were sold in the Caribbean islands, and the ships were loaded with sugar, coffee, cotton, indigo, and rum for the return to France. Sometimes on the home voyage, these ships would stop in eastern North Carolina towns such as Beaufort. They traded a portion of their French and Caribbean goods for local products much needed in France, such as turpentine, tar, and lumber. Michel Paquinet was a part of this economy with his import–export business, and so was Barbe Noire.

On one such commercial voyage in 1717, French Captain Pierre Dossett and his lieutenant François Ernaud were one hundred miles from Martinique with a cargo of four hundred slaves and twenty pounds of gold dust from the mines of French West Africa. Their ship, *La Concorde*, was equipped with sixteen cannons and a crew of seventy-five. Pirate Captain Benjamin Hornigold had two vessels at his disposal. He had twice the men and firepower and overtook Dossett and his crew quickly. Hornigold turned the ship over to one of his crew leaders, Edward Teach, who named it *Queen Anne's Revenge*. Teach had served in the Royal British Navy in

Queen Anne's War, and his pun in the naming of the ship was meant to irritate his former employer, the Crown of England, who was now his enemy.

Barbe Noire used the ship to sail up and down the eastern Atlantic Coast to the Caribbean. He would plunder English, French, Dutch, and Spanish ships. Barbe Noire would regularly confiscate goods such as rum, brandy, silver, gold, fabrics, and jewelry and sell them when he got to his next port. He was a scandalous but wealthy man who lived large. He would also use the ship in part for its original purpose: to transport slaves to sell in the markets. Barbe Noire was a criminal, but the local colonial administration would often turn a blind eye because he was good for business. He would sell his stolen goods at discount rates and stay in town for a while to make merry and plot future escapades with his crew. They would spend money at the inns and taverns and infuse the town's local economy with much-needed gold and silver currency.

Some of the goods Barbe Noire and other French ships brought to Beaufort enhanced the town's culinary scene. Local cuisine was a blend of hearty English fare, enriched with Caribbean products, and often prepared by a female African or Caribbean slave. Such a cook would have infused this combination with foods, spices, and techniques of her own country. This mixture of culinary cultures would become known as "southern cooking," east North Carolina style. It was a unique one, and Beaufort's food scene today continues this culinary melting pot.

Barbe Noire was a dangerous character, but if one worked with him, he and his crew livened things up. He infused the area with a multicultural flair. On Barbe Noire's frequent journeys between French islands such as Martinique and Haiti to towns such as Beaufort and Bath he would have brought with him slaves who spoke French Creole. Their distant descendants still populate the area today. Blackbeard's crew had French seamen in it. They frequented Beaufort and intermingled with the local population. He also had well-chosen Frenchmen on board valuable to his enterprise. Dossett and Ernaud's report of the taking of *La Concorde* testifies that a cabin boy and three of the crew members voluntarily joined Barbe Noire's outfit. He took others by force, including a pilot, a surgeon, two carpenters, two sailors, and the ship's cook. As an entrepreneur, Barbe Noire knew what he was doing.

Barbe Noire's headquarters were in Bath and Beaufort. After he had met his demise, some of his former crew, French included, surrendered and changed their ways. Some of them settled in coastal Carolina to make their way in a new locale. French ancestry in North Carolina comes from many different places. Beaufort's citizenry was diverse since its earliest days; its multicultural heritage is at the heart of French North Carolina.

When I first called the Beaufort Historical Society for information related to the French in Beaufort, a pleasant staff member recommended that I get in touch with Mamré Wilson. She had researched the history of Beaufort and the "French Connection" of Beaufort. As he spelled out her name over the phone, my researcher's heart leaped when he mentioned that there was a French accent on the letter "é." He said, "the one that points to the right." This is the French *accent aigu*, as in Mamré. I was on to something.

When I met Mamré, she told me she added the accent at one point in her life because she liked the way it looked and said it gave the name a touch of French refinement. Her knowledge, not only of Beaufort but also of the French presence in North Carolina, is impressive. As a result, I have named her "Madame Beaufort." Mamré is a kind and generous person. We have had several informative discussions at her home library near downtown Beaufort. She has been a helpful collaborator in moving the project along, and I am grateful to her for it.

Beaufort today is one of the unique towns in North Carolina. It blends the hardy frontier port it once was with Georgian charm. Beaufort has a unique aura created in part by its early French settlers and their descendants. It is a thriving town and one that has kept its past alive through historical conservation. This would warm a French heart since they are a people who preserve their history, as anyone who has traveled to France knows.

In 1995, Beaufort, North Carolina, entered into a partnership with its first French sister city, Beaufort-en-Vallée, located in the Maine-et-Loire region. It is a commune of six thousand people with a millennial history in one of the most beautiful areas in France. In 2002, representatives of the Beaufort Sister City Organization traveled to a sister city celebration. The alliance spawned the international Beaufort Sister Cities Society. It currently has dozens of sister cities named Beaufort throughout the world.

The Beaufort, North Carolina, visitors were hosted in private homes, given tours of the Loire Valley, and were wined and dined in local restaurants. There was a closing ceremony with a banquet, live music, and dancing. There was an excellent camaraderie shared by the Americans and French during the two-week visit. It was one of the most memorable French experiences an American could have. Beaufort, North Carolina, has an extended family in France and wherever there is a town named Beaufort.

The hospitality and generosity of Beaufort's first sister city mirror that of Beaufort, North Carolina. It is one of the most accommodating and cultured towns in the state. The Beaufort sister cities are the essence of French North Carolina. They have much in common: a rich architectural legacy, cultural programs in history, the arts, music, and theater. The location of both towns in fertile agricultural regions enhances their respective cuisines. Most importantly, both have a populace with a generous spirit. Beaufort, North Carolina, owes some of this cosmopolitan personality to its French ancestry.

CHAPTER 8

French North Carolina

Over the years, on trips between Raleigh and the North Carolina coast, I noticed French place names: Lenoir County, Faison, La Grange, Peletier, Beaufort, and many others. I was intrigued and began to research the topic of the French heritage of North Carolina. Some years later, I had the good fortune to meet Lisa Pelletier-Harman, former president of the Carteret County Historical Society in Morehead City. Lisa is a direct descendant of the first Pelletier to come to North Carolina. She has a wealth of knowledge about the history of the French presence in eastern North Carolina. Lisa has been generous with her time and shared with me her insights on the Pelletier family history. The first section of this chapter gives an account of the Pelletier ancestry in North Carolina. It is a blend of Lisa's knowledge and my research.

The influence of the Pelletier lineage in French North Carolina is significant. The name dates back to Warin Pelletier of Normandy, France, in the 1100s. This is the earliest reference of which we know. The name is of Norman origin and signified a furrier, a person who trades animal skins and makes clothing out of them. The family seat was in the county of Houssaye. Some Pelletiers fled the Huguenot persecutions in the late 1600s and migrated to England. Others remained in France and either converted or somehow avoided persecution. The American line of the family begins with the arrival of Jerome Pelletier to Beaufort, North Carolina, just after the Revolutionary War in 1780.

The name Pelletier is not common in America. The branches scattered throughout the United States originated with the North Carolina family. When Jerome stepped off the ship, he wore the uniform of a French naval officer. He had been educated in law and brought with him a private library. Jerome Pelletier came from France by way of Haiti to Beaufort. It is not certain, but was presumed that he served in the French Navy during the Revolutionary War, hence the uniform. As we will see, the naval outfit could have been a ruse. After the war, Jerome settled with his brother Peter in what the French called the *Aux Cayes* region of southwestern Haiti. They owned a plantation and made a handsome profit in the sugar trade. Peter

Peletier (photograph by the author).

remained on the estate in Haiti, where he died. In his will, he left Jerome a tidy inheritance. Jerome cited the amount in his own will as "three thousand Livres Tournois," representing the profits from the plantation (Fisher, *One Dozen Pre-Revolutionary War Families* 72). Jerome eventually put them to good use in French North Carolina.

Jerome wisely invested this nest egg and began to increase his wealth after settling in Beaufort. He was an unstoppable entrepreneur who made a fortune in the years to come. The first mention of him is in a 1786 land deed for a lot in Beaufort. About this time, Jerome married a young local woman, Sarah Dennis. A close friend and business partner of Jerome's was another Frenchman, Guillaume Ferrand. Jerome settled about the same time in the Swansboro vicinity near the White Oak River.

In acknowledgment of their friendship, Jerome named one of his sons Ferrand. In his 1801 will, Jerome appointed "William Ferrand, my worthy friend" as one of the will's two executors. The original will was written in French with the use of an interpreter, George Sanderson. Jerome was a first-generation French American and was not completely fluent in English. When he married Sarah Dennis in 1784, she was thirty years his younger; it was a fruitful marriage. Elizabeth and Peter Pelletier were born before 1790. Mary, William, James, Ferrand, and Reuben were born between 1790 and 1800. Peter eventually rose to prominence and became "Constable of Bogue Sound District" in 1821.

Jerome was appointed juror to the County Superior Court in 1791. He had become an influential citizen of Carteret County in a short amount of time. Jerome and Ferrand set up a business enterprise in turpentine, tar, and pitch, as well as mercantile goods. Coincidentally, the word turpentine is of Old French origin: *terre bentine* from the Latin *terebinthia resina*, "resin of the terebinth tree." It is a small cashew tree in southern Europe that was a source for turpentine. Jerome and Ferrand brought with them their European knowledge of agriculture and distillation, and they were astute businessmen.

Turpentine has been used since ancient times as a solvent and for producing varnishes. It is essential for sealing wooden boats and ships. It was also used medicinally as a topical, and sometimes internal, home remedy. In the 1800s, it was burned in lamps as a less expensive alternative to whale oil. Turpentine also began to be used to make cleaning and sanitary products since people liked its fresh, antiseptic scent. Jerome and Ferrand were on the cutting edge of the new uses of turpentine. Their expertise in traditional purposes and methods were the foundation of this innovation. Moreover, they were part of a thriving maritime economy. They owned hundreds of acres of dense pine forests used to make their tar and turpentine products. It was the perfect place to bring together Old World knowledge and New World technology.

Working on Jerome's thriving plantation were fourteen of his slaves. Some were Africans via Haiti and spoke French Creole. In addition to the French the Pelletiers spoke with French merchants, seamen, and laborers, Creole enriched the linguistic fabric of the Pelletier plantation and production facility. It was a multilingual community since the Frenchmen Pelletier and Ferrand spoke decent English. In addition, some of the Haitian slaves still spoke their African dialects. We will return to the complex linguistic components of French North Carolina in the Crusoe Island chapter and elsewhere.

The location of Pelletier Mills was at Hatchell's Point on Hadnot Creek on the western side of the White Oak River. The spot was initially called Pelletier Point. There was a windmill located there that helped to power the production facility. The Pelletiers owned a thousand-acre plantation between Spooners Creek and Pelletier Creek on Bogue Sound. Lisa Pelletier-Harman lives there today. The family also owned another thousand acres on the New Port River for loading and unloading ships. The plantation on Pelletier Creek was the home place. The family also had a home in Beaufort, "lot number 30," as listed in Jerome's will. Pelletier Creek is still used today for harboring ships during storms.

Ferrand also did well for himself and had equivalent land holdings and a plantation. Today, one can visit the location of the old Pelletier Warehouse on SR 1101, 110 Wethering Landing Road. Nearby is the Primitive Baptist Church, which served at times as a meetinghouse. The church dates back to the 1800s. Jerome and Ferrand would have gone there to attend local and county meetings. The descendants of Jerome Pelletier continued the family business after his passing. The 1850 North Carolina Census Addendum lists Pelletier Mills as one of the largest manufacturers in eastern North Carolina.

Jerome Pelletier was part of the new immigrant French group that came to North Carolina after the Revolutionary War looking for a place

Primitive Baptist Church (photograph by the author).

to live and prosper. By his accomplishments, we know that he was a highly motivated and educated immigrant with monetary resources. Jerome knew how to increase his investments and create success and well-being for his family. He was a convincing communicator and in two languages. Although he was an intelligent and resourceful man, some of his life is shrouded in enigma.

There is no documented evidence to date that Jerome served in the French Navy. One theory is that, as smart and crafty as he was, he wore the naval uniform as a ploy. He wanted to gain immediate attention and respect of the local populace and town officials when he landed in Beaufort. Let us keep in mind that many Americans were grateful to France at the time. Her military support in the Revolutionary War, especially naval, helped the American colonies defeat the British. To see a French naval officer in town must have been quite an event. Jerome's idea worked; he became an adopted son of Beaufort and a key player in the area's economy. He provided a comfortable life for his wife, children, grandchildren, and extended family.

The Pelletier family has burial records and gravesites in Carteret and Onslow Counties. However, Lisa, the most earnest of the family historians, has never been able to locate Jerome's burial site or gravestone. As she tells us, "He's just wrapped in mystery from beginning to end" (Pelletier-Harman). What is not cloaked in mystery is the success of Jerome's descendants. His sons Peter and Ferrand owned a small fleet of merchant ships. They were among the founding citizens of Beaufort, Morehead City, and Swansboro. In turn, their children helped to establish Jacksonville, Peletier, Maysville, Half Moon Bay, and some smaller settlements that were swallowed up when Camp Lejeune was built in 1941.

The Pelletiers were busy people as they migrated southward down the coast. Peter and Ferrand married cousins from the prominent Weeks family (Tamar and Sarah, respectively). Ferrand and Tamar had six children: four boys and two girls; their descendants live in the area today. Many Weeks descend from Ferrand and Tamar. Other Pelletiers married into the Fisher family. Levi Rowe Pelletier married Caroline Arendell, another prominent family in the area. Caroline's family name became that of the main road in Morehead City, Arendell Street. The marriages of Pelletiers into the Fisher and Weeks families helped to spread the Pelletier bloodline in French North Carolina.

The unbroken lineage of the North Carolina Pelletier family is unique. There are hundreds of land transactions throughout the 1800s of Jerome's descendants. The Pelletier Cemetery is on the land of the old family plantation on Bogue Sound. It is one of the state's oldest intact family cemeteries. Tamar Weeks Pelletier is buried there. There are numerous Pelletiers in the Weeks Cemetery near Swansboro. Primrose Fisher has conducted extensive research on the Pelletier genealogy, and this section of the chapter is indebted to his work (Fisher, *One Dozen Pre-Revolutionary War Families passim*), as it is to Lisa's. The French heritage of Peletier is one of the beating hearts of French North Carolina.

Today, Swansboro is an appealing maritime town. The "Friendly City by the Sea'" is a miniature version of Beaufort. Like Beaufort, Swansboro has a history of Frenchness. Its historic district has a bohemian flair; the old salts that hang out at the Yacht Club tavern have not changed much over the centuries. Just across the White Oak River, Pelletier is rich in farmland, marshlands, creeks, and wildlife. Some of the town's land is located in the Croatan National Forest that has some of the most beautiful coastal scenery in the state. The area just west of town, near Hadnot Creek, where Jerome and Ferrand lived and worked, has not changed that much since their time. The nearby French-named road, Petitford, gives us one more trace of Frenchness in Peletier. It is a mélange of English and French words meaning "little crossing."

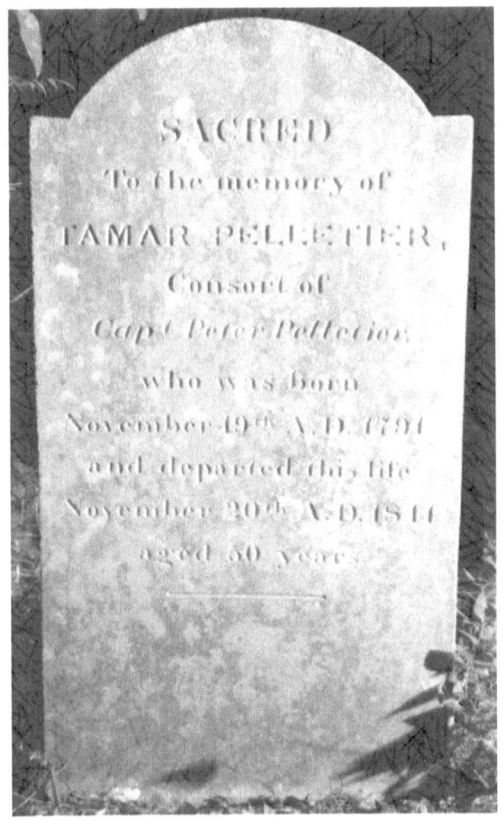

Headstone of Tamar Weeks Pelletier, Swansboro (photograph by the author).

The Pelletiers are integral members of the French North Carolina family. Pelletier Harbor in Morehead City reminds us of this. Even one hundred years after Jerome's landing, the Pelletiers continued to keep the family's lineage intact. They also kept their entrepreneurial spirit alive. Jeremiah Walter Pelletier married Clara Irene Bell in 1886. He ran a general merchandise store in Stella on the White Oak River. The business depended on a riverboat that brought in supplies and fertilizers. Jeremiah ran the business until he retired in the 1920s. There are Bells in the Carteret area today with ancestry that reaches back to Jeremiah and Clara.

The Pelletier House in Jacksonville is a historic landmark and the oldest standing structure in the town. It was built in 1850 by Rufus Ferrand Pelletier in the Greek Revival style. The house is located at Wantland Spring on the banks of the New River. It was constructed as a one-room dwelling and served as a home and office. The house was part of a turpentine lot that was owned by Rufus and his brother William. The house was occupied by a Pelletier, Eliza, as late as 1954. It now belongs to the Onslow Historical Society and is open for public viewing on special occasions. The house is one of simple tastefulness.

Jerome's business partner, Guillaume Ferrand, also made a name for himself and established a prominent family heritage of his own. Land deeds from Craven and Onslow counties document his extensive landholdings. In 1819, he purchased lot number 6 in Swansboro at the corner of Front and Moore streets. On that site, he built the "Old Brick Store." He ran the store for decades and became one of the wealthiest merchants in Onslow County. He also owned taverns, several vessels, a watermill in Hubert, and a turpentine distillery in Swansboro. Ferrand became Onslow County's state senator in 1846. He passed away in October 1847 and rests in the Ferrand family cemetery on Pettiford Creek. The "Old Brick Store" still stands today and is a thriving antique and collectibles shop.

We will now leave Jerome, Guillaume, and their families to delve further into French North Carolina. The small town of today's Hubert, just east of Jacksonville, has some local French history as well as impressive ancestral credentials. The name Hubert has some French in it. The name is of Germanic origin, meaning "bright light." It is also a common name in eastern France. The early French were the Franks, who were Germanic. Many French names were Gallicized from German in the seventh and eighth centuries. In the case of Hubert, his Latin name was Hubertus (656–727 CE). He was a Frankish bishop from the Ardennes region of eastern France. He is a Christian saint and the patron of hunters, mathematicians, opticians, and metalworkers. Today, one can drive by the approximate location of Fernand's watermill on Queen's Creek.

There is a bluff in Jacksonville overlooking Morgan Bay named Frenchman's Point. It is located at the end of the French named Montfort Road on the Camp Lejeune military base. Camp Lejeune was named after the early twentieth-century Marine and war hero, John Archer Lejeune. He was of a French Cajun family from Baton Rouge, Louisiana, another French–North Carolina twist. Just to the south of Frenchman's Point is Sallier's Bay. The latter is a French surname of Latin origin, meaning "salt."

A *sallier* designated a salt and spice merchant or the keeper of a saltcellar. The *sallier* was an essential person in colonial Carolina. He imported and sold precious salt to preserve meat and fish and to make decent cooking

The Old Brick Store, early 1900s (courtesy Jack Dudley, *Swansboro: A Pictorial Tribute*).

possible. We have seen Onslow County land deeds with the name of Sallier. The North Carolina Salliers may reach back to Charles de Sailly of Manakin Town. We saw him in the La Colonie Perdue chapter. At this time, there exists no clear historical evidence to trace this connection, but the search continues.

Both Frenchman's Point and Sallier's Bay point to North Carolina's French past. "Frenchman's Point" today is closed to the public. In 1941, several small towns and their residents were uprooted and relocated throughout Onslow County. There were French North Carolina citizens among them. Once a year, Camp Lejeune invites families and their descendants to the base for a dinner reunion. They revisit old friends, share stories, and walk on the ground of their ancestors.

The 1850 Swansboro census has multiple listings of Ferrand, Foy, Pigot, and Provow. Other citizens of French descent are Brinson and Amnity Ventriss, M. Rongier, William and Rufus Pelletier ("merchants"), John Pettifer ("mulatto, mechanic"), John Fountain, and Ann Marion. The Pelletier and Ferrand families were the largest, but not the only ones, who helped spread French North Carolina beyond the Carteret region. Some other French individuals and families migrated to eastern North Carolina. The Laroque family is a notable one in this regard.

George Paul Laroque was a descendant of the ancient family La Rocque from the Dordogne region in southwestern France. He came to America via Barbados in 1696 and settled in Louisiana to practice as a physician. His son, James, migrated to Lenoir County in the late 1700s. One of the well-known country doctors in the Kinston area was George Paul's great-grandson, Dr. Frederick Laroque. He was known as "Old Doctor Fred" and practiced in the county until the age of sixty, an old age at the time. He married Mary Elizabeth Dunn, and the couple had five children.

One of the sons was Walter Dunn Laroque, who was born in 1850. He began life as a farmer and became a successful dry goods merchant in Kinston. He was a civic leader and a respected member of the community. His son, Dr. George Paul Laroque, named after his great-great-grandfather, was born in Kinston in 1876. He was educated in the Kinston public schools and at the University of North Carolina at Bellevue (coincidentally another name of French origin). After receiving his medical degree from the University of Pennsylvania, he became a successful surgeon.

Today, many Laroques in the Kinston area and elsewhere in the state descend from George Paul Laroque, Sr. Several years ago, I had the unexpected fortune of having a student of Laroque descent in one of my classes. She generously shared the family genealogy with me. It has served as the foundation for the Laroque discussion.

Much of the western movement of the French in North Carolina took place on the Trent River and along the Old Wagon Road. The migration spread from French Town to Pollocksville, Trenton, and finally, Kinston. This was the route LaPierre followed on his road trips as he ministered to his French brethren. From there, the migration continued to Lenoir and Duplin counties (both names are of French origin) and beyond. Duplin

County was named after Sir Thomas Hays, Lord of Duplin, who served on the Board of Trade and Plantations for the Crown in the 1740s. The name Duplin is a common one in the Department of the Loire in southeastern France. The root of the name is a topographical reference from Old French *du plain* ("of the plain"). Duplin's flat farmland is appropriately named. We will return to Lenoir County shortly.

French Huguenots, along with the Welsh, were among the first settlers in the Duplin Precinct. The Duplin County Register of Deeds documents land purchases from English landholders during the years 1749–84 of the following French settlers: Thomas Averett, Benjamin Beverit, Nicholas Bourdin, Rose Caison, Thomas Castellain, Jesse Dardain, John Deverrill, James Dulaney, Elias Faison, John Farrior, Charles Gavin, John Gilbert, Elizabeth Lanier, William Marchant, Jacob Millard, Andrew Nialley, Isaac Pertivant, and Nicholas Pollard, among others.

Wills of Duplin County contain some of the family names we have seen before. This demonstrates the slow spread of French North Carolinians from the Albemarle and French Town westward. Some of the wills with French names are as follows: John Batchelder (1851), Peter Barbre (1783), Mary Blanchard (1848), Richard Chason (1836), Henry Faison (1788), Martha Faison (1843—extensive landholdings), John Farrior (1851—extensive landholdings), Edward Gavin (1850), Bryan Glisson (1825), Thomas Lanier (1787), John Lanier (1799), and Jesse Lanier (1829) (Duplin County Abstract of Deeds, 1784–1813).

Lenoir County was named in honor of the speaker of the state Senate, General William Lenoir, a hero of the Revolutionary War. The Lenoir family migrated directly from France to the English colonies as a result of the Huguenot persecutions. The family moved from Virginia to North Carolina around 1760. William Lenoir was the youngest of ten children. He was self-educated and could read and write English, Latin, Greek, and French. William also spoke French with some fluency. He married Ann Ballard and eventually rose to prominence. The Lenoir coat of arms, "Le Noir de Nantes" ("Black of Nantes"), is named for the largest city in Brittany, Nantes, which we visited in the Beaufort chapter.

Other towns with French names in eastern North Carolina are Angier, Cognac, Faison, Graingers, La Grange, and Maury. La Grange was named in 1868 after the people in the area suggested it in honor of the Marquis de Lafayette. Lafayette was a French general who served in the Continental Army as a volunteer during the Revolutionary War. He is still admired by North Carolinians. La Grange is the name of Lafayette's estate outside of Paris, after which the town is named. Lafayette's role was essential to the American victory. The word *la grange* is also French for "barn" (Latin, *granica*, "granary"). It is an appropriate name for La Grange, North

Carolina, whose rural economy is rooted in agriculture. We will return to Lafayette's 1825 journey through North Carolina in the Revolutionary Allies chapter.

The town of Faison is named after Henri Faison. His father's full name was Henryk Faison Von Deverge. Henri dropped the nobiliary particle when he came to America. He was born in Secan, France, in the Gascony region in 1630. He is listed in the town's register of the Huguenot Church from 1645 to 1648. He emigrated from France to Holland and then to America to escape persecution like so many others. He married French compatriot Rebecca Plouvier in the late 1640s. Her parents were Pierre and Françoise Plouvier. Henri Faison passed away in 1693 in York County, Virginia.

His son, Henry, migrated to North Carolina in the early 1700s with his family and settled at the Trent River colony. He eventually relocated to Duplin County in search of cheaper land. He had the resources to help establish a settlement and gave it the family name. Faison is situated on the coastal plain with level terrain and clay loam soil whose composition is well suited for agriculture. Faison became a prosperous agricultural and manufacturing town in the 1800s. The town was connected by railway to Wilmington and could export its goods. It could also import some of its necessities, and even a few refinements.

The historic district of Faison is rich in architectural beauty. The peaked and semicircular parapets on many of the homes give the town a European flavor. The oldest dwelling, in the Greek Revival style, is that of Elias Faison (circa 1850). The Faison-Williams house (1853) is in the Italianate style. Another home bears the name of a citizen of French Huguenot descent: Thomas Perret (1880). Faison combined the practical utility of a thriving town with the aesthetic value of artistically constructed homes. The combination of these two qualities, in Latin, *utile et dulce*, "useful and pleasing" (in French, *utile et agréable*), is dear to the French aesthetic heart. It is this principle that the Faison family and others followed in the building of this picturesque town.

Further vestiges of French presence exist in other parts of eastern North Carolina (French *vestige*, "mark, trace" / Latin *vestigium*, "footprint, trace"). The Pollocksville Cemetery contains gravesites of several extended French families, among them: Batchelder, Duval, Foy, Geray, and Monnette. There is a street named after the Foys (a family to which we will shortly return). There is a road with the French–Latinate name, Louvnia (a female wolf), and another named Beaufort. Today's Route 58 west from Pollocksville parallels the Trent River. Some ten miles up the river is a special place. It is a tranquil and verdant spot that has a small tributary of the Trent named French Branch, which waters fertile farmland. French North Carolinians just kept migrating up the Trent on their westward expansion.

Chapter 8. French North Carolina

In Trenton, where John LaPierre ministered, there is an abandoned church designed in the local "Carpenter Gothic" style. With its pointed arches and geometrical patterns of stained glass, the construction is reminiscent of the medieval Gothic style of France. This design appears elsewhere in eastern North Carolina and was influenced in part by French colonial carpenters. Although the current church was rebuilt after LaPierre's lifetime, he likely preached at this location. When entering Trenton from the east on Route 58, one comes to Brock Mill Pond (another tributary of the Trent).

The pond was dammed to provide waterpower for a gristmill, which still stands today. Brock Mill was built in 1700. Stand on the banks of the pond next to the building and take in the view. Time has stood still, and the spot is not much different from when LaPierre ministered at the settlement. The Jones County Register of Deeds office in Trenton contains land

Trenton, Carpenter Gothic style (photograph by the author).

deeds from the 1780s and 1790s that document transactions of settlers with names of French origin. Among them are Vincent Amyett, Neil Blanchard, Sugan Dulin, Hare Jarman, Sarah Dillahunt, Henry Maulden, Frederick Foscue, John Giles, Jacob Granade, John Gilbert, and David Fonville. Trenton was, in part, a French North Carolina town.

The historical indicators of French heritage are everywhere in eastern North Carolina. Head west to the intersection of routes 58 and 70, and there is another tiny tributary of the Trent named Frenchman's Creek. Coincidentally, on the land in front of the creek is a clothing store called La Petite Boutique. It sells French and European clothing and fashion accessories. The area around the creek itself is untamed and whispers the past to us when the "Frenchman" lived there. He was most likely a hunter and a trapper living self-sufficiently in the wilderness some three hundred years ago. There is also "French's Creek" in Onslow County named after the French settler Alexander Nicola, whose land deed is dated 1744.

Further west, although the city of Rocky Mount has anything but a French name, it has some French presence. Some of the town's oldest families are the descendants of French Huguenots: Viverette, Pridgen (Purjean), and Chambliss (Chambly de Beauvois). The author had the pleasure of directing an N.C. State study abroad program to France in 2012; one student in the group was a member of the Chambliss family. There are also an area, a street, and a diner named the Benvenue Grill (*bienvenu*, "welcome" in French). More significantly, located in the area is Nash County's most impressive late nineteenth-century mansion of the same name. Wealthy plantation owner Redmond Bunn built the Benvenue House in 1844.

The Benvenue House is a fine example of Victorian architecture that incorporates elements of the French Second Empire style. The house combines a rectangular tower with a steep French mansard roof and is topped with iron trim. It is a blend of English and French elegance. Finally, N.C. historical marker E-31 in Rocky Mount commemorates the Marquis de Lafayette and his 1825 tour of the state. He stayed in the home of Henry Donaldson on February 23, near the location of the marker.

While working on the French heritage of North Carolina project over the years, I had driven by the Museum of Onslow County on Route 24 in Richlands dozens of times without ever stopping to visit. I had learned from Lisa Pelletier-Harman that there had been a French presence there. I needed to explore it. Meeting Director Lisa Whitman-Grice was another pivotal moment in deepening my understanding of French North Carolina. When I explained that I was working on the French presence in eastern North Carolina, her ears perked up.

Ms. Whitman-Grice is a descendant of French Huguenots, the Foy family. She provided me access to archival material on the French in

Rocky Mount, Benvenue Grill (photograph by the author).

Onslow County. Her family branch of Foys had migrated from Maryland. There is also some evidence that another group of Foys migrated to North Carolina with the Manakin Town group. The name in French is Foye (*foi*, meaning "faith"). There were many Foys in eastern North Carolina, as evidenced by the dozen gravestones in Pollocksville; there are others sprinkled throughout the area. The Foys were prominent citizens, and as we have seen, even have a street named after their family. This second Lisa is rightfully proud of her French North Carolina heritage.

Ms. Whitman-Grice introduced me to a local educator and historian, Mr. Dennis Jones. He is referenced in the La Colonie Perdue chapter and appendix 1. Mr. Jones's work precedes mine and is meticulous in its detail. He is a generous scholar and enthusiastically shared his extensive research with me.

Some of it has been incorporated into *The French Heritage of North Carolina*. His expertise in the historical geography of North Carolina is second to none; his knowledge of colonial migration patterns in the state is likewise impressive. We have had discussions at the museum and chatted over lunch, and we engage in ongoing email correspondence. His shared knowledge has served to round out my perspective of the French presence in eastern North Carolina.

Mr. Jones is a descendant of French Huguenots, in his case, the Farrior family. The family name descends from the French "Lafarrier" of the Province of Lorraine in eastern France. The Farrior ancestry reaches back to Henri Lafarrier, the first documented ancestor of the mid–1500s. Pierre Lafarrier, born in 1680, married Jeanne Bisset in 1700. Pierre and Jeanne migrated to America in the early 1700s and settled with their children in North Carolina. He was most likely with the Manakin Town group that established French Town in Craven County. He dropped the French "La" from his name, and it became "Farrier." He was a trader, had several children, and lived a good life.

His oldest son, George, was born in 1720 in Craven County. He married an unknown woman, and the couple had four sons and several daughters. The sons were named John, Benard, Jacques, and Palmier. It seems that George was trying to continue the family's French heritage by giving French names to three of his boys. However, when the children grew up, John and Benard chose to change the spelling of the family name to the Anglicized Farrior. Jacques and Palmier kept the French spelling of Farrier. This difference is evidence that the family had some disagreements in maintaining its French identity. This struggle is typical of the French North Carolina families whose names became Anglicized. John went on to serve in the Revolutionary War. There are numerous Farriors in the state today stemming from this lineage. There is even a Farrior school just outside of Beulaville in Jones County.

In 1795, there was a major hurricane in Onslow County. Much of what existed in and around Pelletier and Swansboro was ravaged by extreme winds, torrential rain, and floods. Many homes, farms, and businesses were washed out. Some residents relocated to Onslow County, a bit more inland and a safer place to settle. There were French North Carolinians among these migrants. The archives housed in the Museum of Onslow County provide a wealth of information about French settlers in the area. What follows is a summary of its holdings about French North Carolina, which I have supplemented with my research. The settlement Half-Moon had many Batchelder residents who were descendants of the original Bachelier family of the Trent River colony. Some settled west of New Bern at Batchelder's Creek on land that became the Fonville plantation. Some Batchelders eventually migrated southward to Onslow County.

There were numerous Rochelles in the area, and there are still some today. Many French sailed from the port of La Rochelle, France. Jacob Rochelle stated in a 1977 interview that he was a direct descendant of three French brothers who settled in Maple Hill in the early 1800s. The location of their former farm is between Burgaw and Jacksonville on Highway 53. The earliest documentation we have is of Ephraim J. Rochelle. His mother was Annie Rochelle.

Ephraim was born in New Hanover County in 1824 and passed away on April 24, 1849, in Onslow County. His son, Ephraim Jr., was a farmer and served in the Confederate Army. In a battle at Malvern Hill, Ephraim was wounded in the leg but survived and left a modest estate to his wife and children.

William Cray came from the French Huguenot colony in Charleston, South Carolina, to settle in Onslow County in 1749. He was of French and Scottish descent. He married a woman of French origin, Mary Magdalene Gignilliat, daughter of Henry Gignilliat and Ester Marion. Mary was the first cousin of the famed "Swamp Fox" Francis Marion of the Revolutionary War. We will return to Francis Marion's military contributions to the cause in the Revolutionary Allies chapter.

The Onslow County Register of Deeds houses land deeds of French settlers as far back as 1782. Some of the names are as follows: Leddy Duval (1772), a transaction between John Fonville and Christian Duval (1782), Arthur Venters (1782), and numerous land purchases by Jeremiah Fonville. There are other deeds from the 1800s of John Grenade, Anderson Gillet, John Jarrot, William Montfort, John Sallier, and several transactions of James Foy. Marriage records of the 1800s document marital transactions of persons of French descent: George Foy, Henry Ferrand, Dempsey Fouse, Israel Faison, Edward Fonville, William Farrar, Jacques Le Maresquier, and Peter Rainguinoire among them. The latter two surnames are elegant French ones for sure.

Other French surnames frequently appear in Onslow County public records such as Lanier, Lemaire, Midgett, Pelletier, Petifer, Rochelle, and Ventois. The Southwest Primitive Baptist Church on N.C. 53 at the outskirts of Jacksonville has several gravestones with French names such as Foscue, Rochelle, and Lanier. The church dates from the early 1800s. Descendants of French Huguenots would have worshiped here.

Richlands not only houses vital colonial records but also has among its historic homes some with the names of owners of French descent. Two notable ones are the Mittie and Agnes Venters House (circa 1910) and the Del Barbee House (circa 1910). The latter is located, coincidentally, or perhaps not, on Foy Street. Both homes have decorative front porches. The Del Barbee House shows exuberant late Victorian detailing with its decorative wrap-around porch, bay window, and metal gable sheathing. Del Barbee was a man of some education who was in charge of the town's mail services. He had the good taste and wherewithal to build a gem of European elegance in the rural heartland of the state.

Other French families settled in the state in various locations as French North Carolinians continued their slow spread southward and westward. For some of them, we do not have as much information to go on as we would like. The Brevard and Fourney families came from Touraine, France, and settled in Lincoln County. Brevard, North Carolina, is named after the Brevard family. It is near today's French-named Dupont Forest. We will return to the French settlers of western North Carolina in the Go West, Monsieur chapter.

Jean Venois (Anglicized to John Vannoy) migrated with a colony of French Huguenots from New Jersey in 1716 and settled on the Yadkin River in Rowan County. The settlement was known as the "French Jersey Colony." He lived near the mouth of Lick Creek at a spot long remembered as the old Vannoy fish dam. The family record of John and Susannah Vannoy, their son Nathaniel, and Nathaniel's son Jesse has been preserved in an old family Bible. Nathaniel was a pioneer settler and sheriff of Wilkes County during the Revolutionary War.

The Prevatt family descends from Pierre Prévot, who migrated from Manakin Town in the early 1700s to settle on the Neuse River in Craven County, not far from New Bern. His eldest son, James, fought in the Revolutionary War. Another son, Thomas, had three sons: Thomas Jr., Peter, and James. They all moved to Robeson County in the late 1700s and settled northeast of the Old Field Swamp near the town of Fairmont. Thomas Prevatt married Sally West in 1797, and Peter took Eleanor Clements as his wife. There is an 1802 Robeson County land deed with Peter's signature. Thomas and Sally had six boys and three girls. Peter and Eleanor had five boys and three girls.

Most of the Prevatts in Robeson County descend from these two families. Two Baptist ministers from the Prevatt family, Furney and F. A. Prevatt, established several churches in the area: Centerville, Claybourne, and Zion's Tabernacle. Several sons of the Revs. Prevatt served in the Confederate Army during the Civil War. Other spellings of the original name Prévot include Prevatte, Privette, and Provo.

Francis Foye was a native of Normandy, France. Like so many of his countrymen, he fled persecution as a Huguenot. He married Serena Miles in Yorkshire and indentured himself to gain passage to America. Francis settled in Baltimore County, Maryland, in 1673. One of his sons married Rebecca Polies, a daughter of French Huguenots. Their son James moved to Craven County, where he died in 1822. James fought in the Revolutionary War at all of the significant battles that took place in North Carolina: Moore's Creek, Guilford Courthouse, and King's Mountain. In the latter conflict, he shot and killed a British officer to help turn the tide in the American favor. In his will, he partitioned out his sizable estate to his immediate and extended families.

The Lanier family name is a common one in French North Carolina. The origin of the name has its roots in Old French and means a type of falcon. The Laniers were originally from Gascony in southwestern France. Some Laniers escaped the early Huguenot persecutions in France and went to London with their families in 1555. Several generations of the London Laniers were royal musicians. Other Laniers remained in France in Rouen and the Normandy region. Nicolas Lanier was born in Rouen in 1542. He was a member of the court of French King Henri II. The name Lanier is a notable one.

The first Lanier to come to America in 1655 was Jean Lanier. He settled in Virginia and bought land there in the same year. Eventually, some Laniers migrated to the Albemarle region in the late 1600s and increased from there. Thomas Lanier relocated from Brunswick County, Virginia, to Duplin County, North Carolina, in 1752. One of his sons, Thomas (1733–87), married Sarah Miles of Onslow County and settled at Cypress Creek near Chinquapin. Over the generations, the North Carolina Laniers have pursued many different walks of life. There are hundreds of Lanier descendants living in Pasquotank and Duplin counties and elsewhere in the state. The Laniers have a long and accomplished French North Carolina family lineage.

René Julien de Vitré was born in 1669 in France's northwestern province of Bretagne (Brittany). William III of Orange bequeathed him a land grant for service in the King's Army at the close of England's "Glorious Revolution" in 1689. He had five sons; one of them, Peter Julien, born in 1712, was a regulator in Orange County. Another son, Isaac, born in 1716, lived in Randolph County. Isaac died in 1778 of a rattlesnake bite and rests in the Billy Trogdon Cemetery. This is an expansive family cemetery of Trogdons with the families that intermarried with them. There are names with French ancestry there. Along with Julien, there are those of Ferree (Feray) and Duffie (Du Fays).

Dr. Armand Jean De Rossett was born in Narbonne, today a resort town located in southwestern France, on the Mediterranean Sea. He was the son of Huguenots who had fled to Ireland: Captain Louis De Rossett and his wife, Gabrielle de Gondin. They sent Armand Jean to Switzerland, where he studied medicine. He received a medical degree with honors from the University of Basel on December 3, 1720. Armand married a woman who descended from a noble Swiss family of the House of Uzes. She was also a Huguenot.

Armand rejoined his parents in Northern Ireland with his wife. From there, he traveled with a small group of Huguenots to the Wilmington area. They settled with the Cape Fear colony. Armand De Rossett and his wife had three children. His daughter Gabrielle French married compatriot John DuBois. De Rossett bought a home in Wilmington on Second Street between Market and Princess streets. He became mayor of the town in the early 1760s. He also distinguished himself during the French and Indian War. He died in 1767 and is buried in St. John's churchyard.

De Rossett's youngest son, Moses John De Rossett, was ten years old when his father settled the family in Wilmington. Numerous generations of De Rossetts stem from Moses and his children. Moses was an officer in the North Carolina militia during the French and Indian War. He served for many years in Wilmington as a county commissioner and a member of the Board of Alderman. He studied at Princeton University and received his medical degree from the University of Pennsylvania. He practiced as a doctor in Wilmington, like his father. His older brother, Louis, also received a medical degree. He, too, practiced as a physician in Wilmington.

The descendants of Dr. Armand John De Rossett were numerous. What is most striking about his legacy is that for one hundred and eighty years, there was an unbroken succession of physicians with the family name De Rossett in Wilmington. A mural tablet at Saint James Church (where Ms. Tryon intended to meet M. Lobbinière) reads, "In Blessed Memory of four generations of the Rossett family." Listed are Armand John De Rossett (1695–1760), Louis Henry De Rossett (1722–86), Moses John De Rossett (1726–86), Armand John De Rossett (1767–1859), and Armand John De Rossett, Jr. (1807–97). The De Rossett family has left an indelible mark on the history of French North Carolina.

The Southern Historical Collection of Wilson Library at UNC-Chapel Hill houses over two thousand items regarding the De Rossett family. Hundreds of letters, shipping records, business transactions, wills, estate papers, military commissions, birth and death records, and De Rossett women's diaries provide an intimate view into this premier French North Carolina family. Of special interest are documents written in French, including a 1671 marriage contract and an 1817 deed of emancipation for one of the family slaves. A final noteworthy item is a charming poem written in 1795 by Armand John, Sr., to a female acquaintance about the fleeting beauty of life.

One more noteworthy family of French descent is that of Devane (Devanne). Thomas Devanne was born in 1700 and died in 1760. He and his family left France, settled briefly in Scotland as Huguenot refugees, and settled at the Cape Fear colony. He brought some wealth with him from France. By 1735, he possessed land grants for nearly two thousand acres in upper New Hanover County near the Black River. He was from a prominent family and married a French woman of nobility, Marguerite de Contin, before leaving Scotland. She was the niece of the famous French Prince de Conti.

Thomas's two sons, Thomas Devane, Jr. (born in 1725) and John Devane (born in 1740), both served as officers during the Revolutionary War and were active in public affairs. Thomas Jr., who inherited the family plantation, was captain of the Wilmington Brigade of the North Carolina militia. John became a member of the Halifax Congress in 1776 and operated a gun manufactory during the war. His grave is located under the Saint James Church, where the Parish House now stands. One of Thomas Jr.'s daughters, Margaret, married the Frenchman James Portivent, with whom she bore six children. The ancestral lineage of the Devane family in eastern North Carolina continues; many Devanes are living in North Carolina today.

Finally, two Huguenot descendants of North Carolina attained fame. The first, Nathaniel Macon (1758–1837), was born in Warren County. His father, Gideon Macon, migrated from Virginia to North Carolina in the early 1740s. He built the "Macon Manor" in Warrenton on Buck Spring and became a successful tobacco planter. Nathaniel was born in this house, which still stands today. He served in the North Carolina militia during the Revolutionary War. Macon became the foremost public figure in the state during the early nineteenth century. He served in the federal House of Representatives for twenty-four years and in the U.S. Senate for thirteen years.

Despite a successful public life, Macon's demeanor reminded his colleagues of Cincinnatus, the model of Roman virtue and simplicity. Like the Roman farmer turned politician, Macon did not seek or welcome political office but served effectively when the people chose him. Nathaniel Macon was a staunch anti-federalist and was referred to as the "Thomas Jefferson of North Carolina." We will meet him again.

William Gaston (1778–1844) was born in New Bern to a father of Huguenot descent, Alexander Gaston, and a Roman Catholic mother, Margaret Sharpe. By the age of eighteen, William had graduated at the head of his class from the New Jersey University at Princeton. He returned to New Bern to study law with François Xavier-Martin and was admitted to the bar in 1789. William rose to prominence as an attorney and judge, and was elected to the North Carolina Supreme Court in 1833.

In 1840, Gaston composed the words to "The Old North State," North Carolina's state song. He was acclaimed in his lifetime for this intellect and his ability as an orator. Gaston was inducted into the nation's most prestigious academic and intellectual group, the American Philosophical Society. The name Gaston derives from the name of the Gascony region of southwest France. It was the name of several counts of Foix-Béarn, beginning in the thirteenth century, and one with a noble lineage. William Gaston is an icon of French North Carolina.

Chapter 9

Entr'acte

The story of French North Carolina will continue as we delve further into its imprint on the history of the state. Although I have frequently referred to family ancestry, I am not a genealogist. Others have carried out French North Carolina genealogical work over the years. I have relied on their efforts to preserve our knowledge of French heritage in the state. As any genealogist or cultural historian knows, there is often inconclusiveness in bringing to light the hidden past or forgotten family history with absolute certainty. This is similar to the challenge of writing the present work.

Over the years, members of the Huguenot Society of North Carolina have carried out significant research on the French ancestry of North Carolina. I am indebted to them. There will be readers of French North Carolina descent whose families I did not mention in the book. You have my apologies and are welcome to share your family history. There will be other readers whose family has been discussed. They will be pleased, but they may have some corrections or additions to their ancestry that they would like to share, and I welcome them. My N.C. State email is dmm@ncsu.edu.

I hope that readers of this book will become collaborators, adding information to the ongoing story of the French–North Carolina connection. It is in this spirit of public humanities that this work has been written. Readers are encouraged to provide documents or information they have to add to our collective knowledge. This book, though not by my original intention, has turned into a public archive. Readers are invited to add to it.

The French heritage is like a patchwork quilt and can be continually embroidered to enrich our understanding of the French–North Carolina connection. The member roster of the Huguenot Society of North Carolina lists hundreds of North Carolina citizens whose ancestors were the French colonial settlers in the state. Some of them are direct descendants of the French immigrants we have met. Among them are Christophe de Breuil, Francis De La Mare, Bartholomew DuPuy, Mareen DuVall, Thomas De Vane, John Fonvielle, Henri Faysann/Faison, John Lanier, John de LaPierre, and William Rochelle. The ancestry of the French settlers in the Albemarle region and those of the Trent River colony and elsewhere is alive and well.

Ancestry gives us comfort that we belong to a larger family group, living and deceased. It helps us keep our personal histories grounded in the past, whether a few generations, centuries, or even millennia, as we have seen in this book. The Huguenot Society is an extended French North Carolina family. I will continue to piece together the historical and ancestral fabric of French North Carolina, so all can know more about it.

The information gathered in the book is sometimes incomplete, for so few factual records have been preserved. When I extrapolated and speculated, I tried to do so responsibly by weaving together the strands of information that we do have. I have also sought to add some missing pieces of French genealogy in the state by tracing French North Carolinians back to French and even Roman ancestry. But not a purely genealogical work, this book has mostly attempted to bring part of North Carolina's forgotten past out of the darkness.

My discussion of English history equals that of France; likewise with migration patterns and the early colonial history of North Carolina. The French rode on the backs of the English colonists who were the ones with the genius and resourcefulness to create the thirteen American colonies. Then, there are the Huguenots and their descendants. These amazing people brought so much to America and North Carolina. By necessity, and somewhat ironically, they blended in with the people of its former country's historical archrival. The French assimilation is, in fact, one of the most harmonious relationships in the thousand-year history of French–English relations.

"Entr'acte" is French for intermission. The writing of this book spans many years, and the first half was written while I was researching the second half. The next part, now that the historical foundation has been established, moves forward in new directions. The focus is more lighthearted, with notable events and compelling personalities leading the way.

I am grateful to those who have helped me with the writing of *The French Heritage of North Carolina* by sharing their time, ideas, knowledge, memories, family histories, and personal experiences. Let us now explore the next episodes of the French–North Carolina connection.

Chapter 10

Revolutionary Allies

Several hundred yards from the Cape Lookout Lighthouse on the sound side at Bartlet Inlet is the location of a fort built by a French naval crew captained by Denis de Cottineau. He and his artillery captain, Jean-Baptiste le Chevalier de Cambray, designed and constructed the fort at their own expense with the eventual support of Governor Richard Caswell.

Fort Hancock, Cape Lookout (photograph by the author).

Chapter 10. Revolutionary Allies

North Carolina played an essential role in the American Revolution, as did France. The French presence in North Carolina during the Revolutionary period is a topic worthy of study. North Carolina had a long history of struggle with the Royal Governors. Culpepper's rebellion was one of the earliest popular uprisings in the American colonies (1667). One hundred years later, at the Battle of Alamance County, Governor Tryon's British militia defeated the North Carolina Regulators, who were demanding fairer taxes and legal representation. This battle was a precursor to the Revolutionary War.

France also played an essential role in the American Revolution. The ideals of the new nation were founded on the ideas of the French Enlightenment, especially in the writings of Montesquieu, Voltaire, and Rousseau (Dunn, *passim*). These ideas were brought to revolutionary fruition by Benjamin Franklin, Thomas Jefferson, and others. Franklin spent crucial years in Paris gaining French support for the American cause. Franklin County, North Carolina, is named after Franklin. North Carolina's revolutionary roots reach deep into the history of the French–American relationship.

France wanted to avenge her defeat in the French and Indian War, after which France lost much of its territory in the American colonies. However, at first, the French did not want to enter into open conflict with England and only helped the American cause indirectly. Over five million *livres* in financial and material support were given to the rebel cause, in secret to the extent possible. Finally, when American victory seemed imminent, the French naval and army forces helped seal the deal at the Battle of Yorktown.

Many French volunteers, inspired by the ideals of liberty and republicanism looking to make a name for themselves, or simply to get on the military payroll, joined the American Continental Army. There was also much trade and shipping between France and the colonies, and French merchant ships and privateers were looking to make wartime profits. In North Carolina, much of this trade activity to support the American cause took place in Edenton, New Bern, Southport, and Wilmington.

Throughout the Revolution, eastern North Carolina was a busy place with commercial shipping of wartime goods and other normal trade activities. Minutes of the North Carolina Council of Saftey (July 21, 1776) underscore the importance of commerce between the French West Indies and North Carolina. Timber, tar, turpentine, grains, meats, and fish were exchanged for arms, ammunition, ironware, and other wartime stores. Other essential goods that had been previously supplied by England were now brought from France by French and American ships. Beyond war goods, clothes, hardware, medicine, eyeglasses, shoes, and an assortment of other items helped keep the citizenry supplied.

A letter of 1782 from French General Le Comte de Rochambeau to North Carolina governor Alexander Martin in which Rochambeau requests that "traders of North Carolina carry flour to Cape François" (today's Haiti) to provide for the French fleet stationed there shows how central North Carolina was in delivering supplies to the French military (Weeks, Vol. XVI, 332). Such trade carried on throughout the war. The town of Edenton was central in this commerce.

North Carolina's second-oldest town, Edenton, was one of the fledgling nation's leading political, cultural, and commercial centers. The state's first colonial capital, it was established in the early 1700s and incorporated in 1722. Edenton today features a historic district vibrant with architectural styles spanning two centuries. The 1767 Chowan County Courthouse is a National Historic Landmark. Once North Carolina's second-largest port, Edenton also provided slaves a means of escape via the Maritime Underground Railroad, before Emancipation. Although located in the heart of the slave industry, there were some enlightened folks in the area.

The presence of the French in Edenton mostly dates from the time of the American Revolution. Young French officers came to Edenton during the war and offered their services to start regiments. The leading families of the town entertained them and hosted social events. This group of Frenchmen tended to be members of the nobility and had social entree into the high society of Edenton. The citizens of Edenton and the French officers had a common enemy in the British, and the latter were welcome.

The local citizens "were quite impressed" with these French visitors (Boyette). France was the center of fine art and culture, and to people in a provincial setting, these educated, handsome, elegant aristocrats were like movie stars. At the receptions and balls, the Frenchmen were, of course, very interested in getting to know the women of Edenton. The latter were accomplished in their own right. They had an upper-class English education, and some were talented musicians. Many of them were politically aware and socially active. The Edenton women were an equal match for the Frenchmen, and enjoyed the social events, but kept them at arm's length.

The Edenton women were also revolutionarily minded. In 1774, led by Penelope Barker, the women of Edenton resolved to stop buying English tea and cloth to protest taxation without representation. The event is known as the "Edenton Tea Party," remembered as the first political movement organized solely by women in the colonies. Penelope and other leading women of the town would have met, talked, and danced with the French officers, their conversations turning at some point to their common cause.

The French volunteers, to their disappointment, were not given the regiments they requested. They either joined existing American regiments or returned to France or the West Indies. Those who remained settled in North Carolina after the war, and we will return to them.

There are other French connections in Edenton that predate the

Revolutionary period. There is evidence of small groups of French settlers in the area before 1700. These Huguenot settlers migrated from Virginia down the Chowan River and through the Great Dismal Swamp. This was the first wave of Huguenots in the 1690s we saw in the Huguenot Migrations chapter; others would follow. There are land patents in Chowan County from the early 1700s of French landowners such as Gilbert, Chevin, Blanchard, and Champion (Hathaway, *passim*).

During the colonial period, French merchants, tradespeople, pirates, and slave traders were part of this burgeoning port. There are cannons on the waterfront given to Edenton by the French government in 1783. The ship *Coeur de Saint Jésus* ("Holy Heart of Jesus") transported them. The famed Wessington House was designed as a "villa in the French style" (State Archives of North Carolina, N.91.9.51). There is just a whiff of historical Frenchness in Edenton, but it is there.

During the 1700s, there were French shops, barbers, tailors, and watchmakers on the Edenton waterfront. A vendor name "La Truchy" brought luxury items from France and North Africa for purchase by the town's wealthier citizens (Hathaway, 7). The women of Edenton's high society looking to refine their colonial homes welcomed French fashion, porcelain, silverware, and other luxury household items, something for which France is still well known.

The Chowan region is inscribed with snippets of French heritage. The former French ferry crossing, *Sans Souci* ("without a care"), not far from Edenton, is another example of the French presence in the area. There is a country road near *Sans Souci* named Paris Trail. There are streets in downtown Edenton with French names such as Carteret and Granville.

Maritime records tell of the constant coming and going of merchant ships to Edenton. They would arrive from Bordeaux, Marseille, and other French ports with such goods as salt, brandy, wine, tools, fabric, candles, and firearms, then return to France with tobacco, barreled pork, lumber, turpentine, and tar. We will revisit Edenton's French commerce and how it benefited the region's economy. Claude Sauthier, as he did for Bath and New Bern, made the first official map of the town. Edenton's French heritage is a meaningful part of the town's history and played an essential role during the American Revolution.

Edenton was the most important port in the state during the Revolution for supplying the Continental Army in North Carolina and northward. Edenton was the center of a bustling trade route between the French West Indies and the northern colonies, and the town prospered. In the 1770s, Philadelphia merchants and their families moved to Edenton, and their presence, along with the many French merchants and sailors, gave Edenton a cosmopolitan flavor. Sugar, molasses, rum, and tropical fruits from

Sans Souci (photograph by the author).

the French West Indies enriched Edenton's alimentary culture. More exotic goods from the Middle East, such as silk, spices, coffee, and cocoa, came in from ships sailing out of Marseille, France, by way of Cadiz, Spain.

There was a wide variety of goods available to the citizens of Edenton, many of French provenance. A Frenchman named Peyrinnant was one prominent merchant of the Edenton waterfront. He oversaw a booming business with his ships traveling to France and the French West Indies. His cargoes of French wine, brandy, lace, silk, jewelry, porcelain, silverware, books, furniture, and fabrics added a level of domestic and social refinement to the town.

Many French mercantile houses sent representatives to the American colonies in the 1770s and some set up shop in Edenton. This was the reason that Stephen Cabarrus, son of a prestigious merchant and shipping family of Bayonne, France (a southwestern seaport), settled in Edenton in 1776. His parents, Etienne Pierre and Catherine Lancereau Cabbarus, sent Etienne Jr. to seek his fortune in America. He studied hard to learn English, Anglicized his name to Stephen, *et voilà*!

Cabarrus quickly established himself as an able businessman and was quite the opportunist. His educated polish, good looks, and French charm helped him win the favor of a widow, Jeanne Henriette Bradley. They were married, and Cabarrus became the owner of her sizeable estate. In her own right, Mrs. Bradley was of French ancestry and from the town of L'Orient, France, a port town in the northwestern province of Brittany. The French–North Carolina connection of Edenton continues to grow.

Cabarrus became a successful merchant and landowner and eventually represented Chowan County in the North Carolina state legislature. He would go on to become speaker of the House of Representatives and was a tireless advocate of education in the state. Education, at the heart of French identity and its long lineage of intellectual culture, was infused into the social arena of North Carolina by the forward-thinking Frenchman Stephen Cabarrus. His brothers Dominique, Auguste, and Thomas eventually joined him and helped manage their elder brother's business interests and continued in the family tradition as successful businessmen.

Other French merchants established themselves in the later 1770s. One was a Monsieur Pucheu, the son of another Bayonne mercantile family. He made a dramatic arrival in 1777 with a "whole Cargo of French folks ... amongst them two very fine ladies with a great many fine things and New Fashions. You have lost your share of the finery. It was all sold the day they came onshore" (Mrs. Jean Blair to her daughter Nelly, Higginbotham, Vol. I, 448). The enthusiasm with which the town's citizens bought up the French luxury items is apparent.

Mrs. Blair goes on to say that Nelly's French tutor Mr. Dermody recently passed away. The teaching of French was taking place among the well-to-do families of Edenton. One of the town's ferry owners was a Frenchman, Augustine Deschamps, and the town had at least one French hairstylist that we know of, a Monsieur André Richard.

Richard had a thriving trade and was able to afford the purchase of the Hatch House on East King Street, a well-to-do neighborhood. Other French professions represented in Edenton were tailors, watchmakers, and fabric merchants. France was an integral part of the town's thriving economy. These French citizens brought their Old World expertise and culture to the town and added a European flair to it.

Government agents also oversaw the trade with France that took place in the state on behalf of the North Carolina legislature. Local commodities such as tobacco, indigo, and flaxseed were traded for military goods from France, such as muskets, gunpowder, flint, and sailcloth. The French agents were often military personnel such as Captain Le Marquis de Brétigny, whom we will soon meet.

In 1778, Edenton had at least a hundred French people living there and "over a dozen French shops" (Cain, 17). Some of the French trading firms were Lory Frères of Nantes, Raimbeaux et Compagnie of Bordeaux, Sebastien Fils et Compagnie of Paris, and Rouilhac et Compagnie. The latter set up its main office in Edenton itself. It was the first international company in North Carolina. The State Archives of North Carolina house account books and correspondence, written in French, of Jean de Rouilhac. These fascinating letters discuss various voyages and their cargoes of his nine vessels. Monsieur de Rouilhac's elegant handwriting and meticulous account books are a marvel to behold. They are also a valuable glimpse into the details of French wartime shipping during the Revolution.

Jean de Rouilhac, account book (courtesy State Archives of North Carolina).

Other names associated with French merchant shipping in Edenton are Benjamin Laporte, Captain Poulard de Rostilloux, merchant Robert Thurbet, and a Monsieur Lacouture. The letters of John Gray Blount, prominent merchant, shipper, and politician of Washington, North Carolina, are testimony to the French in other parts of North Carolina during the Revolutionary period. Blount has some Frenchness to him. The family name derives from the Anglo-Norman French *blunt*, meaning "blond," which stems from the Old French *blund* or "blond" derived from the Latin *blondus*.

Blount exchanged frequent correspondence over many years with French merchants such as John Goelet, Thomas Pasteur, Nicolas Romayne (who conducted business in Southport and Wilmington), and Jean de Rouilhac. He also corresponded with military leaders of French descent,

Chapter 10. Revolutionary Allies

such as John Sevier and James Cole Mountflorence. After the war, in 1791, Blount traveled to Paris with Mountflorence to make North Carolina land deals with French financial speculators.

Blount could speak and write acceptable French and appreciated the refined culture that France had to offer. He took an active part in the election of Thomas Jefferson as president in 1800. Let us remember that the Francophile Jefferson honed his political ideas on the works of French Enlightenment philosophers. Blount's French roots run deep. But alas, both he and Jefferson were part of the slave industry, and their ideals of freedom and equality for all would take two centuries to come to fruition for African Americans, and this is still a work in progress.

Washington, North Carolina, the hometown of the Blount family empire, has a distinctive French heritage to it. French merchant and ship owner Lewis LeRoy, who had migrated from Martinique in the early 1800s, lived in "the most gracious and cultivated home in town" (Lewis and Young, 2). He married Helen Palmer. Her distant ancestors had been French Huguenots. Let us remember that the family name derives from the Old French *palmier*, a palm branch brought from the Holy Land to France during the Crusades. LeRoy's shipping business prospered; his vessels conducted trade between North Carolina, France, and Martinique, continuing the transatlantic exchange of goods, between Old and New Worlds. Around this time, an upscale hotel, named after the Marquis de Lafayette, hosted the many merchants, French among them, who would stay in town on business.

Helen and their daughters became accomplished musicians and experts at needlework. They were cultivated French immigrants, and Lewis was a town leader. French merchants and captains were frequent visitors at the LeRoy house, where they were lavishly entertained (Lewis, 3). The name LeRoy is the Old French spelling for *le roi* ("the king"), and the LeRoys were the royalty of Washington.

The following snippet of Washington history is out of a storybook. In the early 1800s, a merchant ship from Washington sailed into the harbor at Martinique just as a slave rebellion had broken out on the island. Two terrified young boys, one white and one black, escaped to the waterfront and took refuge aboard the ship. Their parents had been massacred in the uprising. When the ship returned to Washington a few weeks later, its captain entrusted the two orphans over to LeRoy, who could speak with them in French.

Lewis and Helen decided to adopt the white boy, John P. Labarbe, and found a home for his friend of blended parentage, Philippe, with a kindly parson who lived nearby, Thomas Bowen. Parson Bowen Anglicized his name to Phil, and taught him English and how to read and write, and Phil became a trusted and valued servant of the family for many years. Washington's French–North Carolina connection is an original one.

Salt was an essential commodity during the colonial period. It was a necessity to preserve meat and fish, necessary for nutrition, and used to tan animal hides. Salt produced in France was brought to Edenton by way of the French West Indies. As the war wore on, there were often shortages, and salt works were established in the Beaufort area. Andrew Mabson set one up at Gallant's Point (both names are of French provenance). He designed salt beds that were flooded with seawater "after the manner of France" (Letter of Cornelius Hernet, May 1776, Weeks, Vol. XII, 740). This is another small way that France played a role in North Carolina during the American Revolution.

The collected papers of James Iredell, longtime North Carolina statesman and a leader of Edenton, shed more light on the town's French activities during the Revolutionary period. One of the best portraits of Iredell is by the French artist Charles Saint-Mémin who also created portraits of Thomas Jefferson and George Washington. Iredell is in prestigious company.

Iredell's letters give us firsthand accounts of family life, politics, and town activities during the colonial period in Edenton. They also give us a glimpse into the French presence there. He had frequent and friendly correspondence with a Monsieur Pucheu. One of Iredell's letters narrates that some Frenchmen complained about doing business with Americans, saying the latter knew little of commercial affairs—the Old World French snobbery at work.

Another letter intimates that although the Frenchmen cut a dapper figure in town, the Edenton women considered them "far too forward," however, "Edenton Ladies are not altogether afraid of French Men" (Higginbotham, Vol. I, 449–50). As we know, Penelope and her girls were independent minded and could take care of themselves. In another letter, Nelly Blair described dining with a Monsieur de Neuville at an inn and complained, "there were so many Frenchmen there, and you know they have not too much reserve" (Higginbotham, Vol. I, 472). As usual with French–American relations, there are mutual likes and dislikes, fascination and suspicion.

Before we leave Edenton, a short literary aside is as follows. James Boyd's historical fiction novel of 1923, *Drums*, captures the French spirit of Edenton just before the American Revolution. The son of a North Carolina squire is sent to a tutor in Edenton to be educated and learn the ways of polite society. Young Johnny Fraser has exciting experiences and encounters with many entertaining people, French among them; he even travels for a spell to England and France. There are dozens of references to the French and France in *Drums*. One of the most entertaining scenes is an encounter with Johnny's gruff inn proprietress in Paris, Madam Legaude, as she comes to his room to collect the rent, "Madam Legaude, huge-bosomed, hairy-faced, filled the doorway demanding her rent in advance." She comes to like Johnny though, acts maternally, dismisses the rent, and calls him "un galant homme"—a good man (Boyd, 336).

Another amusing episode is when Johnny seeks passage to London on the French ship, *Hirondelle*. When he meets Captain Lautrec, the latter exclaims, "Monsieur Desires!" and then calls on his cabin boy, "Pierre! Cognac!" Johnny and the captain come to terms for passage as Johnny sips "the thick, fiery liquid with grateful shudder" (Boyd, 272). Boyd sought to be as historically accurate as possible in his background information. The *Hirondelle* is, in fact, one of the ships used by Rouilhac in his enterprise, as witnessed by his account books. The *Hirondelle* is also referenced in other French shipping records and made many voyages to and from Edenton during the 1770s. There are many French words interspersed in the novel's dialogues, showing the presence of the French in Edenton. Finally, other sons of the landed North Carolina gentry were studying in Edenton and traveling to London and Paris to receive their education and social training. Boyd thus gives us a vivid entry into the Frenchness of Edenton at the time.

Three critical battles of the American Revolution took place in North Carolina: Moore's Creek, King's Mountain, and Guilford Courthouse. The first battle of the American Revolution was, in fact, the Battle of Moore's Creek that took place on February 27, 1776. A Patriot North Carolina militia led by Colonels Richard Caswell and James Moore defeated a Loyalist army marching to rendezvous with a British force stationed near Wilmington. Although a minor engagement, this early victory helped delay the British invasion of the southern colonies for several years and gave time for the North Carolina militia to prepare themselves. It also boosted Patriot morale in the southern colonies.

Militia members of French descent participated in the battle. Francis Marion Fonvielle was the great-grandson of one of the original French settlers in the early 1700s, John Fonvielle. Later during the war, there is some evidence that he served as an interpreter for Le Marquis de Lafayette. Other militiamen of French descent were Peter Ballard, Abraham Gamelian, John Mallady, Manuel Cozier, John Devore, Elias and James Faison, Charles and Samuel Gavin, and Abraham Moulton.

On the Royalist side in the battle were John Bethune (who served as a chaplain), Samuel Diviney, Robert Gillies, Captain Thomas Amy, Philomel Arnet, Uriah Blanchelle, Captain Ephraim Brevard, John Devane, Ebeneezer and Kilbee Faison, Peter Fontaine, James Foy, Peter Mallet, John

Perret, and Lieutenant Henry Vipon. It is interesting to see how the French colonists of the early 1700s had been integrated into the social fabric of colonial North Carolina over the generations and ended up on both sides of the conflict.

The bay of Cape Lookout at the start of the Revolution was an excellent port, but without fortifications. In February 1778, French privateer Captain Denis de Cottineau steered his frigate, *Ferdinand*, into the harbor and noted the site's potential. Cottineau's ship, one laden with supplies to help the American war effort, had been damaged en route in an engagement with the British. His ship needed extensive repairs, and he decided to build a small fort to protect the vessel and his cargo.

Onboard the *Ferdinand* was the handsome and dashing Jean-Baptiste le Chevalier de Cambray, an artillery captain with an engineering background. De Cambray surveyed the area and deemed that Cape Lookout provided a strategic military position to project Cottineau's ship as well as the coastline for the North Carolina Continental Army. De Cambray and Cottineau undertook the construction of the fort, mainly at their own expense. Such generosity was to support the American cause, but also to provide a haven for future French mercantile commerce in the area.

Cottineau donated six cannons, two swivel guns, ammunition, and assorted firearms. In return, he and de Cambray requested letters of introduction to the Continental Congress asking for commissions in the Continental Army. The fort was completed and garrisoned in May 1778. Cottineau named the fort in honor of the owner of the land on which the fort was built, Enoch Hancock. As he prepared to leave North Carolina, Cottineau made claims for some of his expenditures and was awarded nine hundred and forty pounds by the North Carolina General Assembly. His letters to the assembly, written in near-fluent English, are housed in the State Archives and make for fascinating reading.

The location of the fort was at Barden Inlet. Significant research and exploration was conducted in the 1950s to determine the exact location of the fort but was inconclusive. Anecdotal information of residents of the former settlement Diamond City on Shackelford Banks has indicated the general site of the fort. Two of the residents remember swimming there as boys in the early 1900s (Day, 97). They found remnants of the old fortifications, breastworks, bricks, scraps of metal, and French coins. On a visit in 2017 to the spot these residents described, the author found rusty iron spikes and remnants of a wooden rampart that could have been the foundation of the fort.

Fort Hancock protected the area from British ships. It never saw military action though it was often sighted by British vessels who steered clear of any potential engagement. Cottineau and de Cambray played a small but

Chapter 10. Revolutionary Allies 135

Location of Fort Hancock (photograph by the author).

meaningful role in North Carolina's coastal defenses during the Revolution. De Cambray subsequently was made a lieutenant colonel in the Continental Army. He eventually garrisoned in Edenton from where he would lead troops in the Southern Campaign. After the war, he was honorably discharged in 1783. Cottineau received a commission in the Continental Navy and participated in several engagements. He died in 1808 and was buried at the Colonial Park Cemetery in Savannah, Georgia. Cottineau and de Cambray are two French North Carolinian heroes of the Revolutionary War. A final aside on the French heritage of Cape Lookout is that the current lighthouse built in 1859 has a Fresnel lamp. It was developed by the French physicist Augustin Fresnel and was the premier lighthouse apparatus of the nineteenth century.

The Battle of King's Mountain took place nine miles south of King's

Mountain, North Carolina, on October 7, 1780. The Patriot militia defeated the Loyalist militia commanded by the British and inflicted heavy casualties on the latter. A decisive key to the battle was when the "Overmountain Men," three separate militia from Virginia, Washington, and Sullivan counties (then part of North Carolina), surrounded and decimated the Loyalists. Leading the militia from Washington County was John Sevier. The British commander Patrick Ferguson was killed while trying to break through Sevier's battle line, and the British surrendered soon after.

Sevier was the son of a Frenchman, Valentine "The Immigrant" Sevier, who had migrated to Baltimore, Maryland, in the early 1740s. Religious persecution, as for so many others, had driven Valentine Xavier (his name before it was Anglicized) from France. He became a successful tavern keeper. His eldest son, John, distinguished himself as a military and political leader. He was one of the founding fathers of Tennessee and was elected its first governor in 1796. He played a vital role in the British defeat at King's Mountain. Unfortunately, his brother Captain Robert Sevier was mortally wounded in the battle. French blood spilled on Carolina soil in the fight for independence.

The Battle of Guilford Courthouse of March 15, 1781, marked a turning point in the war. General Nathaniel Greene weakened Lord Charles Cornwallis's army at the battle in a series of bloody skirmishes and strategic retreats. Cornwallis lost 27 percent of his men. Seven months later, he would surrender at Yorktown, marking the end of the war. Several notable Frenchmen fought at Guilford.

Charles François Sevelinges, Le Marquis de Brétigny, was a dashing young nobleman from Soissons, France, who came to Philadelphia in July 1778. On January 1, 1779, he wrote to General George Washington and petitioned for the rank of brigadier general and the command of an independent French company. The Continental Congress appointed him at the level of lieutenant colonel, which annoyed de Brétigny. He considered the rank below his station since he had served in France under the command of Louis XVI's brother, the famed Comte d'Artois. Nevertheless, he accepted the appointment and eventually led a detachment of North Carolina militia dragoons at Guilford and performed his duty.

De Brétigny also served the revolutionary cause in North Carolina in another vital way. Congress commissioned him to carry dispatches to French Admiral Jean-Baptiste D'Estaing in the Caribbean. He then led a small corps of French volunteers to defend South Carolina. Before the Battle of Guilford Courthouse, he was commissioned by the North Carolina General Assembly to sail to Martinique for the purchase of food provisions and war supplies. It was a dangerous journey since the British fleet was always looking to attack and plunder American and French ships. This

Chapter 10. Revolutionary Allies

The Battle of Guilford Courthouse at Guilford Courthouse National Military Park (photograph by the author).

successful voyage as a purchasing agent helped supply and sustain General Greene's troops.

De Brétigny's corps was comprised of a few dozen horse soldiers, experienced dragoons, who made the ride with him from South Carolina to Guilford. During the battle, de Brétigny's detachment was composed of his French dragoons and those of the North Carolina militia. He was positioned on the left flank, and his men helped to inflict heavy casualties on the British. This small French–North Carolina alliance on the battlefield shows the cooperation of French and Americans as they fought for their shared ideals of liberty and equality and similar desire to expulse the foreign intervention of a common foe.

At the end of the war, in 1793, Congress paid over twenty-three hundred pounds for the war supplies he had provided on credit and formally thanked de Brétigny. He went to New Bern and either paid off his debts, lived large, or a combination thereof. He died later that year, forgotten and destitute. His plight points to the underside of the French presence in North Carolina at the time. Although they appreciated the efforts of Cottineau, de Cambray, and de Brétigny, folks in North Carolina did not care much for the French.

Appointment of Le Marquis de Brétigny (courtesy State Archives of North Carolina).

Many of the French volunteers were deserters, adventurers looking for profit, scoundrels, and worse. They were a rough bunch and not the refined officers of Edenton or the caliber of de Brétigny et al. With the French and Indian War not too far in the past, folks in North Carolina generally did not like the French. On a national level, although Jefferson and Franklin were pro–French, John Adams was wary that the French secretly wanted to supplant the English as colonial overlord.

The people of North Carolina were grateful to the nation of France but did not care for individual Frenchmen. A 1787 account of the French in Washington, North Carolina, for example, exclaimed, "[t]he People, in general, despise them heartily" (Cain, 17). Similar to American attitudes today, many of us love France's ideals and culture, but not so much the French. A French proverb says that there are two sides to every coin. This is the core of the French–American relationship.

Another French colonel who fought at the Battle of Guilford Courthouse was François Lellorquis, Le Marquis de Malmédy. He served with distinction in the battle. He had been a cavalry lieutenant in France and, after migrating to America to seek his fortune, enlisted in the Continental Army in 1776 as chief engineer of defense works. He was known to have a

Chapter 10. Revolutionary Allies 139

temper, and when he was appointed colonel the next year, he protested, as had de Brétigny, complaining to General Washington himself that the rank was beneath his merit and experience.

Malmédy also had a run-in with Nathaniel Greene about military strategy and the former's failure to complete a mission to obtain supplies and militia from the North Carolina legislature. Greene, however, commended him after the Battle of Eutaw Springs for "great gallantry and good conduct" (State Archives of North Carolina, GASP Jan-Feb 1781). Malmédy commanded a small cavalry unit at the Battle of Guilford Courthouse and carried out his orders successfully. Always quick to anger, which made him a fierce fighter, he was killed in a duel in 1781. The North Carolina legislature awarded the equivalent of three thousand two hundred and fifty dollars to his estate. *Au revoir Monsieur Malmédy.*

Other French officers and soldiers fought at Guilford and elsewhere in North Carolina during the war. Lieutenant Chevalier de Vallier received a mortal wound in a *rencontre* with a British piquet at Guilford. A Colonel Armand commanded a small independent French corps near Edenton. Ordinary soldiers such as Lewis Simon, Jean Lapplanty, and Jean Battice Fromentier served in the Second North Carolina Battalion. They were described as speaking "pretty good English" (Cain, 16) and having swarthy complexions and long dark hair, making it likely they were from southern France. Indeed, other French fought in North Carolina during the war. Militia rosters list the French names Boudin, Brevard, Decarouet, Delamar, Devane, Fontaine, and Fonvielle, among others. Most returned to France or the French West Indies afterward, but some stayed and settled in eastern North Carolina. French family names in the area testify to this.

James Cole Mountflorence is a unique figure. He was a native of France and became an American patriot, land agent, and lawyer. He studied at the University of Paris and served as an officer in the French army for nine years. He came to America in 1778 and was appointed captain of a regiment of French volunteers in the North Carolina Continental Line. The regiment did not pan out, and he ended up in New Bern. Mountflorence then petitioned for an appointment as a French interpreter for the state, but this did not work out. A string of bad luck, but he persisted in making his way in life.

James then became a schoolmaster at the New Bern Academy. His classical French education served him well. He taught mathematics, and a smattering of French, Latin, and geography. The New Bern Academy had adopted a model of a well-rounded and thorough education for its citizens in 1764. It is the oldest public school in North Carolina. The teaching of the French language and culture was an integral part of educating an enlightened and informed citizenry. A Gaspar Beaufort taught French there in the

1770s. Although he taught there only a year, Mountflorence was part of the academy's forward-thinking educational mission.

After his teaching stint, Mountflorence served as a supply officer for General Greene's army and was commended at the end of the war for carrying out his duties with "diligence and activity" (Traxler, 1). After the war, he operated a supply store in Warrenton and became a successful land agent. As mentioned earlier, he contracted at one point with the Blount family and traveled to France with them to promote and sell western North Carolina lands. That must have been a great trip. Blount was a wealthy man, and accommodations would have been first class. North Carolina goes to France in style with its French North Carolina tour guide and interpreter Mountflorence.

In the mid-1790s, Mountflorence moved back to France and served as a private secretary to various American diplomats. His bilingualism and knowledge of both the United States and France made him a valuable asset to the American diplomatic corps. Although he spent the rest of his life in France, he described himself as an American citizen; such was his love of our country. Mountflorence was our revolutionary ally. He also helped develop the educational and economic landscapes of North Carolina. He is a true French North Carolinian, and we will see him again.

French events during the war in New Bern took a nasty turn at one

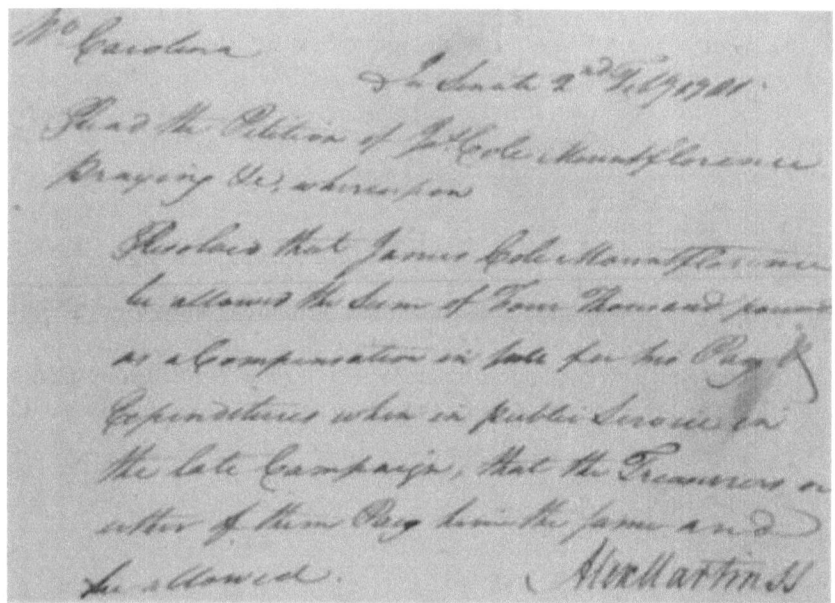

James Cole Mountflorence, compensation for service (courtesy State Archives of North Carolina).

Chapter 10. Revolutionary Allies 141

point. In 1778, in a letter to Governor Richard Caswell, Colonel Chariol de Placer offered to raise a regiment in New Bern composed of former French sailors and other natives of France and the French West Indies living in New Bern and other ports of the state (Weeks, Vol. XIII, 129).

There was an abundance of unemployed Frenchmen looking for work, yet they were not all upstanding citizens. An eyewitness account of a traveler, Elkanah Watson, described his experience of being "turned from tavern to tavern, every house filled with French adventurers" (Cain, 14). This is a hint that there would be some backlash against the French. Nevertheless, Chariol had a plan and began to gather his men for the "French Refugee" regiment, as it is referred to in North Carolina military rosters.

He got a good start and enlisted French officers, men of prominence, to serve as the core of his regiment, and they set about recruiting. Sureau du Vivier, Laval Belvieu, Martin de Breteuil, Le Baron de Bonstetien, and James Cole Mountflorence, among others, were part of this group. Chariol's officer quarters were set up in the house of a Frenchwoman, Mrs. Edouard (Dill, 341). Chariol found it difficult, however, to create an entire regiment in a foreign land. Moreover, many of these unemployed French sailors were disaffected deserters and not eager to enlist in a foreign war. Some of these Frenchmen were also rough around the edges, had some unpleasant encounters with the locals, and sparked anti-French sentiment—this discouraged other refugee Frenchmen in eastern North Carolina from joining Chariol's regiment.

Chariol may have been his own worst enemy in his failed enterprise. During the recruitment process, one of his sergeants enlisted a young French sailor, Julien Laborcet. A local shipper James Davis, Jr., claimed that Laborcet was his indentured servant. Word got around town quickly and infuriated its citizens. James Davis Sr., one of the town's leaders, led an angry mob to the schoolhouse that was being used as a barracks for the French recruits. He threatened, "to put every Frenchman to death, in town, or drive them out of it" (Rankin, 182). Davis and his gang forced their way into the building and gave the French recruits a good beating with cudgels.

After this incident, it was near impossible for Chariol to continue with recruitment. The North Carolina General Assembly recalled his commission. The ability and loyalty of Chariol and his officers were not questioned, but there were not enough "privates of the French Nation" to create a viable regiment (Rankin, 183). Shortly afterward, Chariol returned to France. He had spent one thousand pounds of his own money. It was unfortunate that the revolutionary cause did not benefit from the regiment he could not raise. It was a bump in the road of the French–North Carolina alliance.

In 1782, North Carolina Governor Alexander Martin addressed the General Assembly to praise and thank the French, calling them a

"Magnanimous Ally" (Weeks, Vol. XVI, 295). With the Chariol incident in the past, by the end of the war, France had a growing economic and cultural influence in New Bern. The teaching of the French language, and interest in its culture, was growing there and elsewhere in North Carolina. The many French *immigrés* who sought their fortunes in North Carolina after the Revolution and, as we will see, in the wake of the French West Indies slave rebellions in the 1790s, provided numerous opportunities for the citizens of New Bern to learn French. In 1787 a Madame Bruin taught French and art appreciation. A Monsieur Galliard taught French "grammatically" as his 1795 advertisement boasted (Watson, 177).

In the 1790s, there were enough French businessmen in New Bern that the French newspaper, *Courier de l'Amérique*, published in Philadelphia, was offered to subscribers of the *New Bern Gazette*, whose editor was François Xavier-Martin. Xavier-Martin was a leading intellectual figure in New Bern and helped keep its European ties alive.

On October 19, 1898, the one hundred and seventy-seventh anniversary of the British surrender at Yorktown, the French flame still burned strong in New Bern. Students of the New Bern Academy and the public grade schools honored Lafayette with readings and songs. There was a special address by Professor Thomas Foust, one of the state's leading educators, which underscored the importance of French–American friendship and political alliance (Watson, 552).

After the American Revolution, French–American relations deteriorated rapidly and culminated during the infamous "XYZ Affair." North Carolina was involved in quelling the affair. It is a complicated story, and the following is XYZ in brief. During the war, a Franco-American alliance united France and the United States against the British. However, by the late 1790s, France and the United States almost went to war with each other. The United States had refused to offer aid to France during the French Revolution. Incensed, France went on a naval offensive and illegally seized over three hundred American ships between 1797 and 1798.

To settle this conflict, President Washington sent a diplomatic mission to France. The American diplomats met with three French agents who were known as Messieurs X, Y, and Z to protect their identity. Our friend, James Cole Mountflorence, was one of the intermediaries during the negotiations. The French agents demanded that the United States pay two hundred and fifty thousand dollars to France and provide a twelve-million-dollar loan, and they would stop seizing American ships. This infuriated the United States, and tensions were high.

Three of North Carolina's most prominent congressional representatives, Nathaniel Macon, Joseph McDowell, and Robert Williams, were of the levelheaded opinion that the proposed bribe was not offered by the

French government, but by these rogue agents. They encouraged President Adams to avoid war and to build up rather the U.S. naval force to protect American ships from the French. After three years, thanks in part to the efforts of the North Carolina senators, things quieted down when France and the United States signed the Treaty of Mortefontaine. French–American relations immediately improved.

As we know, Macon was of French Huguenot descent, and this may have been a factor in his ability to understand France and help end the crisis. His colleagues McDowell and Williams had also fought in the Revolutionary War in North Carolina side by side with the French and saw their significant potential as an ally rather than as an enemy. The French–North Carolina connection did well in keeping this young country out of an unnecessary war.

One of the most exciting aspects of French North Carolina uniqueness is the imprint on the state left by Le Marquis de Lafayette. Marie Jean-Joseph Roche Yves Gilbert du Motier, Marquis de Lafayette, was the French rock star of the American Revolution. He was known in the United States simply as Lafayette. He was a French aristocrat and military officer and volunteered to fight in the American Revolutionary War. He commanded American and French troops in several battles, including the Siege of Yorktown.

Lafayette funded French troops at his own expense and distinguished himself in several battles. He was a child of the Enlightenment and filled with enthusiasm and devotion to the causes of liberty and "the rights of man." He was a close friend of General Washington himself, who called him the son he never had. *Lafayette and the American Revolution* (Freedman) is an essential and enjoyable introduction to Le Marquis. Lafayette will leave his mark on North Carolina.

Nearly fifty years after the war, in 1824, the U.S. Congress requested in a unanimous resolution that President Monroe invite Lafayette to visit the United States. The purpose was to commemorate the fiftieth anniversary of the American Revolution, to revive the patriotic spirit of America that had begun to dissipate, and to instill the essence of the Revolution in the next generation of Americans. Lafayette was now an elder French statesman and a prominent international figure. He arrived in the United States in August 1824 and, over the next fourteen months, visited each of the twenty-four states and all the principal cities. Lafayette was received everywhere with reverence, tokens of affection, and public celebrations.

Lafayette's visit to North Carolina in 1825 is a notable French North Carolina event. His entourage consisted of himself, his son George Washington Lafayette, personal secretary Auguste Levasseur, North Carolina delegates, and militia escort, seven coaches in all. It was a rough winter journey, and the North Carolina roads were poor at the time. Lafayette was a hardened war veteran, though. He had also been made resilient by his years in prison when he had been on the wrong side of politics during the French Revolution, so he could handle it. The grueling journey was softened by how he was feted graciously at all of his stops in North Carolina. There were parades, artillery salutes, veterans from the war who met and dined with him, banquets and balls, and schoolchildren reciting poems and singing songs to celebrate his achievements.

Lafayette's first overnight stop in North Carolina was Murfreesboro on February 26. He missed a ball in his honor when the carriages became stuck in the mud. The group had a difficult time, as Levasseur recounts. Upon arrival, Levasseur tells us, "we were very amply compensated by the cordial hospitality of the inhabitants" (Levasseur, 303). Lafayette stayed at the Indian Queen Inn, had a late dinner there, and received visitors. The historic district of Murfreesboro has homes that are over two hundred years old. One of the grandest of them is Melrose, erected in 1805, that still stands today. It is just a few blocks away from the location of the Indian Queen Inn on Broad Street. Lafayette would have passed by the home and was perhaps even entertained there.

The next day the group traveled twenty miles to Northampton Courthouse (now the town of Jackson) to be greeted by the official state delegation from Raleigh. The town had prepared a formal dinner, and guests took turns in expressing their appreciation of Le Marquis. Jackson has a small portion of French heritage. The Faison House, built circa 1790, is one of the oldest houses left in Jackson.

The Faison family was of French Huguenot ancestry. They migrated to North Carolina in the early 1700s and became successful in the eastern part of the state. The Faison family of Jackson were among the town's leading citizens and would most likely have attended the Lafayette dinner. The town of Faison, North Carolina, which we have visited, testifies to the Faison family's French heritage, as does the Faison House in Jackson.

The next morning Lafayette traveled to Halifax and was received by the official state welcoming committee. He stayed overnight at the Eagle Tavern, where a banquet was held in his honor. The town of Halifax was established in 1760; it was a river port, county seat, and social center. It also had a thriving agricultural economy. Markets operated in the town, and the inns and taverns did a brisk business. Today the Eagle Tavern stands, as does the Tap Room, a colonial pub. They date from the late 1700s. Lafayette and his group enjoyed the hospitality and conviviality of these establishments.

Halifax has a special place in the history of the American Revolution. In 1776, the "Halifax Resolves" were adopted. It was the first official action by an entire colony to recommend independence from England. During

Chapter 10. Revolutionary Allies

Lafayette at the Eagle Tavern (photograph by the author).

the war, Cornwallis briefly occupied Halifax before his northward march to Yorktown. Halifax thus had important symbolism for Lafayette.

After the Revolution, Halifax entered a golden age of prosperity and culture. Elegant homes were built, and the town was a thriving one. It was at the peak of its success at the time of Lafayette's visit. There were settlers of French ancestry who were part of this era. French war veterans had also made their homes there after the Revolution. The Halifax County Register of Deeds has land transactions from the 1780s of Earl Granville, Thomas Corbin, Charles Pasteur, Henry Montfort, and William Fuqua. There are towns nearby named after French communities, such as Macon, Gaston, and Severn. The French presence in Halifax County is small, but it is there.

We have mentioned that Lafayette and his entourage were enjoying dinners and banquets on his North Carolina tour, so what was offered for food and beverage? Wines, beers, hard ciders, and exotic punches were standard offerings on the drink menus of North Carolina taverns. Liquor-based toddies were popular after a long day of travel. The drink's potency and warmth, and the addition of nutmeg or other spices, made toddies particularly welcome in colder months.

Lafayette's North Carolina tour took place in late February, and it had been a cold and often rainy trip. They must have enjoyed some of these American toddies. And the culinary offerings! Although the Frenchmen were used to refined European cuisine and had been dining at upscale venues in New York and Philadelphia, they enjoyed North Carolina cooking. They helped themselves to copious servings of smoked ham, trout, duck, butter beans, potatoes, cornbread, apple cobbler, sweet potato pie, and more.

After Halifax, the party traveled through Enfield. On the way, they would have passed Bellamy's Mill. The name is a transformation of the French, *bel ami*, a "good friend" that a gristmill was to colonial settlers. Lafayette and company crossed the Tar River at the falls in Rocky Mount and stopped briefly in Louisburg for a pit stop and to water their horses.

Louisburg is an integral piece of the French–North Carolina connection. The town is in Franklin County, named after Benjamin Franklin, who secured our support from France during his years in Paris as America's premier diplomat. The town takes its name from Louis XVI. Although hesitant during the war's early years, Louis, and his queen Marie Antoinette, would eventually authorize financial and military support for the American cause. A related aside about the name Franklin is that it originates in the French-Anglo word *fraunclein*, a landowner of free but not noble origin. It is an appropriate one for Benjamin Franklin since he rejected the very concept of nobility and fought tirelessly for his country's freedom.

From the late 1700s to the early 1800s, settlers of French descent came to the Louisburg area. The Franklin County Register of Deeds contains land transactions of Jenkins Devaney, Mary Mabry, Charles Blanchard, Amos Linort, Harrison Macon, and Solomon Bachelor. Today, the downtown area and the main building of Louisburg College have touches of European design, reminding us of the town's French heritage.

Continuing south on Louisburg Road, Lafayette and his entourage

Chapter 10. Revolutionary Allies 147

spent the night at Colonel Allen Rogers Tavern at Rogers Crossroads. Today, one can visit the location at the intersection of Forestville Road and Louisburg Road just north of Raleigh. The tavern no longer stands, but Lafayette would have stayed there, close to this crossroads. The next morning, the group continued to Raleigh down Louisburg Road and was met at Crabtree Bridge by Raleigh officials. The original bridge no longer exists, but one can visit the crossing at Hodges Street and Wake Forest Road and see the bridge built in 1952 at the very location of the one over which Lafayette traveled.

Crabtree Creek Bridge (photograph by the author).

Lafayette traveled down Wake Forest Road, passing through the Mordecai plantation, and arrived at the home of Thomas P. Devereux on Halifax Street where a local cavalry unit met him and his party. It is coincidental, perhaps not, that the Devereux family name is of French descent. The family's name dates to the eleventh-century town in Normandy France, D'Evreux (i.e., "from Evreux"). A few hundred yards from Halifax Street, Devereux Street commemorates the family name. Two blocks north, the Mordecai House, at the corner of Wake Forest Road and Lafayette Road, recalls Le Marquis's visit to Raleigh.

The cavalry unit, the Raleigh Blues, then escorted Lafayette's coaches down Blount Street to the Governor's Mansion, where state officials and prominent local citizens awaited him for a reception. In the evening, there was a formal ball given at the Governor's Mansion, and the Marquis "was very complimentary in his remarks as to the beauty of the Raleigh ladies" (Haywood). Those Frenchmen. Over the next two days, Lafayette was hosted at several celebratory events in Raleigh and was entertained to his delight.

He visited the state capitol and stopped to admire the statue of his comrade George Washington. Thomas Jefferson and Nathaniel Macon commissioned the original Canova statue (and let us remember their French connections). During his visit to Raleigh, Lafayette was reunited with Colonel William Polk, who had seen action at Guilford Courthouse. He and Lafayette had fought together at the Battle of Brandywine. Polk invited Le Marquis to breakfast one of the mornings Lafayette was in town at his North Street home.

Today, the French-inspired Lafayette Village in North Raleigh reminds us of Le Marquis's visit. On a more somber note, a freed slave who lived from 1826 to 1891 is buried in Raleigh's Mordecai neighborhood at the Oak Grove Community Cemetery, two miles from the downtown area that Lafayette visited. His name is Lafayette Ligon. Le Marquis, as we will see, was a key figure in France's abolishment of slavery during the early 1800s. The French–North Carolina connection always has its unexpected ways.

There are a few more tidbits of interesting information about Lafayette's visit to Raleigh, much of it from Levasseur's journal. He calls Raleigh "a pretty little town of 2,700 citizens, half of whom were of the Colored race, free or enslaved" (Levasseur, 308). We will soon return to the role slavery played in Lafayette's life and career.

Another French North Carolina tale out of a storybook is as follows. The night before the group arrived in Raleigh, one of the horses bolted and hit a tree trunk. In the carriage was General Daniel of the North Carolina militia. He was unconscious, and Daniel's colleague General Williams got out his lancet and wanted to "bleed him on the spot" (Levasseur, 304). Bleeding was a medical treatment at the time but could save as well as kill a person. As General Daniel was starting to recover, Lafayette's son George insisted against Williams's plan. The group agreed with Lafayette Jr. and took General Daniel to a nearby farmhouse to spend the night. The next day, Daniel had recovered and joined the group in Raleigh for the celebrations, "tenderly expressing gratitude for [George] having saved him" (Levasseur, 305). George Lafayette was thus inducted into the pantheon of French North Carolina heroes.

After leaving Raleigh, Lafayette's party journeyed south down the Old Stagecoach Road (today's Route 401), escorted by the Mecklenburg Cavalry, to Fayetteville for the famed commemoration, the centerpiece of his journey through North Carolina. Lafayette's visit to Fayetteville has been

Chapter 10. Revolutionary Allies 149

Lafayette Ligon (photograph by the author).

better documented than the rest of his trip through North Carolina. The state's oldest newspaper, the *Fayetteville Observer*, announced the travel tour of Le Marquis in its first issue on January 13, 1825. Lafayette would arrive six weeks later.

Fayetteville was one of the first towns in the newly independent United States to adopt Lafayette for its name (minus the French article "La"). It was the only town named after him in the United States that he visited. Levasseur wrote in detail about the visit in his travel log of the journey. His eyewitness account of the two days Lafayette spent in Fayetteville is informative. Fayetteville also has strong revolutionary roots. In 1775, a group of fifty-five citizens signed a document of freedom (a year before the Declaration of Independence) known as the "Liberty Point Resolves." As he crossed the Clarendon Bridge, Lafayette passed by Liberty Point. Fayetteville was an appropriate place to take Lafayette as its namesake.

Today, the "Lafayette Trail" in Fayetteville marks the places Lafayette visited with twelve bronze markers. Although in town for only two days, Lafayette was honored at several receptions and met as many citizens as time allowed. The day he arrived, the "weather was dreadful," and the "ladies dressed in all their finery" rushed out in the pouring rain across the muddy street for the "pleasure of gazing" upon Le Marquis (Levasseur, 305). Even in his sixties, Lafayette was still a spectacle to behold. Moreover, true to form, North Carolinians would not let bad weather stop the show.

Le Marquis addressed the populace from a stage that had been erected at the Town House, a symbolic place since North Carolina had ratified the U.S. Constitution there. Chief Justice Toomer praised him for undying faith in "the principles of liberty and the rights of man" (Levasseur, 305). There was an elaborate military review in the town square and artillery fire to salute Le Marquis. The French instructor of the Fayetteville Academy at the time was a Monsieur Laising, "a native of France and a gentleman of talents" (Coon, xiv). One can surmise that he would have been there to greet the Marquis in their native language.

A ball and a farewell dinner in his honor were held at the newly built "Lafayette Hotel," where the rooms had been decorated with evergreens and flowers. Lafayette was treated royally in his new hometown. His legacy lives on, not only in the streets and buildings of Fayetteville but also in the "Lafayette Collection" of Davis Memorial Library at Methodist University. The collection includes letters, monographs, books, commemorative medals and plates, maps, prints, paintings, and other items dating from Lafayette's lifetime. Nineteen original letters, written by Lafayette or concerning him, several of them to George Washington, are part of the collection.

One of the gems of the collection is a print depicting Lafayette's interview with Louis XVI and Marie Antoinette before his departure for America. This was the meeting when Lafayette failed to enlist their support for the American cause. He came to America anyway, defying the king's orders, and at his own expense, to help the Americans. He was nineteen years old at the time.

Fayetteville remains proud of its French heritage as witnessed today by its long-standing "Lafayette Society." It was founded in 1981 to honor and promote awareness of Lafayette's contributions to freedom and human rights. On a lighter French North Carolina note, Fayetteville boasts the Bordeaux Center, named after Bordeaux, France, complete with its own Eiffel Tower. Since 1964, the Bordeaux Center has been one of Fayetteville's favorite places to shop and dine. Bordeaux is one of the most beautiful and culturally rich cities in France. Fayetteville has been proactive in maintaining its French heritage for nearly two hundred years.

Fayetteville's French roots go even deeper. Since 1933, Fayetteville and the town of Saint-Avold, France, have been sister cities. Saint-Avold is in the Lorraine region in the northeast corner of France (where Joan of Arc was from). The Lorraine National Cemetery, just north of town, is the final resting place for over ten thousand American service members who died in World War II. It is the largest American military cemetery in Europe. There are numerous North Carolinians buried there, and the transatlantic circle of freedom is complete, France and North Carolina allies forever. American and French blood has been spilled on the ground of each other's country in the quest for freedom. North Carolina is a part of this legacy.

Lafayette's 1825 journey through North Carolina is the capstone of revolutionary French North Carolina. The state's hosting of him is a key moment in the French–North Carolina connection. One of the fascinating historical French North Carolina objects is a compass and sundial housed in the North Carolina Museum of History. French ensign Gabriel du Brutz carried the compass/sundial during the siege of Yorktown that ended the war in 1781 when Lord Cornwallis surrendered to a coalition of America and French forces. Du Brutz sailed on the *Souverain* of the French fleet under Admiral Comte de Grasse, a key figure in the American victory.

Lafayette's regiment also played a vital role in this victory. Before the French Navy and American Continental Army hedged him in at Yorktown, Cornwallis was seeking safety in a retreat to North Carolina, perhaps to Halifax, where he had already garrisoned. Lafayette's regiment of eight thousand men blocked the neck of the peninsula at Williamsburg, thus cutting off Cornwallis's retreat to North Carolina. Lafayette certainly thought back to those days on his visit to Halifax.

This was the start of a new world for the American colonies, and the French helped make it possible. After the war, du Brutz made his home in Fayetteville when the town's name was still Cross Creek. Unfortunately, du Brutz died in 1824 and missed being united with his brother-in-arms to celebrate his French North Carolina legacy, of which he was a part. His gravesite was commemorated, though, in 1825, the year of Lafayette's visit, and the *Fayetteville Observer* reported the event. One wonders if Le Marquis had time to visit Gabriel.

Today, there are dozens of streets and place names named after

Lafayette in cities and towns throughout the state. The town of La Grange was named in 1868 after the people in the area suggested it in honor of Lafayette. He was still remembered and admired by North Carolinians nearly one hundred years after the American Revolution. La Grange was the name of Lafayette's country estate outside of Paris, Château de la Grange, and his French North Carolina legacy lives on.

There is one final part of Lafayette's American and North Carolina tours that leaves us with the larger picture of the significance of his travel through the southern states. In the early 1800s,

Compass and sundial, Gabriel du Brutz. (Courtesy North Carolina Museum of History)

Lafayette became an active liberal politician and helped shape a new egalitarian society in post-Napoleonic France. Although he had seen some slavery firsthand during the Revolution, during the 1825 southern tour, he was immersed in what he referred to as "the cloud of evil which o'erhangs and shadows the South" (Jones, 60).

Lafayette was an ardent supporter of the abolishment of slavery, and France did so decades before the Civil War. His 1825 trip opened his eyes as to what his heart told him to do: take "all men are created equal" to the next level. Levasseur plays a role in this. He states that North Carolina was not an advanced state, the cause of which "must be attributed to Slavery" (Levasseur, 307). As a personal attaché to a man of Le Marquis's stature, Levasseur was not only highly educated but also a grandchild of the Enlightenment. His generation of intellectuals helped make France into a Republic. Lafayette was a key political figure in this achievement.

Let us remember Justice Toomer's praise of Lafayette's commitment to liberty and human rights. How true, but Justice Toomer's recognition is ironic since the Frenchman Lafayette was more true to these ideals than the former southern colonists whose economy thrived on enslaved people. France has its own history of slavery but abolished it decades before U.S.

Chapter 10. Revolutionary Allies 153

Emancipation, thanks to the efforts of people like Lafayette, Levasseur, and others. Lafayette's trip through the American South reinforced his belief that freedom should be for all. *Vive la Liberté!*

A final irony is that the most recent version of the Lafayette Hotel burned to the ground in 1995. The neighborhood had become over the years a low-income one populated by African Americans. Some of them are likely to have been descendants of the slaves that Lafayette witnessed on his Fayetteville visit. Before the fire, the hotel had been a homeless shelter, and some of its residents accidentally started the fire. Could Layafette ever have imagined the plight of what were to become of the freed slaves?

On the other side of the coin, there was a positive side to Lafayette's experience and opinion of the South. He admired the South's "sons who are the most patriotic and enlightened, the most generous and hospitable" (Jones, 60). Closer to home, Levasseur commends the North Carolina militia that was vital in several critical battles of the Revolution. In Georgia, Lafayette laid the cornerstone for a monument to General Nathaniel Greene (let us remember Guilford Courthouse), who had been one of his commanders and whose memory Lafayette cherished. On a personal note, Greene's daughter Martha lived for a year with the Lafayette family in Paris in the early 1800s, another twist in the French–North Carolina connection.

One should keep in mind that Lafayette was the last surviving general of the Revolutionary War, so his American tour was a landmark event for the U.S. Congress. President Monroe had also invited him to help establish good relations with young Republican France. North Carolina played a significant role in this episode of American history, as it did in the Revolutionary War.

The pendulum of French–North Carolina relations has always swung between rivalry and friendship. The French–American relationship, always paradoxical and often ambivalent, waxes and wanes between appreciation and animosity. North Carolina's French connection is a microcosm of this dynamic.

Throughout its history, North Carolina has been involved with France in meaningful ways. This chapter shows the many facets of this French North Carolina history and prepares future stories about the French connections of North Carolina. Other patriotic uprisings in the transatlantic world in the early 1800s are on the way. Some will have repercussions for French North Carolina.

Chapter 11

Crusoe Island

Southeastern North Carolina is an area with a significant French footprint. In the early summer of 1664, a group called the "Barbados Adventurers" led by John Vassall settled in the Lower Cape Fear region. He was the grandson of a French religious refugee of the same name. The latter was from Normandy, France, and had been a merchant and mariner in the late 1500s before fleeing France. His grandson John III took up his seafaring ways. Unfortunately, Vassal's colony never prospered, and the settlement was abandoned in 1667. This small trace of French presence in the area opens the way for other instances of the French phenomenon in southeastern North Carolina.

In the mid–1720s, settlers started to migrate to the Cape Fear region. Some came from South Carolina, where they had been unsuccessful at farming. Other colonists came from England, Scotland, and Ireland. Some of these were Protestants seeking religious and economic freedom. There were French Huguenots among the Scottish settlers. The former had fled France and found a haven in Scotland before migrating to America. Some of the South Carolina group were French Huguenot families who had settled in South Carolina earlier in the 1700s.

South Carolina planter Maurice Moore granted land to these new groups of settlers. Moore's name has traces of French ancestry. The English surname Moore comes from the personal name "More," which derives from the Old French *maur*, meaning "moor." Moore's first name Maurice is French derived from the Latin *Mauricius* that was subsequently adopted into other languages. His son, Maurice Jr., married Anne Grange, a name of French origin, as we learned in the French North Carolina chapter. Maurice Moore was also responsible for overseeing the construction of St. Philip's Church at Brunswick Town at the very place where John LaPierre preached. The French–North Carolina connection grows.

Land deeds in New Hanover County attest to French property owners throughout the 1700s. In 1739, Flavell Grainger and Gallard Lyon completed a land transaction. Armand and Lewis De Rossett purchased several hundred acres in 1779. Other names of landowners who were French or of French descent are as follows: Bellamy, Borchard, Colville, Devane, Dumay, Foy, Grainger, and Le Guion. The name Bellamy frequently appears in land deeds. The elegant Bellamy Mansion is a highlight of Wilmington's historic district. The number of French names at the Hanover County Register of Deeds is, of course, minimal compared to those of the other immigrant groups, but the French presence is there.

Thirty miles south of Wilmington, Southport also has some French heritage. Like Wilmington, Southport was a maritime port and had its share of French trading ships and their crews in town. Some of these sailors stayed and lived out their lives in the Southport area, along with the aforementioned French settlers. The Old Smithfield Burial Ground is a trove of French names attesting to the French citizens of Southport. The names are as follows: Bellamy, Napoleon Bonaparte Brown, Caison, Fountain, Fulcher, Mary Gamache, Gilbert, Giles (from Saint Giles of southern France), Guy, Hardee (Hardi), Jannette, LeHew (Leheu), several Pivers, Prioleau, Vernon, and Vitou.

The Brunswick County Register of Deeds in Bolivia has the following land deeds with names of French origin: William Grissett, Daniel Bellume, Lewis Dupree, George Clewis, D. J. Bordeaux, E. Vannon, and M. Vernon. The etymology of "Grisette" is the name of a gray (*gris*) French cloth. Grisettown is not far from Southport, as is the French-named town of Shallotte (French, *échalote*). Just south of Southport is the community named Bonaparte Landing. The name Clewis has an interesting French North Carolina story to which we will return, as we will to Southport.

Between 1791 and 1810, more than twenty-five thousand refugees arrived in the United States from the French colony of Saint-Domingue, today, the nation of Haiti. The Revolutionary ideals of France and the United States were now put into play in the French plantation slave colonies. Hundreds of thousands of slaves took up arms under such revolutionary heroes as Toussaint Louverture and won their independence after years of violent and bloody rebellion. The consequences for the southern states in the United States were serious ones, and complex. What follows is the situation in brief.

The influx of French refugees into the United States were mainly plantation owners and their families, along with their slaves. There was fear in the United States that the "French blacks" (Foreman, 3) would incite slave rebellions to spread from the West Indies. There was, in fact, an aborted rebellion in Louisiana that drew the attention of neighboring states. In the mid–1790s, several southern states banned slave importation from the rebellious colonies. In 1794, North Carolina legislators passed the "Act Against West Indian Slaves," whereby slaves could not be imported from

Saint-Domingue. South Carolina and Georgia did likewise. Nevertheless, French-speaking slaves found themselves in eastern North Carolina one way or the other, often as the property of their French owners.

A 1795 petition from the French Republic to the North Carolina General Assembly asks permission for French political refugees from Jamaica and their slaves to land in Wilmington. The letter, written by Monsieur P. Manguy, pleads their case as they were in a "deplorable situation" (State Archives of North Carolina, PC.1629). These refugees were well-off plantation owners and their families. They were among the lucky ones who had escaped with their lives. They and their slaves would have spoken French. Some of these French refugees settled in North Carolina with their slaves and enriched the linguistic fabric of the English spoken Down East.

There are slave deeds that attest to the slave ownership of French landowners in the Cape Fear region. A partial list of the landowners follows along with the name of their French-named slave when it could be identified: Armand De Rossett, W. Gaillard (Chloé), Blake Portevint, E. Vernon (César), Thomas Devane, J. Guerrard, Avery Fonvielle, J. Virdien (Marinette), J. Lalamme (Clovis), J. Foy (Jean-Pierre), and L. Poirier (Charlotte). North Carolina slaves came from a variety of places. Some were from the French West Indies (today's countries of Haiti and Guadaloupe) and French West Africa (today's countries of Cameroun, La Côte d'Ivoire, and Sénégal). We will return to a later wave of immigration of Africans to North Carolina in the French North Carolina Today chapter.

Research conducted by Catherine Mennear (MA, N.C. State University, 2003) has indicated significant instances of French language influence Down East (Mennear, *passim*). A few cases are as follows. The double negative, for example, of Down East dialect, "I don't do nothing," is a literal translation of the French, *Je ne fais rien*. "Y'all" may derive from the French plural of *vous tous*. A feature of the early Ocracoke dialect was the absence of the word "do" in places where it is used today. "Sit not here" is the translation of the French, *t'assieds pas là*. Finally, the delightful expression, "I caught me *beaucoup* fish," is a French North Carolina novelty for sure. Mennear delineates other examples of the "interlanguage" of Down East dialect that included French influence. The mix of immigrants from the British Isles, French settlers, and African slaves (both English- and French-speaking) led to the particular character of English pronunciation, grammar, and vocabulary Down East. We will return shortly to the French North Carolina language question.

Now for the heart of our southeastern North Carolina story. It is a fascinating and controversial one. In 1804, the exact date we do not know, a group of French families, led by Dr. Jerome Prosper Formy-Duval (1760–1821), landed in Southport. Formy-Duval was from Tours, France. He was a

Chapter 11. Crusoe Island

royalist and had to flee France at the outbreak of the French Revolution in 1789. He emigrated to Saint-Domingue and established a profitable sugar plantation. Toward the end of the slave rebellions, when all was lost for the French, he managed to escape with five or six families as his entourage. It was a hasty retreat as the group fled for their lives in an open fishing boat. A French merchant ship headed to Wilmington spotted them and picked up the refugees.

The captain of the ship learned of the harrowing experience of Formy-Duval and company. However, he was fearful of taking them as far as Wilmington, where he traded regularly. If word got back to the rebels in Saint-Domingue, this would put both his shipping enterprise and life at stake. He thus set the fugitives ashore at Southport (then called Smithville). He advised them to find passage up the Waccamaw River and find refuge in the swamp, and so they did.

Formy-Duval and his French entourage must have taken some of their wealth with them from Saint-Domingue. They most likely met some of the French settlers living in Southport and had the means to pay for a guide, boats, and the provisions, tools, and weapons needed to survive in the swamplands. When Formy-Duval and his group arrived at the swamp settlement, they met the inhabitants already living there. The islanders welcomed them apparently since this is where Formy-Duval and his entourage settled.

Nearly a hundred years before, Portuguese pirates had escaped from Spanish pursuit and lived on the Waccamaw island with English settlers. These were the original inhabitants along with other former pirates, mutineers, and those fleeing the law, who had made their way to Crusoe Island, from Southport up the Waccamaw River as did Formy-Duval. There were French among them. It was a multicultural settlement of linguistic diversity, unique at the time in the North Carolina rural complexion of the early 1800s.

Dr. Formy-Duval and his companions bought land and established themselves near their new neighbors in the place eventually named Crusoe Island. Formy-Duval's training as a doctor would serve him and the settlement well. He became an essential member of the community, and the family increased and prospered. There are hundreds of Formy-Duval descendants living Down East today. Detailed genealogical research has been carried out, census records show the growth of the family over the last two centuries, and there are numerous Formy-Duval headstones in the area. Of note are those of Formy-Duval's son and a descendant who served in World War II.

Today, the Lake Waccamaw museum houses items that belong to Dr. Formy-Duval: a wooden chest, his overcoat, his walking stick, other

Crusoe Island (photograph by the author).

personal items, and, most importantly, a metal mortar and pestle that he used to make homemade medicine. Formy-Duval served as the physician for his French companions and other members of the Crusoe community. One fascinating object in the collection is a *lignum vitae* bowl (Latin, "wood of life"). It is the hardest wood in the world. Resin from the wood was used since Roman antiquity to treat a variety of medical conditions, from coughing to arthritis. The bowl is a symbol of the resilience Dr. Formy-Duval had to survive his harrowing experiences. Through it all, he finally succeeded in making a decent life for his family and their descendants.

Crusoe Island is an area surrounded by the swamps and the Waccamaw River. Until the 1980s, the only way to get on or off the island was by a shallow-bottomed boat. Today, the only way in or out of Crusoe Island is an isolated dead-end road. Crusoe Island is still an excellent place to hide. It is hard to find unless one asks a local. This served the French North Carolina refugees well as they wanted it to be hard, if not impossible, to be tracked down by the Haitian revolutionaries, or even the French government.

The Crusoe settlement is located on a small rise of land bounded on three sides by the Waccamaw River and on the fourth by Green Swamp. Although it is not technically an island, these boundaries left its residents relatively isolated, as they pretty much are today. They made their living by fishing, subsistence farming, shingle making, basket weaving, hunting, and trading furs in the nearby town of Old Dock. Today, the island has not changed much since the early 1800s. The homes are not the original ones but are nestled in similar locations in the lush greenery of the island. It is a natural paradise, a hushed place, and one feels transported back to the time of the refugee Haitian settlers.

Living on Crusoe Island (photograph by the author).

Crusoe Island's isolation and residents' distinct style of speech struck some visitors over the years as French-sounding. This led to speculation as to the community's origins. Some have suggested that such frequent Crusoe Island surnames as Sasser and Clewis were Anglicized versions of DeSaucière and Cluvières. Some Clewis descendants, however, dispute this theory and claim that their Crusoe Island ancestor was George Clauss of Germany. There are no other known family names of German origin on Crusoe Island, so this latter theory is tenuous. Other islanders claim their ancestry as English, but there is evidence of French heritage too.

Descendants of another early settler, Laspeyre Long, claim that the family is of English origin. However, one member of that family, Eva Long, did genetic testing in the 1980s and found that her DNA had strains of French, English, and West African ancestry. This latter strain could be from the descendants of Haitian slaves that Formy-Duval and his group brought with them during their escape from Saint-Domingue. Moreover, does the name Laspeyre not have a French ring to it? Other common names in the community, some we have seen throughout French North Carolina, such as Forney, Duvall, Dubois, and Dupree, are clearly of French origin.

The name Crusoe Island itself is a mystery. It may derive from, due to its island-like isolation, a reference to Robinson Crusoe in the Robert Louis Stevenson novel. More plausible, however, is the compelling case put forth by Charles E. Patton that "Crusoe" was the Anglicized name of "Crousilleau," the name of Formy-Duval's plantation in Saint-Domingue. Land deeds from the early 1800s, some of which are Formy-Duval's, show this linguistic mutation from "Crousilleau" in the spelling to "Croossous Island" (Patton, 27).

The travels of adventurer and explorer Kinchen D. Council made some observations and insights about the Frenchness of Crusoe Island (MacNeill, *passim*). In the early 1900s, Mr. Council met and interviewed Mr. Buck Clewis and other of the island's fifteen hundred residents to unravel the mystery of the origins of Crusoe Island. In the course of his research, Council estimated that about half of the islanders were of "the French strain" (MacNeill, 5). In his conversations with the French descendants, he noticed specific interpersonal characteristics that belong to the French: "a swiftness to perceptions, a lithe grace of speech, and an inborn hunger for something that is beautiful" (MacNeill, 5). These qualities are the heart of French self-identity.

The link with France and Crusoe Island is further supported by the similarity between chimneys built in the Columbus County settlement and those of Normandy, France. Mr. Council was a well-read and worldly man and could appreciate the French penchant for aesthetic design. He saw a glimpse of this in the rough swampland settlement of Crusoe Island. One night in his reading, he came across a picture of a nineteenth-century French farmhouse in Normandy. Its chimney looked like the ones in Crusoe Island, which were unique in North Carolina.

Mr. Council admires the artistry of the Crusoe chimney as follows: "[T]he sticks were completely hidden by a white plaster of pinkish chalk, and the lines of the chimney molded into a smooth curve. The tip of the chimney was a smooth, chastely decorative one" (MacNeill, 3). The Crusoe Island chimneys were more than just sticks and mud; there was an artistic style to them that harked back to France. The French North Carolina settlers brought some of their ingrained homeland and cultural history

Chapter 11. Crusoe Island   161

with them. Mr. Council also noted the islanders' penchant to enhance ordinary life with beauty, at the heart of the French aesthetic ideal. Instead of wearing neckties, the men wore necklaces of colored beads, for example, showing, perhaps, the Caribbean influence brought by the French settlers and their West Indies slaves.

Let us return to the question of the French language at Crusoe Island. Council tells us that Mr. Clewis's speech, and that of the other islanders, "is pitched high against the roof of the mouth, like a Frenchman's, and their syllables are clipped and precise" (MacNeill, 6). Pocahontas Wight Edmunds, in *Tales of the North Carolina Coast*, provides an intriguing comment on the local dialect and its similarity to French, "by the way they linger on the last syllable" (Edmunds, 139).

These observations prepared the way for the more scientific research carried out by Amy Lavonne Gannt (MA, N.C. State University, 2000). It supports the remarks of Council and Edmunds about the unique flavor of the islanders' speech. Gannt has shown clear evidence of a French linguistic inflection in the local speech of Crusoe Islanders. The geographical isolation of the island created social and linguistic isolation. As such, remnants of early local speech characteristics have survived.

Gannt interviewed Crusoe speakers and analyzed their speech patterns to show that the Crusoe English dialect has some of its origins in the French language (Gannt, *passim*). Linguistic data is more scientific than historical analysis or even the similarity of chimney design. Gannt's work provides evidence to support the hypothesis of Crusoe Island's French ancestry. The linguistic and phonological qualities of English are complicated, and what follows is her research in brief.

Some key pronunciation characteristics of Crusoe speakers are as follows. The way the islanders pronounce the voiced alveolar nasal consonant in words such as "none" and "month" is characteristic of French pronunciation. Likewise, with their turning diphthongs into monophthongs (i.e., two syllables are blended into one). The word "fire" in Southern English is usually stretched into two syllables, whereas the islanders pronounce it as one syllable (the French word for fire is the one-syllable *feu*). Finally, what Gannt defines as the frequent "prevocalic consonant cluster reduction" (Gannt, 58) of Crusoe speakers also points to French pronunciation. Gannt's fieldwork recorded numerous instances of the unique French pronunciation of Crusoe Islanders. Like headstones and land deeds, the scientific analysis of language is a reliable historical document that rises above legend, hearsay, and scholarly speculation.

From the American Revolution to the French Revolution, and finally, to the Caribbean Revolution, the broader meaning of democracy and human rights was finally recognized. Let us remember that the Marquis de Lafayette worked tirelessly to promote these ideals. Ironically, Dr. Formy-Duval was twice on the wrong side of history. The first was as a member of the aristocratic ruling class at the time of the French Revolution when he had to flee for his life or face the guillotine. The second was as a wealthy sugar plantation owner, of which he reaped the benefits of privilege for over a decade before the slave rebellions turned his life upside down once again.

    How he ended up where he did, in the swamplands of eastern North Carolina, established himself anew, and with success, is extraordinary. Of all the people we have met in France, he may be the most intriguing. The case of Crusoe Island remains, however, somewhat enigmatic. What seemed to unite those who settled there was that most of them had fled one difficult situation or another. Whatever the reasons, they chose to live in their isolated community rather than in the more prosperous settlements along the coast. Because of this isolation, their French manner of speaking English has remained constant over two centuries. The Crusoe Islanders are prominent members of the French North Carolina family, and many people in eastern North Carolina have Dr. Formy-Duval's aristocratic French blood running through their veins.

Chapter 12

Notable Names

The following individuals are essential players in the French–North Carolina connection: François Xavier-Martin, André Michaux, Maréchal Peter Ney, and Dr. Sidney Weller. They all left their unique mark on the cultural history of the state.

François Xavier-Martin (1762–1846) was born in Marseille, France, and was of Provençal descent. We have met him several times before, and now it is time for the full story of his French–North Carolina connection. He was the third son of a prosperous merchant. In 1780, he sailed to the French island Martinique where he worked for his uncle's shipping business as an assistant. The next year, his uncle went bankrupt and returned to France. François wanted to make his own life, so he sailed to New York City, where he stayed briefly before moving to New Bern to seek his fortune. He was without means and had no marketable skills and little knowledge of English. François took whatever jobs he could find—teaching French, delivering the mail, and finally working in the print shop of Mr. James Davis. He trained as a typesetter, which is how he learned and improved his English.

Xavier-Martin was industrious, and he eventually established his own printing business. He published many books (school manuals, almanacs, translations of French novels, and legal pamphlets) as well as the *North Carolina Gazette*. He studied law and was admitted to the North Carolina bar in 1789. In 1806, he was elected to the North Carolina General Assembly, where he served for two years before leaving North Carolina for Louisiana after he had been appointed attorney general by President James Madison. He went on to become one of the foremost legal experts in the United States. Quite an accomplishment for our French North Carolina immigrant who did much to educate and enrich the citizenry of New Bern for over twenty years.

The *North Carolina Gazette* was first published in 1751 and was the first newspaper printed in North Carolina. It announced local news but focused mostly on international news. It was the lifeline to the outside world for

New Bern's citizens. James Davis ran the newspaper for many years with his son Thomas and partner Robert Keith. The latter taught François the trade, and he learned it well enough to become the newspaper's owner and publisher from 1786 to 1798. It was under his guidance that the paper's subscribers could also buy a subscription to the *Courier de l'Amérique*, published in Philadelphia.

As discussed in the Revolutionary Allies chapter, there were enough expatriate French living in New Bern at the time to warrant such an opportunity. Xavier-Martin devoted a good deal of space in the paper to European news and especially current events in France. In the mid-1790s, he published several articles about French military campaigns in Europe. An etymological aside is that the word "gazette" came into English via seventeenth-century French from the Italian word for the cost of a newspaper (*gazeta*, a coin of small value).

Xavier-Martin also translated and published seven French novels, including three by Marie-Jeanne de Riccoboni, one of the most popular novelists in France during the mid-1700s. Her most well-known work, the *Lettres de Fanni Butlerd*, is in the epistolary (letter writing) style and examines the psychology of love and Marie-Jeanne's progressive ideas on men and women. Of Xavier-Martin's choice of novels to translate, Madame Riccoboni's are the best of them; the others were popular romance novels of the day for the general reader and of inferior quality.

Xavier-Martin's translations became best sellers in New Bern. He printed these novels and made a profit on them while disregarding copyright laws. In his defense, international copyright laws were not very rigorous at the time, and François Xavier-Martin would do anything for a buck. Unfortunately, slave owners who were buying, selling, or looking for runaway slaves paid for most of the advertisements that supported the *Gazette*. Alas François, the unsavory side of French North Carolina.

Let us take a closer look into the Xavier-Martin–Madame Riccoboni association, and give women more of their due in the French–North Carolina connection. One of Xavier-Martin's most popular translations of Riccoboni was *Jenny; or, the Distress of Love* (*Histoire de Miss Jenny*). The story is about a woman trying to conquer her female identity in a male-dominated society. Madame Riccoboni promoted very progressive ideas about the rights of women. It is interesting to see her work catch on in New Bern. Xavier-Martin, perhaps inadvertently, perhaps not, brings these modern ideas to the female readership of New Bern (the biggest consumers of these novels).

As we have seen, more women started to be educated after the Revolutionary War in New Bern; it was a cosmopolitan city, and such ideas were taking hold. It is noteworthy that Madame Riccoboni was born in

1713, three years after the founding of New Bern; she and the town are contemporaries. Moreover, one part of the *Gazette* was the "Distresses and Grievances" section in which subscribers could submit their problems and complaints. Distress and grievance are what Madame Riccoboni's heroines are all about. Men, for example, betray Jenny and the heroines of her other novels time and again. She stays strong, however, overcomes her problems, and survives. Her resilient female identity would have appealed to the New Bern female readership. Women struggled mightily in the masculine tenor of life in early America for their equality. Madame Riccoboni's modern notions of women were unique for the time of their appearance in New Bern. Her work promoted a balanced relationship between men and women. François is to be commended for bringing Madame Riccoboni's work to light in the United States.

Madame Riccoboni was a beautiful, highly educated, and vivacious person. She was an actress as well as a writer, and most of the heroines' problems in her books express firsthand experiences. Unfortunately, she lost her royal pension after the French Revolution and died in poverty. This is the opposite trajectory of Xavier-Martin, who began his career penniless and ended up a wealthy man. His sale of the translated works of Madame Riccoboni's work, in part, was part of his success. It is a sad French North Carolina irony. Xavier-Martin was also a dour person and quite the opposite of the charming and vibrant Madame Riccoboni. Their French North Carolina relationship is thus a paradoxical one in more ways than one.

As a scholar's aside, one thing that should be mentioned concerns conducting library and archival work in France; to carry out fact-finding there is a scholar's experience second to none. The French save everything having to do with their past, and their librarians and archivists are experts in what they do and are extremely helpful. Some of the writing of this book relies on archival work conducted in France. This is where the author researched Madame Riccoboni and her *Histoire de Miss Jenny* as well as some of the Huguenot families we have met.

We have learned that Xavier-Martin published the first comprehensive historical studies of the colonial period in North Carolina, *The History of North Carolina from the Earliest Period*. It is a worthy study; however, in all of Xavier-Martin's publications, there are stylistic errors that expose his imperfect proficiency in English, and the carelessness of a man who published copiously and rapidly. He was a bachelor his entire life and a tireless worker. He amassed a good deal of wealth over the years but was known as a miser. He was even arrested in 1786 for failing to pay a disputed debt he owed to fellow Frenchman, Monsieur J. Coulougnac. Xavier-Martin finally paid the debt and was released from jail (Weeks, Vol. XVIII, 693–95).

Before coming to New Bern, Xavier-Martin served for a brief time in the Virginia militia toward the end of the Revolutionary War. It is thus fitting that he had the opportunity to meet President George Washington in New Bern during the latter's 1791 tour of North Carolina. The town even entrusted Xavier-Martin with an appointment to the receiving committee for the president. The president's stay in New Bern, where he was comfortably lodged in town and entertained at Tryon Palace, delighted Washington. Xavier-Martin always remembered the several days he spent in the president's company as the most memorable of his life.

Sadly to say, François Xavier-Martin's life ended miserably. He became blind in his later years and chose to live in poverty in New Orleans toward the end. When he died, his estate was worth four hundred and fifty thousand dollars, a fortune at the time. He had become one of the top legal experts in the United States but was also a Scrooge, whom most people disliked, especially in his final years. Nevertheless, François, even with his flaws, is part of our French North Carolina family.

André Michaux (1746–1802), famed French explorer, naturalist, and writer, left a remarkable imprint on French North Carolina. By the late 1700s, France was running out of its most crucial natural resource, wood. It was needed for heating homes, storing wine, making warships, and more. In 1785, Louis XVI called Michaux to Versailles and offered him a commission to search for new trees in the dense forests of the United States. Michaux was given a generous salary and status equal to that of an ambassador. He traveled hundreds of miles in the American wilderness, by horse and by foot, for eleven years, searching for trees that might thrive in France. He was an educated student of the French Enlightenment, yet also physically hardy enough to brave the American wilderness.

Michaux and his son François André propagated seedlings in portable greenhouses and sent them back to France by the thousands (over five thousand to Versailles alone). He also conducted exploratory research and made significant botanical discoveries. From 1789 to 1796, Michaux made five forays into North Carolina. In 1787, he and a group led by Cherokee guides explored the border area of North Carolina, South Carolina, and Georgia. They camped near Highlands and Cashiers. In 1789, he traveled to the area around Morganton. Here he made one of his essential botanical discoveries near present-day Mount Holly. This was the Bigleaf Magnolia tree; it has the largest leaves (three feet long) and flowers (up to sixteen inches wide) of any North American tree.

Just outside of Morganton, Mr. Waightstill Avery lodged Michaux and his son at Swan Ponds plantation. Avery was Princeton educated, had served in the American Revolution, and was the first attorney general of North Carolina. His Ivy League education had taught him French, and he was the perfect host for Michaux. Today, curiously, there are several roads near Swan Ponds with the French names La Fôret Drive, Du Mont Drive, and La Bellevue Road, which recall Michaux's visits to the area. The creator of La Fôret ("Forest") did well in adding the correct French accent, not always the case with French place names in the United States, and also using the article "La," which gives an air of French authenticity.

André Michaux at Swans Pond (photograph by the author).

In the same year, Michaux also traveled to the Wilmington area and back out west to Black Mountain, where he collected more than twenty-five hundred seedlings of trees and shrubs. His journeys then took him to other states, but he returned to North Carolina in 1794 and climbed Grandfather Mountain. In his journal, Michaux tells us that when he reached the summit, he celebrated the moment by shouting out, "Long live France! Long live America! Long live liberty!" and then sang the new French national anthem, *La Marseillaise*, at the top of his lungs, with the North Carolina mountain wind blowing through his hair (Deleuze, 33). It is one of the most memorable events he recorded in his journal.

Other areas visited by Michaux in North Carolina were Halifax, Fayetteville, Salisbury, Linville Gorge, and Table Rock (near Morganton). He saw more of North Carolina and its natural beauty in a few years than most North Carolinians do in a lifetime. Many plants have been named after André Michaux. One of the most remarkable is the rare and lovely

Carolina lily (*Lilium michauxii*). North Carolina adopted this lily as the state's wildflower in 2003. It grows throughout North Carolina and is a delicate beauty to behold. Michaux also discovered the Catawba rhododendron near today's town of Belmont. One can see these scarlet rhododendrons in their glorious display at the Daniel Stowe Botanical Garden, not far from where Michaux discovered them.

Near Toxaway, Michaux identified one of the rarest wildflowers in North America, the *Shortia galacifolia*, popularly known as the Oconee bell. Beyond such botanical discoveries, one of Michaux's essential contributions to the mountain folks of western North Carolina was showing them how to collect and produce ginseng commercially. Many North Carolina mountain families started selling ginseng root on the Chinese market, where it was valued for its medicinal purposes as a potent antioxidant that boosts the immune system. The sale of "sang," as the locals called it, became a viable cash crop for many mountain families.

Housed in the Jardin des Plantes in Paris are displays of seeds gathered by Michaux on his American explorations. One of them is of the red oak collected in western North Carolina. Some of these North Carolina red oaks were planted in this royal botanical garden established in 1635 during the reign of Louis XIII. The descendants of these seedlings thrive there today in this transatlantic migration of North Carolina's natural beauty. André Michaux is an elite member of French North Carolina who did much to bring the state's botanical richness to light. *Merci, Monsieur Michaux.*

One of the most mysterious French North Carolina stories is that of Maréchal Michel Ney, Duke of Elchingen. It has perplexed historians since his death in 1846. The son of a successful barrel maker from eastern France, Pierre Ney, he rose through the ranks as a soldier in the army, and became a member of the elite French cavalry (the "hussars") and eventually the field marshal of Napoléon's Grande Armée. He was a true war hero, a decorated veteran of numerous battles, wounded many times. He was called *le plus courageux de tous* ("the bravest of the brave") by Napoléon himself. Ney was a tall man with flowing red hair, a commanding presence, loved and respected by his soldiers. He had cool courage, expert military skill, and served Napoléon with distinction.

After Napoléon's defeat at Waterloo, Ney was on the wrong side of politics. He was put on trial for treason by the new French government, found guilty, and condemned to death by firing squad. Now, the legend begins. What follows is a synopsis of a complicated story, and many have written about it. There is some evidence that Ney faked his death on December 7, 1815. His execution was held at dawn in a remote area of the Luxembourg Gardens (not the usual place for executions). The firing squad had, perhaps, been bribed to fire blank cartridges or to shoot over his head, and Ney had blood packs hidden in his shirt that he burst as they fired. When the rifles went off on the signal, Ney fell forward. This is counter to such executions when the body is thrown violently backward. There was also no customary final shot to the head delivered after the rifle volley. Ney was then put on a stretcher and whisked away to a hospice where he would "die" the next day.

Rumors quickly spread that this was a mock execution and that a substitute corpse had been placed in the casket and buried in a simple grave at the Père Lachaise Cemetery in Paris. Conspiracy theorists maintained that some military officials, still loyal in their hearts to Napoléon and Ney, hatched this plot and then smuggled him out of the country. The firing squad could also have been former soldiers of Ney who were easy to persuade in the charade. After the faked execution, Ney was taken to Bordeaux and took a U.S. ship to America. There is some truth to yet doubt in this theory. An interesting French North Carolina coincidence is that Bordeaux is the same French port city from which Lafayette sailed to the American colonies for the first time in 1780.

Six weeks later, about the time it took for a transatlantic voyage, in January 1816, a man named Peter Stuart Ney arrived in Charleston, South Carolina. It is no coincidence that his destination was Charleston. We know that the French had populated the city since early in the state's history. There may have been French contacts who could help him get settled and begin a new life. The tall redheaded immigrant resembled the Maréchal and spoke English with a French accent. He boarded with residents in the coastal area of South Carolina, living simply out of a trunk and earning a living as a schoolteacher. Ney always seemed to have more money though than a teacher's salary paid back then (around twenty dollars per month). He was trying to remain incognito, and then some French expatriates recognized him one day in Georgetown, South Carolina.

For the next few years, to keep his identity secret, Ney moved from small town to small town in South Carolina, Virginia, and North Carolina, and earned a living as a schoolmaster. He was well versed in French, Latin, and German, and could teach math, history, and geography. He would move on to the next town when folks became suspicious of his identity, fearful of being apprehended or assassinated by French government agents.

Around 1819, Ney settled in Cleveland, North Carolina, and became Rowan County's premier teacher, training young men to enter Davidson College. He was well liked by his students, and the daily school routine always began with a military flair when Ney paraded and inspected the students each morning, mixing soldierly discipline into his scholastic regime. Ney was also an expert equestrian and skilled swordsman, characteristic of the French hussars. He was a voracious reader of books on French history and newspapers in which he paid particular attention to news from France. He wrote in the margins of books on the Napoleonic Wars and the French Revolution, adding his commentary whenever there, in his opinion, was an inaccuracy. His students said in interviews after his death that he seemed to have firsthand knowledge of French battles.

Peter Ney's schoolhouse (courtesy the Raleigh *News and Observer*).

In 1821, upon hearing news of Napoléon's death, Ney burned a large number of papers to hide his identity, attempted suicide with a knife, and was miraculously saved by a local physician. Asked what had prompted him to take his life, Ney replied, "Napoleon is dead. My last hope is gone" (Quynn, 165). If Ney had been spirited out of France in 1815 to return and fight another day when the Bonapartists returned to power, that option had vanished.

French veterans of the Napoleonic Wars who had fled to the United States and settled there would recognize Ney as the Maréchal when they passed through town (Gerard, 17). Peter Ney also liked to drink a bit, and when intoxicated enough, he would start speaking French and tell war stories from his years under Napoléon's command. Quite often, however, after

Chapter 12. Notable Names 171

he had sobered up the next day, he would deny such claims, careful of protecting his secret.

Ney was careful not to make public claims about his past but would confide the truth to his drinking companions, *in vino veritas!* (Latin, "in wine, there is truth!"). The folks in Rowan County knew, or wanted to believe, that Peter Ney was Le Maréchal, and covered up for him, so appreciated he was. Keeping this legend alive also made the citizens of Rowan County feel like they were sharing in the glory of Ney's prestigious past.

In 1846, on his deathbed, he raised himself on his elbow and made the public acknowledgment that he was indeed Maréchal Ney: "I will not die with a lie on my lips, I am Marshal Ney of France" (Gerard, 21). His attending physician, Dr. Thomas Graham, noted that he had many shrapnel and sword scars, bullet wounds, and a musket ball in his left calf that had never been removed. There was also a deep scar on his left arm, at a spot similar to a severe wound the Maréchal had received at the siege of Mainz in 1794.

Ney is buried in a cemetery at the Third Creek Presbyterian Church, and his headstone reads, "[a] native of France and soldier of the French Revolution under Napoleon Bonaparte." The plaque lists Peter Ney's age at seventy-seven years, making the year of his birth 1769, the same as that of Maréchal Ney.

There is, thus, evidence that Peter Ney was the Maréchal. His father's name, after all, Pierre, is French for Peter. Yet, if the latter was the Maréchal and wanted to hide this identity, why did he not change his name altogether (Quynn, 170)? It is possible that Peter Ney, like many other expatriate Frenchmen living in the United States at the time, used the false French war hero pedigree to his advantage in making his way in America.

Others have maintained that Peter Ney was, in fact, the Scottish-born Peter Stuart McNee, who had served in Napoléon's army and thus had some of the firsthand knowledge that Peter Ney espoused. The historian William Henry Hoyt has asserted that the true Maréchal Ney did not escape the firing squad. He also found an 1820 application for citizenship filed by Peter Stuart Ney in South Carolina and a record of his baptism in Scotland. Yet, Hoyt's research is inconclusive; he could never provide enough evidence that Peter McNee had ever traveled to the United States, or was the same man as Peter Stuart Ney of Rowan County, North Carolina.

Let us turn the coin over one more time. In 1815, the deceased Maréchal Ney was carried away and buried quickly after the execution, and in secrecy. There was no ceremony for a man of his stature, and his devoted wife Aglaé did not attend. Decades after Ney's death, when his body was moved from its simple grave to the current monument in Père Lachaise, the gravedigger Dumesnil claimed that the coffin was empty when he went to exhume the body (Mace, 1). Perhaps the corpse that replaced the Maréchal's was never buried. Peter Ney used to wistfully intimate that he had left a wife in France whom he loved very much. He had hoped to reunite with Aglaé one day, but as we know, his plans did not work out.

The mystery has yet to be unraveled. Analyses of handwriting samples of Peter Ney and the Maréchal were compared in 1895 and 1934 and deemed to be of the same hand. His body was exhumed twice. In 1887, as reported in the Raleigh *News and Observer*, over three hundred people, many physicians among them, attended the event. Maréchal Ney had a silver plate in his skull and an anklebone that had been nicked by a bullet. The physicians tried to identify these details, but their findings were inconclusive. One of them made a plaster cast of his skull. In 1936, another exhumation was carried out, but there was also no consensus. Would DNA analyses of Peter Ney's body and Maréchal Ney's descendants unravel the enigma?

Whether Peter Ney was an imposter or not may never be known. Whomever the gentleman buried in Rowan County is, he certainly put on a good show, and has kept people talking and writing about him for a long time. In this, Peter Ney is a French North Carolina legend. One thing about Peter Ney's legacy, though, has no doubt; he taught for several years as a lecturer at Davidson College, which is not far from Cleveland. In 1840, Peter Ney designed the seal for the college, which is a hand plunging a dagger into a coiled snake surrounded by the Latin motto *Alenda Lux Ubi Orta* ("Let Learning Be Cherished Where Liberty Has Arisen"). Davidson College today houses the Peter Ney Collection: books annotated by Ney, some of his letters, poems, and personal belongings, and yes, his plaster skull. *Au revoir, Monsieur Ney.*

When Giovanni da Verrazzano explored the North Carolina coast in 1524, he wrote in his journal of many grapevines he had seen growing naturally. He compared them to the grapes of Lombardy, Italy, and thought they would make great wines. His observation is the beginning of French wine culture.

About twenty miles from Halifax, North Carolina, rises Medoc Mountain. It reaches only an elevation of three hundred and twenty-five feet after three hundred million years of erosion of what were initially volcanic peaks. The slopes of the mountain were long used for agriculture. Ample streams provide a steady water supply. In the 1800s, the property belonged to Dr. Sidney Weller, an acclaimed farmer and educator, who used the land for the cultivation of grapes and the production of wine.

Weller named the mountain "'Medoc,' after the celebrated wine province in the Bordeaux region of France, Médoc" (Helsley, 37). Note that Weller Americanizes the name by dropping the French *accent aigu*. Weller produced highly regarded wines known as "Weller's Halifax." He also promoted advancements in the American systems of grape cultivation and winemaking.

Chapter 12. Notable Names 173

Weller named his enterprise Medoc Vineyards, one of the first commercial wineries in the United States. He cultivated indigenous black and white muscadine grapes, along with other varieties. By 1835, Weller was producing sixty barrels of wine per year and sold his wines from one to six dollars a gallon. By 1840, North Carolina was the premier winemaking state in America, with Weller in the lead.

One of Weller's true inspirations is his champagne made from scuppernong grapes. This is the perfect blend of France and North Carolina. French monks first produced champagne in the Middle Ages. The Scuppernong thrives prolifically in North Carolina and was the first cultivated wine in the state. Hence, the harmonious blend of French Old Word discovery and technique and New World innovation and use of the natural resources at hand.

Weller passed away in 1854. Paul Garrett purchased the vineyards, and he and his family continued to produce wines into the early twentieth century until North Carolina implemented prohibition in 1909, which put North Carolina wineries out of business. Garrett went on to create a nationwide wine empire, and he started with what Weller had established and brought the doctor's genius to the next level. Garrett's ultimate homage to Wellner was to take top honors in a 1904 national wine exposition for his sparkling Scuppernong, yes, a descendant of Weller's champagne.

Today, driving through Medoc Mountain on a cool spring morning, one can revel in this peaceful, off-the-beaten-track state park and its cloak of intimate green beauty. Weller's former land has a natural aesthetic beauty to it that recalls the horticultural elegance of his vineyards, as witnessed in the paintings of them displayed in the park's visitor center.

In 1829 Weller purchased three hundred acres of this farmland at a dollar fifty per acre. The land was of poor quality, hence the bargain price. Weller was a self-professed "book farmer" who read many journals (and wrote for them) about new farming methods and experimental techniques. Weller's ideas were innovative at the time. Instead of searching for more fertile lands, typical of North Carolinians at the time, Weller advocated for crop rotation, plant propagation, and enriching the soil with creative plantings and natural fertilizers. He thus took this substandard land and made it into an agricultural marvel.

Some of Weller's techniques he learned from French practices, and this is one reason he so ably produced quality wines. In the 1820s, the Frenchman Nicholas Herbemont, a pioneering viticulturist, had perfected the art of American winemaking on his farm in South Carolina. Weller learned from his writings and "was cultivating grapes using the methods of Nicholas Herbemont" (Helsley, 35). Moreover, if one remembers the Pangaea effect, the climate and conditions of Medoc Mountain, North Carolina,

Wild grape vine, Medoc Mountain Park (photograph by the author).

are not too different from those of Médoc, France. Thus, the marriage of knowledge, environment, and climate, so crucial for successful winemaking, was vital to Weller's success, and to French North Carolina wine.

By 1850, Weller was cultivating over two hundred types of grapes, concentrating on the Scuppernong and other native varieties. As a physician, he understood the benefits of the responsible consumption of organically produced wine, whose grapes were locally sourced, important for today's food and wine culture in the United States. Weller also educated North Carolina farmers about winemaking and created the State Agricultural Society and the North Carolina State Fair. At the annual fair, Weller's pioneering wine production equipment and techniques would have been on display and his wines available for purchase. Beyond being an educator, he was also an excellent businessman and saw the economic benefit that winemaking could provide for the state.

Sidney Weller was a pioneer in the wine culture of North Carolina and the United States. In the wake of his efforts, other vineyards started cropping up. Dr. Joseph Tongo, a French Canadian who had read some of Weller's articles on winemaking, established a vineyard and viticulture school on his Diccoteaux plantation near Wilmington in the 1850s. In the 1870s, the French Canadian Eugene Morel planted European grape varieties and established vineyards near Ridgeway, North Carolina, in Warren County. North Carolina census documents attest to the presence of French Canadians in the area, along with French farmers who had migrated to Canada before coming to North Carolina to work the vineyards.

Chapter 12. Notable Names

In the 1890s, Bordeaux Vineyards, just west of Fayetteville in Cumberland County, could boast of over five hundred grape-bearing vines. Doubleday Vineyards, a large vineyard of nineteen thousand vines in Polk County, hired the French horticulturist Alexis J. Lamort to help establish its enterprise. North Carolina wine culture would blossom through the second half of the twentieth century until today. It owes its success and legacy to Dr. Weller's pioneering adaptation of French winemaking into the wine culture of French North Carolina. In the French North Carolina Today chapter, we will explore further the French heritage of North Carolina wine.

The stories of Xavier-Martin, Michaux, Ney, and Weller deal with very different individuals and circumstances. Nevertheless, they lived in North Carolina around the same time and are united as quintessential members of the French–North Carolina connection.

Chapter 13

Le Pied du Mont

The Piedmont of North Carolina owes its name to precolonial French trappers, who were among the early European explorers in North Carolina. *Le pied du mont* translates from the French as "foothills." The Piedmont region has a significant French heritage intertwined with other parts of North Carolina history. Originating in the eastern part of the state with the arrival of the Huguenots, French North Carolinians gradually migrated westward.

We have already visited Raleigh during Lafayette's visit. Let us look closer at the French North Carolina heritage of the state capitol. The Raleigh Academy, a private school for young men and women, opened in the early 1800s. In 1804, the principal teacher was the Rev. Marin Detargny, a Frenchman who had been educated at Princeton University. He taught languages (French, German, Italian, and Latin), and also stenography and the writing of shorthand.

In 1827, Peter Le Messurier was one of the instructors and had a "considerable reputation as a classical scholar and teacher" (Coon, xvii). One of the school's subscribers was a John S. Raboteau, who paid the five-dollar annual subscription that year. Among the predominantly Anglo-Saxon families, there were some French living in town, and their children would have attended the academy so they could receive the classical education they would have had in France. As we have seen in New Bern and Fayetteville, many of North Carolina's early educators were French. The teaching of a classical curriculum, with French as a central component, was taking hold in the state, but why?

For many, the study of French is the gateway into a world of history, geography, and the culture of Europe. France is located at the heart of Europe, and learning about it branches out to antiquity, and two thousand years of intertwined world history. French architecture, art, geography, and culinary traditions are admired and emulated throughout the world. Learning French is also a portal into enlightened thinking, and into the technical areas of mathematics, science, philosophy, and masterpieces of literature. Aesthetic beauty, manners, and refinement are what also made France so civilized and prosperous a country. Since the late 1700s in North Carolina, the most forward-thinking and successful of its citizens understood this in one way another.

We briefly met Thomas Devereux (sometimes spelled with a French twist, Devereaux) during Lafayette's visit to Raleigh in 1825 and learned that his family name stems from the French Middle Ages, the town of Evreux. Devereux's plantation was located in today's Brooklyn/Glenwood area, between Peace Street and Five Points (called Bloomsbury at the time). His grandson, Colonel John Devereux Jr., inherited the sizeable family estate and ran it successfully at first. He had received a Yale education and had a genuine love of books and learning throughout his life. He was a southern gentleman farmer, but even his Ivy League education did not sway him from the evils of owning a slave plantation.

In 1842, John Jr. married Margaret Mordecai, to whom we will shortly return. Devereux was a quartermaster during the Civil War, responsible for supplying the North Carolina troops. He was an eminent member of the community and was sent with the Raleigh delegation to arrange terms for the city with General Sherman in 1865. After the war, like many of his kind, he struggled to maintain the estate, and upon his death in 1886 had debts of two hundred and fifty-seven thousand dollars. His wife Margaret was obliged to sell the home, located on today's Wills Forest Street, along with all of its land, to settle the estate's debts.

The Mordecai family also has some French heritage. Margaret's grandfather Moses Mordecai was born in New York City; his grandfather belonged to one of the original three hundred Jewish families to migrate to the United States. He became one of Raleigh's premier lawyers and plantation owners, a man of wealth and cosmopolitan taste, and kept his Jewish faith throughout his life. The Mordecai House contains notable household items of French provenance: crystal, china, silverware, and engravings. Moses would have enjoyed French wine, brandy, and cordials when socializing with guests. One of his daughters, Margaret, as we know, married a man of French ancestry, John Devereux, Jr.

Another daughter, Ellen, Margaret's half-sister, received her early education at home from a governess of "one of the northern states" and then attended a seminary in Philadelphia. There, she became "a thorough French scholar, possessing knowledge of many of the masterpieces in that language … and was a wonderment to all who knew her" (Murray). Ellen Mordecai went on to become one of Raleigh's most admired and philanthropic citizens.

After the Civil War, Ellen helped slaves freed by her family when they were struggling to get by. Her benevolence, wit, and charm have their roots in her liberal education, of which French was a vital part. She even taught school for some years in Raleigh and must have surely imparted her passion and expertise in French literature to her students. At the age of eighty-six, she dictated memories of her life to her granddaughter, one with a French name, Anne Valleau Morel, yet another French North Carolina concurrence. Anne was a descendant of the Guerard family, whom we have seen elsewhere in French North Carolina, at Brunswick Town. Today, the lovely gardens of Mordecai House commemorate Ellen's beautiful soul and cultured spirit.

The papers of Mr. John Julius Guthrie provide another of Raleigh's interesting French–North Carolina connections. His correspondence of 1866 with the French pharmacy, Grimault & Company of Paris, gives us a peek into French North Carolina just after the Civil War. At the time, Guthrie was editor of the *Raleigh Daily Progress,* and the 1866 letter is a request from Monsieur Grimault with financial terms for a series of advertisements in the paper. France was one of the world leaders in pharmaceutical production in the nineteenth century, and the residents of Raleigh would benefit from its products. And indeed, there were veterans of the war who had been wounded and needed medicinal help.

The deal between Grimault and Guthrie is a precursor to international commerce and the pharmaceutical industry of the Triangle area that would blossom in the late twentieth century. As an aside, the Guthrie surname is Scottish and has been in recorded existence since 1299, a year when the Laird of Guthrie was sent to France to bring William Wallace back to Scotland. Just another small ripple in the French–North Carolina connection.

The Guthrie collection also contains a printed image that belonged to Guthrie's son, Joseph A. Guthrie. It is a portrait of Joseph's great-uncle, with "Le Comte de Dijon, France" written on the back of the image. The connection with the Comte de Dijon cannot be clarified more in terms of family genealogy but is an intriguing discovery. Once again, as is often the case in the research of French North Carolina, primary documents and clear evidence are often hard to come by. One gathers what is available and makes informed speculation. In this light, there were surely other French people living in Raleigh after the Civil War. Still, records of their lives are unknown unless someone uncovers new information hidden away in an archive, library, or attic.

Even a small cross-section, for example, of Raleigh land deeds in Wake County, shows evidence of families of French descent (and some who may have been French). The 1886 land deed roster contains the following French names: Barbey, Batchelor, Blanchard, Chamblee, Chavers, DeCarteret (Undine), Devereux, Dupree, Faison, Fonville, Laffoon (Frances), Lanier, Menard, Moncure, Montague, Privette, Purefoy, Rochelle, and Rocher.

Chapter 13. Le Pied du Mont

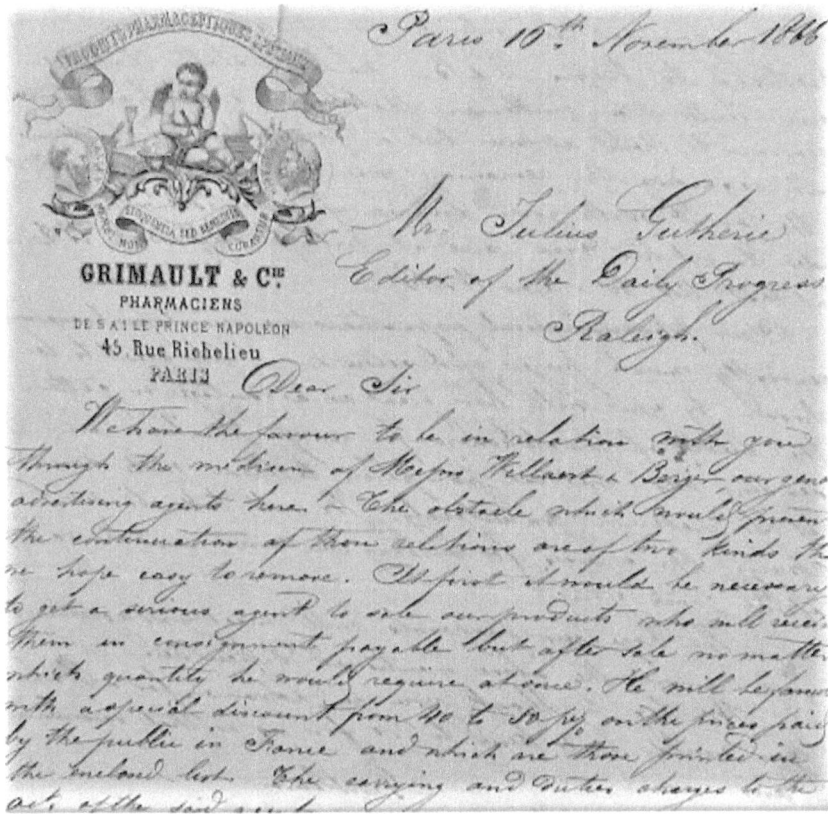

Julius Guthrie's correspondence with Grimault & Company (courtesy State Archives of North Carolina).

There has always been a small pocket of French Americans living in Raleigh and Wake County. One could search the land deeds for any other year and find a sprinkling of French names.

One Raleigh family we do know quite a bit about is that of Edouard Besson (1835–78). The boxes of his family papers housed in the State Archives are a French North Carolina treasure chest. Edouard Besson was a native of France and a Raleigh tailor. His family was from Vernon, France, about forty miles from Paris, the town near which Monet's Giverny is located. Such a beautiful part of France is fitting since the name Edouard Besson itself is *très français* and has a poetic cadence when spoken in French. His parents, Juste Edouard Besson and Caroline Poudfry Besson, were a successful bourgeois family, and Edouard was well raised and educated.

The Besson collection contains numerous letters, baptism records, school certificates and workbooks, photographs, anecdotal details of the family's transatlantic history, and more. It gives us a glimpse into a typical nineteenth-century French bourgeois family, yet this one is unique in its connection to North Carolina.

Babette Besson correspondence (courtesy State Archives of North Carolina).

Edouard came to the United States at the start of the Civil War. He had been touring the Americas on family business (his father had stock in the Panama Canal project). His journey eventually took him to New York City, and he ended up in Richmond, Virginia, where he was detained indefinitely as a foreign national during wartime. While in Richmond, Besson worked as a tailor and made uniforms for Confederate officers. In 1863, he married Babette Ziegler, a native of Germany who had immigrated to Richmond in 1856. The name Babette is French and comes from the Hebrew "God is plentiful." A woman of German heritage with a French first name that stems from Hebrew is an interesting cultural blend. Babette had spent time in France and had family members living in Dieppe, so she and Edouard were a good match.

After the war, Edouard and Babette moved to Raleigh and opened a tailor shop on Fayetteville Street. They had five children and lived there until 1874. The Bessons were vital members of the Raleigh community and provided fine-tailored clothes for the men and women of Raleigh's elite. Raleigh was a thriving and charming city in the late 1800s, and the Bessons were essential members of the community.

The Besson children were baptized at the old Saint Mary's Chapel between 1866 and 1873. They received sound educations, both at school and home, and were also trained to play musical instruments. Raleigh school records show them to be excellent students. Edouard and Babette wanted their children to be cultivated for success. In 1874, Edouard and his family returned to France to be closer to his ailing mother and to settle the family estate. Babette also missed her beloved grandfather in Dieppe. The Bessons lived in Paris until 1878, the year Edouard died.

So far, the discussion in *The French Heritage of North Carolina* of men has far outweighed that of women since there is far less information about them in the history books and archives. That is about to change. After Edouard's death, Babette Besson returned to Raleigh with her children and oversaw a successful milliner and clothier business to support them. She had inherited a portion of her husband's estate and had the resources to set herself up.

Babette did well, lived in a nice neighborhood on West Edenton Street, and continued to watch over the education of her children. She must have been a strong and resourceful woman and became a respected member of the Raleigh community. One of her sisters came to live with her, so she had some help. One must ask, though, why did Babette return to Raleigh? She must have felt like it was home. Her children had been born there, and she knew people. Moreover, as we know, the burgeoning United States was also a land of opportunity for many Europeans.

Babette Dorothea Besson is buried in Raleigh's Oakwood Cemetery. She is a patron mother of French North Carolina, Maman Besson. Near Babette in Oakwood rest five of her children, Edward (Edouard Anglicized), Charles, Josephine, Jeannette, and Camille (the daughters' names are very French). Four of the children predeceased their mother, one of the hardest things for a parent to live through. *Pauvre Maman!*

In 1897, Babette's daughter Marie Besson became engaged to Mr. William Linehan who also worked in the clothing business on Fayetteville Street. A local wedding announcement proclaimed, "the bride is one of Raleigh's most accomplished young women" (State Archives of North Carolina, PC 1568, 3B, 2078). William was a successful businessman. He and Marie went to New York City for their honeymoon and, upon return, built their home on the corner of Blount and East Jones streets. Maman Besson must have been happy to see Marie so well settled.

Marie Besson, although she had married into an Irish family, did not forget her French roots. The French cultural organization, the Alliance Française (AF), was established in 1883 to promote French language and culture abroad. Louis Pasteur and Jules Verne, among others, helped establish the organization. The Raleigh chapter, the first in North Carolina, was established by Marie Besson in 1915 and would go on to become today's Alliance Française de Raleigh-Durham-Chapel Hill.

There would have had to be enough French and Francophiles in Raleigh to warrant the establishment of a local chapter of the AF. Moreover, Marie Besson Linehan did things right. She received a heartfelt letter of appreciation from the president of the AF. In addition, in 1918, two aristocratic French couples, the Marquis and Marquises de Polignac and de Courtivron, visited Raleigh on a diplomatic visit. They were on tour to express France's gratitude for the American effort and sacrifice in World War I. Their visit was a big event for Raleigh.

The elegance of the marquises made quite a sensation at a women's club luncheon, which many members of the Raleigh AF attended. The Raleigh *News and Observer* covered their visit on the front page: "a profusion of longleaf pine, pine cones, and flags of the Allies and Confederacy decorated the auditorium of the Woman's Club when the members entertained and honored the Marquise de Courtivron and the Marquise de Polignac" (January 16, 1918). A curious aside is that the fathers of both marquises served in the Confederate Army during the Civil War. Their sons now returned to the land they fought for to celebrate the French–North Carolina connection in Raleigh.

Raleigh's French footprint is significant and unique. We will return to it as well as to the growth of the Alliance Française in North Carolina, the French role in the Civil War, and French North Carolina's participation in World War I. From Raleigh, the French–North Carolina connection would spread southward and westward.

Twenty miles south of Raleigh is the town of Fuquay-Varina. First known as Piney-Woods, the town is named after its founder, a Revolutionary War veteran, Frenchman William Fuqua (sometimes spelled Fuquay). His French name was Guillaume Fourquet, and there is evidence that he served under Lafayette in the Virginia Continental Army. In 1804, he purchased one thousand acres from one of the original land grant recipients, Mr. Jesse Jones, for five dollars per acre.

William and his wife Mary had already purchased land in Chatham County. We have previously seen his land deed from Halifax. He thus had resources at his disposal and was buying up North Carolina land and building a family dynasty. His Fuquay plantation home was somewhere in the area of today's Pine Street and Judd Hills. William and Mary had three children, and the Fuquay genealogy branched out from there. William passed away in 1814. His will names his children, Isum, Louisa, and Stephen, as inheritors of his estate. There is a direct ancestral line between William and Mary's children and the many Fuquays living in Chatham County, and elsewhere in North Carolina, today.

In 1858, William's grandson discovered a mineral spring that was believed to cure physical ailments. This put the community on the map;

hotels were quickly built around the spring, and out-of-town visitors boosted the citizens' prosperity. The town was called at the time "Fuquay Springs," and would be joined with the neighboring community of Varina in 1963. In 1870, Sarah Fuquay bequeathed her property to her daughter. Sarah was William's granddaughter, keeping the family lineage intact.

Hillsborough, North Carolina, thirty-eight miles to the west of Raleigh, has some small French heritage. The historic home, Sans Souci, a French place name we also saw in Edenton, adds a bit of Frenchness to the town. There is another French-named landmark home, "Bellevue." In the Old Town Cemetery are the headstones of Marie Estelle and Anne Vasseur Brown from the 1850s. The French Vasseur family had settled in Halifax in the early 1800s, and one of the daughters, Mary Louisa Vasseur, married Mr. William Brown, who then moved to Hillsborough with her around 1830. Marie Estelle and Anne were their French North Carolina daughters.

In between Raleigh and Hillsborough, the crown jewel of the city of Durham is Duke University. Julian Abele was one of the foremost landscape architects of the early twentieth century in the United States and designed the university's two campuses between the years 1925 and 1932. Abele was from a prominent African American family in Philadelphia, a tolerant city with a prosperous Black middle class, and he had received a top-notch education. Julian was working at the firm of Horace Trumbauer in Philadelphia while completing his degree at the University of Pennsylvania. He was a visionary who also had the skills to implement planning and design.

Julian could draw masterfully, and when he completed his degree, Trumbauer helped fund a tour of Europe for him. He wanted Abele to have a firsthand experience of European Gothic and Renaissance designs that he had studied at Penn. Abele spoke fluent French and audited classes at the Ecole des Beaux-Arts in Paris. Black writers, artists, musicians, and students were welcome in Paris. The Ecole was, and still is, one of the premier art schools in the world. As an auditor, Julian attended various *ateliers* (studios and workshops), sketched, and absorbed the classical culture of Paris and France. This experience was pivotal in his design of the Duke West Campus and its neo-Gothic design.

Abele, of course, incorporated design motifs from the other countries he visited, particularly England, which informed his conception of the Georgian redbrick East Campus. The West Campus, though, was built with local limestone that was hand-carved by stonecutters—much like Notre Dame de Paris was built over a thousand years ago. The Duke West Campus, thus, has its small part of French North Carolina history. Duke University went on to have one of the top academic French programs in the United

States. Its renowned French scholars surely felt at home in Abele's creation. We will return to them in the French North Carolina Today chapter.

Just north of Durham is the town of Rougemont (formerly Red Mountain). How Red Mountain had its French name change in the late 1800s is still a mystery. There is a commune in central-eastern France and a municipality in southern Québec of the same name. The latter's topography has a striking similarity to its North Carolina counterpart. Just north of Rougement is the French-named community of Ca-vel. It is possible that this was a French Canadian community, and they changed the name of Red Mountain to Rougement in memory of their homeland.

There is another theory of the name's origin. In the 1880s, the wife of the first railroad superintendent in the village, in a moment of Francophile inspiration, named the town Rougemont. Perhaps she knew some of the French speakers in the area. The real reason for the French-naming of Rougemont is still uncertain, and the search continues.

Near the top of Red Mountain, the sculptor and artistic visionary Robert Mihaly has built one of the most original structures in the Piedmont, the Castle Mont Rouge, a playful inversion of the town's name. The castle is an architectural curiosity in its eclectic blending of styles: French-styled towers, copper-covered cupolas, Middle Eastern minarets, and medieval gargoyles remind us of a French fairytale castle. There are some female hooded figures on the tallest steeple that "call to mind [{French sculptress}] Camille Claudel's *The Prayer*." (Mihaly). Castle Mont Rouge brings a unique touch of French North Carolina to rural Durham County.

In the 1890s, Sanford, North Carolina, became one of the largest producers of brownstone materials in the United States. In February 1890, the contractor William H. Smith of Marquette, Michigan, visited Sanford to inspect brownstone deposits and found them to be of excellent quality. He admired the Sanford brownstone's vibrant reddish-brown color and suspected there would be a market for it. Smith immediately leased a site southwest of downtown and brought in twenty-five stonecutters. The stone was shipped on the Cape Fear and Yadkin Valley Railway to Wilmington, where he was supervising the construction of the new Federal Building. Black stonecutters comprised most of the workforce at the Smith quarry. By 1891, Smith's enterprise began to take off, and he supplemented his work crew with French stonecutters he brought in from France via Wilmington.

These men knew the craft and art of stonecutting, and many came from generations of family stonecutters. They were the cream of the crop. They worked side by side with the Black workers, and they all got along just fine. Most white locals would not work with African Americans during Jim Crow, but it was no problem for the French. The local press commented on these French newcomers as follows: "[a]s a rule, they are very reserved

Chapter 13. Le Pied du Mont

Castle Mont Rouge (photograph by the author).

and well behaved ... sometimes they gather in knots on the streets, and it is interesting to hear their French, but it is more entertaining to hear their 'Inglis'" (Pezzoni, 54).

On one hand, it must have been somewhat of a culture shock for these Frenchmen in rural North Carolina. On the other hand, perhaps not; many of them were from areas in the French countryside, not too different from Sanford. Still, this was quite a cultural and linguistic divide between the French and the Sanford folks. In any case, the French workers got along with them and did well for themselves.

In 1895, the Detroit attorney Frank Aldrich purchased the Smith quarry and hired Smith to oversee its operation. At this time, Sanford brownstone was the most sought after in the country, and the town prospered. The Aldrich quarry provided brownstone foundation blocks, window trim, and archway *voussoir* blocks (Old French, "rounded stone"), including columns and foliated capitals for the entrances of public buildings. Aldrich had contracts throughout the southeastern United States, even as far as Chicago and Washington, DC. New Bern City Hall was the quarry's most significant project in North Carolina; it is a neoclassical beauty to behold. There are other examples of the beautiful work of the French artisans in Raleigh, Goldsboro, and Gastonia.

In the 1970s, a residential neighborhood on today's Walden Street replaced the original Smith brownstone quarry. The streets are steeply sloped since they were built on the excavation created by the quarry. The cut stone would have been taken down Fields Drive on a track to the Sanford Depot Station, and then shipped out of state for building. Sanford was a prosperous town in the 1890s, and the French stonecutters helped make it so. Smith's Frenchmen created the most excellent Sanford brownstone work. The most noteworthy among them were master stonecutters John "Frenchy" Gonella and his colleague Antoine Jules Bellet.

Frenchy Gonella married Miss Minnie Rackle in 1892. The ceremony was held at the home of her father, William Rackle, on Hawkins Avenue. Rackle himself was a successful stonecutter and had done some work on the Vanderbilt mansion, Biltmore, in Asheville. In 1893, Gonella had a house built at 402 Hawkins Avenue. One can visit this peaceful, charming neighborhood today. It has not changed much since the 1890s. The property has a simple but elegant stone fence carved and assembled by Frenchy. He did quite well as a French immigrant and integrated himself into the social fabric of Sanford. He was a skilled artisan, hard worker, good citizen, and caring family man.

In 1895, Gonella received honorable recognition at the Atlanta Exposition for a doorway and an urn he had carved. It is located today in Sanford's historic district at a private residence, "[s]culpted in three blocks; it features a basin carved to suggest a partially opened flower head" (Pezzoni, 55). It takes great skill to create such detail in stone. Gonella went on to have his own entrepreneurial success as a partner in the Carrington-Gonella Brownstone Company, also known as the Lost Creek Quarry.

The Lee County Courthouse (1908) features brownstone column bases and Ionic capitals that were carved at Gonella's quarry under his supervision. Gonella also designed and carved the brownstone trim on the Sanford Railroad Depot Building as well as window lintels and other façade trim of Sanford commercial buildings. His craftsmanship is artful and precise, and has a Spartan elegance.

The year of 1908 is also the same year that Frenchy placed an advertisement to sell his share of the quarry in *The Stonecutters' Journal* that read "For Sale Cheap." The massive Romanesque brownstone buildings of the 1880s and 1890s went out of style at the turn of the century, and it was harder to make a living in the brownstone business. On one hand, there is no evidence that Frenchy sold his share in the quarry; he may have remained a partner until after World War I when the quarry closed. On the other hand, there is evidence of a Gonella Brothers Quarry, about a mile south of Sanford near the Seaboard Airline Railroad. In any case, Frenchy kept grinding along.

By 1927, the last of Sanford's brownstone quarries went out of business. Frenchy opened a shop for carved brownstone grave monuments and other architectural ornaments. His work yard and shop were located at today's H & H Auto Parts on 215 Carthage Street. Frenchy lived until 1943, and phone directories in the years after his death always have a few Gonella listings in it. Frenchy's legacy lives on in his descendants, but especially in the works he created. He was not only a craftsman but an artist. He taught his trade to many apprentices over the fifty years he lived in Sanford, and some of them were Black.

The Buffalo Presbyterian Church cemetery in Sanford has seven Gonella headstones, and other brownstone markers carved by French stonecutters for themselves and their families. Four of them are of the Bellet family. Antoine Bellet worked alongside his compatriot, Gonella, for many years. He was not as prolific as Frenchy but could hold his own. His daughter Clara married another Frenchman, Charles Trebuchon, who was most likely another of the French stonecutters; it was a close-knit group. Clara Bellet Trebuchon lived in Sanford until her passing in 1983; the author wishes he had been able to meet with her for an interview.

Gonella's masterpiece is the grave marker for Minnie and himself, which he erected in 1906 when Minnie passed away. This marker shows exceptional brownstone craftsmanship and artistic design. It is a tall monument on a rusticated base with molded cornice, arched top with engraved filigree, and a crescent bas-relief with a five-point star. Gonella's initials are artfully intertwined on the base. The French have been artistic stonecutters for over a thousand years. John Gonella and his fellow stonemasons brought French aesthetics into the heart of Lee County. A final word about John Gonella is the heart-rending headstone he carved for his granddaughter Mary who died at the age of four months in 1909.

Now for some final Sanford French tidbits. Also buried in the Buffalo Cemetery are John Gerome and Virginia Formy-Duval (let us recall the name from Crusoe Island) and Dennis Couturier, who was perhaps another French stonecutter. There are more French names in other cemeteries in Lee County. Marquette, Michigan, was a mining town where William Smith received his training; the town was named after Jacques Marquette, the French Jesuit missionary who first explored the region in the 1600s. After much research, how William Smith had the knowledge of French stonecutters and the necessary contacts to hire French stonecutters, has not been discovered. We can surmise, however, that he must have had a

Frenchy and Minnie Gonella (photograph by the author).

Chapter 13. Le Pied du Mont

working knowledge of stone masonry in France and spoken enough French to communicate with the foreman of his *équipage français* ("crew"). On a humorous note, there is a vintage boutique in downtown Sanford, named with a French pun, Redoux Home Vintage.

South of Sanford is the legacy of one of the most original members of the French North Carolina family, the famous wrestler and actor André the Giant. His real name was André René Roussimof, and he was a behemoth of a man at seven feet four inches tall, weighing close to five hundred pounds, and wearing size twenty-six shoes. He was the dominant wrestler in the 1970s and 1980s and defeated Hulk Hogan for the World Federation Heavyweight Title in 1988. His most famous film role was as the gentle giant Fezzik in the 1987 film, *The Princess Bride*.

André was raised in a small French farming village, Moliens, about two hundred miles north of Paris, France, and lived a quiet pastoral life as a child. It is thus appropriate that he purchased a two-hundred-acre ranch in the Sandhills during the early 1980s. The landscape of his Ellerbe estate is reminiscent of André's childhood farm. At his Ellerbe estate, André enjoyed looking after his cattle, playing with his dogs, riding around on his Honda ATV, and entertaining guests. André was a lover of good food, a prodigious beer drinker, and the host of many raucous parties. André loved nothing more than to roast a pig and knock back some cold ones with his buddies. He got along with the folks in Ellerbe and would drive to Dixie Burger every morning for coffee and to chat with the locals. This larger-than-life Frenchman, a wealthy man, loved the peace and simple life of rural North Carolina.

André died in Paris, France, in 1993, and one of his last wishes was that his ashes be scattered on his Ellerbe farm. His family had planned to bury him near his father in Moliens, yet they honored this last request, and André became one with the North Carolina soil. His former wrestling foe Hulk Hogan gave a tearful eulogy at the memorial ceremony held at the ranch. His close friend Frenchy Bernard spread André's seventeen pounds of ashes, on horseback, over André's favorite places on the ranch. Today, one can visit the André the Giant display in the Rankin Museum in Ellerbe and drive by his former ranch on Route 73. As a final aside, about twenty miles southwest of Ellerbe is the site of a historic colonial community named Paris. Yes, French North Carolina always has its surprises.

Moving westward, the town of Badin has a unique place in twentieth-century North Carolina history. It is a mill village with a French flair built in conjunction with an aluminum plant on the Yadkin River by a French company, L'Aluminum Français. In 1912, the French engineer Adrien Badin came to the Yadkin River Valley, where it runs just west of the Uwharrie Forest. Badin was from Salindres, France, where he owned a chemical factory. He went to the United States looking to expand his enterprise. Badin thus established the Southern Aluminum Company as a subsidiary of L'Aluminum Français and became its president. Monsieur P. Bunet of Paris was his vice president; they had a plan and went into action.

Early in the spring of 1913, the French began construction of the dam at the narrows of the Yadkin River to provide power for the planned aluminum processing plant. Badin also started the development of a village a mile and a half south of the dam. The town was designed by a New York architectural firm in consultation with Badin and his associates. They collectively created the town based on the principles of attractive design, usefulness, and progressive features such as running water, a sewer system, electricity, indoor bathrooms, and fire hydrants for managers and hourly workers alike. It was an innovative concept for the time.

The Badin *Fleur-de-Lys* (photograph by the author).

By 1917, Badin had a hospital, twenty-room school, theater, and several commercial buildings. The housing and cultural facilities were available to white as well as Black workers. This was progressive and unique at the time in North Carolina. The town blends European design with American home amenities. Its design concept is also indicative of French American liberal principles that provided a level of racial equality and a humane existence for its employees. Driving through Badin today, one can feel its French flavor in the houses, gardens, picket fences, narrow lanes, and small entry bridges over rock-lined storm drains.

Unique to Badin were the four-apartment quadruplex homes built to house the French workers. They were a design popular in France at the time and provided a level of comfort and simple elegance for the Badin employees and their families. In early 1914, the French also completed an impressive residential structure that would eventually become the Badin

Clubhouse, and ultimately the Badin Inn. It had a shingle roof, steam heat, hot and cold running water, showers, and numerous rooms equipped with private baths.

The building's purpose was to provide accommodations for the technical staff as well as office employees. Badin and his colleagues were getting ready for the business to take off. The Badin Inn, not surprisingly, also has an aesthetic flair to it. The graceful wraparound porch, supported by Doric columns, was designed to be cool and shady. There are wooden lattice infills between the brick piers of the lower foundation. Shed dormers and French doors give the building a sense of graceful decorum.

In 1914, the French workers, many of whom were in the military reserve, had to leave the United States at the start of World War I. Construction was suspended, and because of wartime need, the French government prohibited capital from leaving the country for private foreign investment. By this time, the French had completed the initial work at the plant site, the company's main office, machine shop, storage room, and four baking furnaces. They also had purchased parcels of land that were to be flooded to create Badin Lake.

Unfortunately, Adrien Badin died while serving his country during World War I and never saw the finished town named after him. It is a

The Badin Inn (photograph by the author).

French North Carolina tragedy, for sure. His son, Ferdinand Badin, however, a Parisian engineer, was invited by the town to visit Badin in 1976. Until then, he had seen only faded photographs of Badin and the work his father had undertaken. Ferdinand expressed his appreciation of the opportunity in a *Charlotte Observer* interview. Adrien is remembered today in his hometown of Salindres by an impressive commemorative monument.

The Alcoa Company purchased the unfinished mining and production site in 1915, completed it, and operated an aluminum processing plant from 1917 to 2002. It was an American success for which the French had paved the way. Today, the town and the Badin Historic Museum are a must-see, not only for the French–North Carolina connection but also for the history of hydropower in North Carolina.

W. P. Marseilles of Paris was Adrien Badin's general manager. There is a photograph in the Badin Historic Museum of Monsieur Marseilles and his wife being escorted in an automobile to the house that was built for them in 1913. It is a charming image. Madame Marseilles is standing up in the back seat; she and W.P. are looking over their shoulders with joy and

Monsieur et Madame Marseilles (courtesy Badin Historic Museum).

pride on their faces. It is the only single-family house of its size erected by the French, and it still stands today. Adrien Badin and Monsieur and Madame Marseilles are an integral part of the French heritage of North Carolina. From Badin, we will see French North Carolina spread westward, as far as the Tennessee border.

Chapter 14

Go West, Monsieur

French remnants are sprinkled throughout western North Carolina. We have already met two notable members of French North Carolina, André Michaux and John Sevier, whose lives are intertwined with the area. Let us take a closer look at Monsieur Sevier since his life is significantly involved in the history of the state.

The French Broad River got its name from early European settlers, one of the two broad rivers in the area that flowed from North Carolina into French territory in eastern Tennessee. The river was named French Broad to distinguish it from North Carolina's Broad River. The French Broad flows west through Transylvania County and into Tennessee, passing through communities of French settlers, hence the river's name. In the 1700s, the North Carolina and Tennessee borders were not divided as they are today. The land west of the Appalachians belonged to North Carolina. Several counties in eastern Tennessee today were in the northwestern corner North Carolina at the time.

The river starts in the Pisgah National Forest at Balsam Grove and meanders for seventy miles through western North Carolina. On the Appalachian Trail, at Hot Springs, it flows into Tennessee. There was much river travel, back and forth, on this river route, and among these travelers were French trappers and explorers. Near Sylva is the town of East Laport, a French trading post in the 1700s. A trading post was the lifeline of the frontier, where furs would be traded in exchange for survival necessities and household provisions.

Now, for the tale of Monsieur Sevier. In 1784, John Sevier and fifty of his fellow frontiersmen signed a document in Jonesboro (near the border of today's North Carolina and Tennessee) to declare their independence from North Carolina and become the fourteenth state of the United States. Sevier was at the lead of this loosely organized rogue territory, named "Franklin" in honor of our Francophile founding father and revolutionary, Benjamin Franklin. Sevier even wrote to Franklin for his backing, but the latter chose not to get involved. The establishment of a new state without federal consent was too controversial for Ben. Eventually, Sevier was arrested and imprisoned for treason in Morganton. When released, he decided to abandon the statehood idea and moved on.

As the State of Franklin disintegrated, a series of vicious and bloody battles between the frontiersman and the Cherokee ensued. Sevier and the settlers eventually defeated the Cherokee and destroyed many of their villages. Cruel treatment for the very people who had shown the early European explorers the area's routes and trails. Yet, those were the times.

Sevier went on to become the first governor of Tennessee in 1796. Let us not forget that he was the hero of King's Mountain. That is some notoriety and success for a first-generation American, the son of his French immigrant father, Valentine Sevier. Let us keep in mind too that the Sevier family in southeastern France had been prominent for centuries as landed nobility. John thus came from noble stock and had leadership in his blood. This French American separatist had a following; among them were some French, hopeful for a new life in the United States.

The French Broad River runs through what briefly was the State of Franklin and today's Sevier County and Sevierville in eastern Tennessee. This was the area of the French communities. Most of the early settlers, of course, were English and Scottish, but there were Germans and French among them. There was enough French presence in the area for the river to be named after them. Today, the Old French Mill still stands in Dandridge, Tennessee, on Douglas Lake into which the French Broad River flows, a testimony of these French settlers.

The French Broad runs through a county subdivision of Jackson County, East Laport, indicating the North Carolina French traders' river route. There is some linguistic confusion in the spelling of the name "Laport." It seems to be a combination of the feminine *la porte* (door) and the masculine *le port* (port). Since the town was on the river, and the gateway to Tennessee, it is thus some of both. The French Broad also runs through the town of Brevard. In medieval England, clerks would write *brevets*, short accounts of events, or various transactions. The word stems from the Old French word for short or brief, *bref*. A clerk was called the *brevetour*. This is the etymology of the name Brevard, a small North Carolina town that has the culture and charm of a French village. The town's namesake is Ephraim Brevard, who played an important role in the Revolutionary War as one of the signers of the Mecklenburg Declaration of Independence. Although an old Anglo-Saxon name, it is one with French roots.

Other vestiges of French heritage abound in western North Carolina. Beyond East Laport and Brevard, there are French towns and place names as follows: Baton, Blantyre, Calvert, Collettsville, Lenoir, Marion, Olivette, Quebec, and yes, Sevier, not far from Morganton where John was briefly imprisoned. Most of these French-named places are in the former failed State of Franklin, showing the French presence in the region led by John Sevier.

There are western North Carolina land deeds from the 1700s with the following French names: James Huppert, Francis Robert Jourdan, Francis Levashue, Isaac Lenoir, John Montreville, *et oui*, Monsieur John Sevier. The list is not exhaustive, and more deeds with French names are housed in county courthouses throughout western North Carolina. One other place name remains to be mentioned, and it is Rendezvous Mountain (French, "appointment" or "meeting"). It is of historical importance since this is where Sevier's mountain men gathered before hiking down to the Battle of King's Mountain.

In the late 1940s, the DuPont Forest, east of Brevard, was named after the French-owned DuPont-Nemours Company. The DuPont dynasty descended from Pierre Samuel DuPont de Nemours of Paris, France. Pierre came to the United States in 1799 at the close of the French Revolution. His son, Éleuthère Irénée du Pont de Nemours, had been trained as a chemist (studying with the renowned Antoine Lavoisier), and he went on to become one of the giant industrialists of the United States in the nineteenth century. The DuPont family became one of the most prominent and wealthiest in the United States during the twentieth century.

In 1956, the DuPont de Nemours Company purchased seventy-six hundred acres of land from North Carolina to build and operate a production facility for cellophane and photographic film. Its production facility brought many jobs to the area and remained in operation until 1996 when it sold its land to the state at the bargain price of three hundred dollars per acre (a little over two million dollars). Today, with its waterfalls and nature trails, DuPont Forest is one of the natural wonders of the state.

Guion Farms is in the heart of the DuPont Forest. It is a tranquil habitat of pine trees, birdwatching trails, peaceful cascades, and other gems of nature. We may remember the Guion family lineage. The Guion ancestor who first came to the United States was Louis Guion of La Rochelle, France. He was a Huguenot and an *écuyer* (a riding master but one who also carries the shield of a knight, the *écu*). He migrated to New Rochelle, New York, in 1687. Other Guions followed Louis to the United States and Québec in the early 1700s. The extended family grew, and some members traveled southward over the years, ended up in North Carolina, and established roots. Today many Guions live in North Carolina, and the name Gwynn is the Anglicized version of the name.

North of DuPont Forest, to the west of Morganton, is the summer colony and winter ski resort community Little Switzerland. It has been called the jewel of the Blue Ridge Parkway and was named as such due to

Chapter 14. Go West, Monsieur

its topographical similarity to the Swiss landscape. A "little Switzerland" is a Romantic aesthetic term to denote an area with inspiring natural scenery attractive to tourists. Although more than half of the Swiss population speak German, French is spoken by nearly one-quarter of its citizens. Switzerland thus has a French cultural heritage of which Little Switzerland, North Carolina, is a part.

Not far from Little Switzerland is the Spruce Pine mining district. Bon Ami, French for "good friend," is a brand of household cleaner developed in 1886. The feldspar needed to make Bon Ami was mined in the Spruce Pine area near today's Emerald Village. Bon Ami has been one of the most successful cleaning products in the United States for over one hundred and thirty years. Why the product's inventor, J. T. Robertson of Manchester, England, gave it a French name is a mystery.

When Bon Ami first appeared on the market, people did not know how to pronounce the French, "bone-ah-me." Variations were (and still are today) "bone-aymee," "bo-nam-ee," etc. Perhaps this was Robertson's marketing ploy; the name is unforgettable and a subject for conversation. A newly hatched chick has been the advertising symbol for Bon Ami since the 1800s. Baby chicks do not scratch the ground for food as older chickens do. Bon Ami is an effective but gentle cleanser that will not scratch hard surfaces, hence the metaphor.

A 1980 Bon Ami advertisement proclaimed, "[n]ever underestimate the cleaning power of a 94-year-old chick with a French name." A bit sexist, even for the 1980s, but one that can bring a chuckle. *Oh, là là!* French-named Bon Ami is part of the history of North Carolina mining and the French North Carolina landscape. The Bon Ami mine is closed today, but the company continues to source its feldspar from the Spruce Pine mining district.

Twenty-five miles south of the city of Asheville, and ten minutes from Hendersonville, is the village of Flat Rock, where there is an impressive remnant of French North Carolina, the Chanteloup Estate. Count Marie-Joseph Gabriel St. Xavier de Choiseul was born in France in 1787. He was a cousin of the future King Louis-Philippe I, who ruled from 1830 to 1848, and was thus part of the extended royal family. There were many illustrious members of the Choiseul lineage in France. In 1831, Gabriel accepted the post of French Consul of Charleston, South Carolina, a position he held until 1856.

Many Charlestonians and Europeans had begun to vacation in Flat Rock, and Gabriel and his wife Sarah visited friends there during the spring of 1831. Immediately impressed, he purchased over two hundred acres of land to build a summer home for him and his wife Sarah, their son Charles, and two daughters Louise and Béatrix. Gabriel Choiseul's responsibilities in

Charleston kept him away from Flat Rock except for the summer months. His wife Sarah, however, lived there comfortably year-round. The climate was better than Charleston's, there was an educated community, and it was a better overall environment for her children.

Sarah thus oversaw the building of Chanteloup, an elegant French country manor that she impeccably furnished and decorated. Chanteloup was initially called "The Castle" since it was made entirely out of stone and sat on a hill, similar to the rural castles of France. The French name Chanteloup can be roughly translated as "sings the wolf." Chanteloup's French name, though, has a deeper connection to France. There is a Chanteloup castle in Tours, France, in the Loire Valley that was purchased by Louis XV's prime minister, Le Duc Etienne-François de Choiseul, in 1761. Chanteloup was one of the most elegant of eighteenth-century French estates, and the duke was Gabriel's great uncle. That is quite a French–North Carolina connection. Today, the Rue de Choiseul in Flat Rock commemorates the town's royal French heritage.

Sarah was well educated, a woman of informed taste, and known for her warm, vibrant personality. She enjoyed living in Flat Rock year-round to raise her son and daughters. Charles became the first surveyor in

The Chanteloup Castle, Flat Rock (courtesy State Archives of North Carolina).

Chapter 14. Go West, Monsieur 199

Henderson County and did well for himself. Louise and Béatrix were also well educated and opened a school called the "school of the Misses Choiseul" (Cuthbert, 78). Sarah de Choiseul passed away in 1859, and there are no definite facts as to how she died. Mysterious circumstances surrounded her death. Some have said that she died of an unspecified illness, others that she and Gabriel had a heated argument and he pushed her off a balcony. Sarah rests today in Saint John in the Wilderness Cemetery in Flat Rock.

There are other tragic stories about Chanteloup. Charles died in battle during the Civil War in 1862. Despondent over the death of his wife and son, Gabriel left Charleston and returned to France in 1862, where he died in 1872 in Cherbourg. His daughters were left alone in the home; they struggled to get by, and almost died of privation. In 1864, marauders attacked and plundered the mansion, and the Choiseul sisters had to flee Flat Rock. They went to Greenville, South Carolina, where they presumably lived with family friends. We do not know how they lived out their lives, but both returned home to be buried near Sarah and Charles, the latter whom we will meet again.

There is one final thought on Gabriel and Sarah. After Sarah's death, Choiseul returned to Charleston, and married a young French woman, Mademoiselle Houard, before returning to France to finish out his years. A marital argument could have broken out between Sarah and Gabriel about an affair Choiseul was having, he lost his temper and disposed of his wife. However, this is purely speculative, and Sarah's tale remains an unsolved French North Carolina mystery.

Also, a final aside about Louise and Béatrix: Gabriel's estate was valued at two million dollars upon his death. It is apparent he abandoned his daughters, and one can only hope he supported them from afar while they lived in Greenville. However, there are no records of this, and we do not know how they subsisted; perhaps they opened another school. Their gravestones do not indicate that they ever married. The Misses Choiseul are the mysterious heroines of French North Carolina.

There is a legend about Chanteloup that Sarah's ghost still wanders the gardens of the estate as confirmed by previous owners. Sarah was a countess, the royalty of France, and her spirit lives on. One can stroll by Chanteloup today to bask in its French ambiance. *Au Revoir, Sarah.* We will return to Gabriel and Charles Choiseul in the Vive le Sud! chapter.

A final item about Chanteloup: in 1898, Lucie and Martha Norton of St. Louis (named after Louis IX, thirteenth-century French king who led two crusades to the Holy Land in 1248 and 1270) purchased the home. They were friends of the Vanderbilts and engaged Frederick Law Olmsted, the premier landscape designer of the day, to reconfigure the gardens and grounds. Biltmore architects and builders were brought in for renovations and updates. After the 1898 restoration, people called Chanteloup the "Baby Biltmore." Chanteloup today still displays a Biltmorian charm. Biltmore, of course, is the French crown jewel of western North Carolina, and we will examine its French heritage in the Biltmore chapter.

The most significant town in western North Carolina's French heritage is Valdese, founded by the Waldenses in the late 1800s. Much has been written about the Waldenses, whose complicated history spans nearly a thousand years, and what follows is a brief overview to prepare for a discussion of Valdese's French heritage.

The Waldenses were the Huguenots before their time, hundreds of years before the Protestant Reformation. The Waldensian movement began in Lyon (southeastern France) during the 1170s. The group referred to as "The Poor Men of Lyon" was organized by Pierre Waldes (Valdés in French), a well-to-do merchant who gave away his property in 1173. He became a self-professed minister and preached apostolic poverty as the path to spiritual perfection.

Others of the group's tenets became the core of Calvinism (French Protestantism started in Geneva by the French theologian John Calvin in the 1500s). They are as follows: all adherents of the faith are ministers, the congregation is the Church, Catholic lavishness, corruption, tyranny is to be rejected, and most importantly, one can speak to God on one's own by reading and reflecting on scripture. The movement started to spread, but

Valdese, town mural (photograph by the author).

Chapter 14. Go West, Monsieur

Waldes and his followers were excommunicated in 1184, and they were forced to leave Lyon. In 1215, the Catholic Church officially declared the Waldenses heretics, and they became the target of intense persecution for centuries. Eighty Waldenses were burned alive in Strasbourg, France, for example, that very year.

Waldes and many of his followers, to avoid persecution, started communities in the Cottian Alps that form the border between France (the Savoie region) and Italy (the Piedmont region). The French also refer to the area as *La Vallée Vaudoise* (Waldensian Valley). It is an area not easy to access or travel through, and this gave the Waldenses some geographic protection. However, they could not stay safe forever, and from 1487 to 1689, the Waldenses fought over thirty wars in defense of their faith.

Two of the most infamous are as follows. In 1545, the army of Francis I—yes, the renowned French Renaissance king who funded the discovery of the Carolina region—attacked the valley, and there was a *horrible* massacre of thousands of men, women, *and* children in the commune of Mérindol; the author chooses not to go into the disturbing details. The French monarchy was staunchly Catholic and wanted to purge such a "heretical" ideology, and would stop at nothing to do so.

Then in 1685, Louis XIV—yes, the great "Sun King"—revoked religious freedom for French Protestants, as we have learned. In the following year, Louis sent an army to eradicate the Waldenses, a form of religious genocide. These people just would not go away. The Waldenses had fortified their villages and fought back bravely for six weeks before succumbing. Two thousand Waldenses were killed, two thousand recanted their faith (at least in word) and accepted Catholicism, and eight thousand were imprisoned, half of whom died of starvation and sickness.

Nevertheless, some Waldenses survived and continued their ways, hiding in the mountains. They were self-sufficient people and skilled farmers, winemakers, and artisans, who made their tools, clothes, and whatever else they needed. They were diligent and extremely resourceful individuals who had an inner strength made resilient by centuries of oppression. Their Latin motto *Lux Lucet In Tenebrus* ("Light Shines in Darkness") reflects their fortitude.

After the French Revolution, in the early 1800s, the Waldenses were granted religious freedom. However, enduring years of discrimination and persecution, they were impoverished and barely able to survive. Throughout the 1800s, many started to migrate to France, Switzerland, Uruguay, and finally to the United States (New York, Boston, Chicago, and elsewhere, and yes, to Valdese, North Carolina, in 1893).

Many folks in North Carolina with whom I discuss Valdese think the Waldensian immigrants were of purely Italian heritage. At least half of the

Waldenses of Valdese were of French ancestry. In 1555, John Calvin himself sent Pastor Jean Vernou from Geneva, Switzerland, on an evangelical mission to lead worship services in the Vaudois. Vernou reported back to Calvin about the magnitude of the Waldenses' faith. He was commissioned to return with other French-Swiss ministers to tend to the Waldensian faithful.

Many of the Waldensian preachers were thus French throughout the centuries, and this had an impact on the traditions of its faith. Moreover, the first Waldensian Bible (1535) was prepared in French by Pierre Robert Olivétan, Calvin's cousin. Olivétan bypassed the Latin Vulgate used by the Catholic Church and worked directly from Hebrew and Greek texts of the Old and New Testaments, respectively. This choice, of course, further incensed the Church. Olivétan's Bible, as written for the Waldenses, is considered the first French Protestant Bible.

Let us also keep in mind that Valdés was a Frenchman from Lyon. Therefore, the French presence in the Waldensian movement has always been a strong one. The language used in the Waldensian Church in Valdese for official colony and church records and worship services was conducted in French for many years. As an aside, with this Waldensian Swiss connection, the proximity of Valdese to Little Switzerland is a fortuitous French North Carolina consonance.

The common language of the Waldenses was a vernacular form of Provençal, a Franco-Italian dialect that dates from the early Middle Ages. It was the language of the renowned traveling poet musicians, *les troubadours*. The French sometimes refer to the Waldensian dialect as *le patois vaudois*. Waldes had the New Testament translated between 1175 and 1185 into this language. Some Waldenses also spoke French, some Italian, and others a bit of both. This was true in the Middle Ages as well as for the Waldenses of Valdese, North Carolina. Waldensian language, history, and culture is thus a hybrid one, with a strong French component.

In May 1893, Valdese had its first settlers. The year before, the president of the Morganton Land and Improvement Company made arrangements to bring Waldenses looking to settle in the United States to the area of today's Valdese. Two French Waldensian delegates, Jean Bounous and Louis Richard, inspected the land in Burke County. They were skilled farmers who were looking for suitable agricultural terrain for the colony. They disagreed on the land's suitability, but Dr. Tron was eager to relocate the Waldenses and decided to move forward on the land deal and establish a colony.

In late May 1893, twenty-nine colonists led by French-Swiss Dr. Charles Albert Tron, a pastor, philanthropist, and president of the Waldensian Emigration Committee, after a sea voyage from France on the SS *Zaandam* to New York City, arrived on the Southern Railway to Burke County.

Chapter 14. Go West, Monsieur

Tron was multilingual and spoke English, although his brethren only knew the languages of their homeland. The Valdese Corporation comprised of Waldenses, and the Morganton Company was established, and Dr. Tron oversaw the purchase of ten thousand acres for twenty-five thousand dollars, mostly on credit.

Tron's party consisted of eleven men, five women, and thirteen children. Members of the Morganton Company, their families, and a small group of curious locals greeted them. What a culture shock it was for the Waldenses to be relocated from their beautiful valley to the North Carolina wilderness. The land had yet to be developed, there was no housing, and they lived primitively at first. This small group had just completed a grueling journey over the Cottian Alps to Switzerland, then underwent a dangerous ocean voyage, and a long train ride to Valdese. All they had were some luggage with all they owned (not much), the clothes they wore, and lots of hope and faith. Let us keep in mind that our colonial French Huguenots arrived at North Carolina in a similar condition two hundred years earlier.

The task of this first group of Waldensian settlers was to clear the land and provide lodging and food for the arrival of future colonists. They worked hard at it, and with some help from folks in the area, made gradual progress. In August 1893, two hundred more settlers arrived, and they began to build their new lives; other immigrant Waldenses would follow. At first, the situation was challenging, and they found that living off the land as they had done back home was difficult. The soil was not the best for farming, the distribution of the farms required the colonists to live at a distance from their neighbors, and there was a language barrier that impeded communication with the residents of Burke County. Dr. Tron gave English lessons to the settlers when time permitted.

These first Waldensian settlers made some progress in farming and operated a steam-powered sawmill to build their homes and make money selling wooden boards. This was quite a challenge for these peasant farmers who had never seen a sawmill, and how hard it must have been for the women to put food on the table and tend to the children. Mrs. Jean Garrou, an original settler, told in a 1939 interview of her "tears and her children's efforts to comfort her in her homesickness for the valleys" (Watts, 25). Nevertheless, Madame Garrou, and as always, the Waldenses persevered.

In June of the same year, the settlers celebrated the first loaf of bread baked in their new community oven. Funds for the oven were raised by the Waldensian women who had visited nearby churches, wearing traditional Waldensian costumes, singing French hymns, and sharing their stories. The people of Burke County took note of the hardships and spirituality of the Waldenses and were generous in their support.

Let us take a moment to discuss the Waldensian children. We have not spent enough time on *les enfants*, and this is a select group. They made up the majority of the first group of colonists. They bore the difficulty of their journey with their parents and suffered through this traumatic experience. When they arrived in Valdese, they were exhausted, hungry, and scared. These thirteen children are the core of the first generation of French North Carolina Waldenses. They were the future and would succeed in building a prosperous town that preserved the community's cultural heritage and make their parents proud. These children worked side by side with their Elders to survive and then did so much more. A photo in the schoolhouse from the late 1890s shows the Waldensian children settling down for a nap in their tiny wooden shelves. These are hardy and disciplined children for sure, the future citizens of Valdese.

The Morganton Company wanted the Waldensian venture to succeed, so in 1894 they contracted to open a hosiery mill to help them become financially stable. The mill was a sweatshop, typical of the time, but the Waldenses bore the burden and made it a success. They eventually opened their own textile mills. The Waldenses then started to build their European community in the heartland of North Carolina. Although the land was

Naptime for the Waldensian school children, at Valdese Trail of Faith (photograph by the author).

Chapter 14. Go West, Monsieur

poor and rocky, they cleared it, found ways to produce crops, and in a few years, there were cultivated fields, houses, stores, a school, and a church.

Dr. Tron kept a handwritten account of the daily meetings of the settlers in French. The abbreviated French title of the document is *Documents à la Fondation de la Valdese Corporation, 1893–1894*. He also kept a large account book, *Le Grand Livre* ("The Great Book"), with all of the legal and financial arrangements made by the Waldensian colonists. Dr. Tron's record-keeping gives a firsthand glimpse into the origins of the colony. The French language was the beating heart of the Waldensian enterprise.

In 1894, the Rev. Barthélemy Soulier arrived to assist in the governance of the growing community. Dr. Tron returned to the Cottian Valley to recruit more colonists. Soulier was a wise and influential leader, and Valdese flourished. He promoted industry over farming as the principal source of income for the Waldensian community. In 1901, the Waldensian Hosiery Mill opened and went on to become one of the leading hosiery manufacturers in the United States. This ushered in an age of prosperity for the Waldenses and the other residents of Burke County.

In 1913, a yarn factory, the Valdese Manufacturing Company, was established, and the town became a hub of the American textile industry. The first colony of three hundred people had paved the way for the future success of the Waldenses of Valdese, which by the 1930s had become a thriving textile town with a population of forty-six hundred. The town and its people basked in this hard-earned halo of their success, a French American dream come true. Valdese was also the largest Waldensian community outside of the Cottian Valley at the time. A collage of photos from the early 1900s in the newspaper *Leslie's Weekly* gives us a fascinating glimpse into Waldensian life of over a hundred years ago. It is available for viewing in the photographic archives of the Wilson Library at UNC-Chapel Hill.

A historical aside to tie things together is that the town where the Waldenses originated, Lyon, has been a textile center for centuries. Many of the Waldenses had been trained as weavers and carried this trade with them to their homes in the Cottian Valley, and ultimately to Valdese. The success of the Waldenses' textile enterprises in Valdese is thus an appropriate one, informed by their long tradition of expertise yarn and fabric production, with its roots in medieval France.

The Waldenses of Valdese united with the Presbyterian Church in 1895, since they share the same fundamental governance and theology, and completed the Waldensian Church in 1899. Its members constructed the church in the Romanesque style of Italy and France. The church is made of stuccoed masonry, with bold sculptural forms, clean-cut arches, restrained pilasters, and a tall corner tower. Its design is sparse and pure, and in the shadows of the Blue Ridge Mountains, it evokes the Waldenses' homeland.

The simplicity and strength of the Romanesque style is a metaphor for the people who built the Waldensian Presbyterian Church and have worshiped in it for over one hundred and twenty years.

In 1915, the Rev. Henri Garrou sailed from Europe to become the lead pastor at Valdese. This might have been the golden age of Valdese. A thriving American frontier community, but one that maintained its ties to the Old World, a little French Italy in North Carolina. Garrou arrived for the Christmas celebration; he took part, offered prayers, and spoke with the children. The church windows were adorned with greenery; two tall trees were laden with decorations and gifts. The schoolchildren recited and sang in three languages, French, Italian, and English. Madame H. F. Martinat was the church organist.

The settlers had built an appealing town and "acquired a real talent in the art of house building" (Watts, 78). They were harvesting enough wheat and Indian corn to feed their community and decided to open a bakery. They had also created some excellent vineyards, learning that the grapevine grew the most easily of all their crops in this new agricultural environment. Garrou arrived a little over twenty years after the first Waldenses and gave us this eyewitness account of Valdese's success. They were now into the second and third generations, well established, and their families would continue to grow from there. Unlike our colonial French Huguenots, there were enough Waldensian colonists to provide more possibilities for marriage, and the community's French and Italian heritage would remain intact for longer.

To visit Valdese today is a unique pilgrimage, a journey filled with perseverance and faith. The flowered brick sidewalk on Main Street transports one into the unique heritage of these amazing people. The topography and architecture speak of the Cottian Valley. Eventually, the Waldenses learned how to succeed agriculturally, and made excellent wine, a product, like bread, that was dear to the French and Italian Waldenses. In 1929, Jean-Pierre Augusta Dallas from Villard Pellice in the Cottian Valley started to make wine, as did other Waldenses. His winemaking operation grew into one of the area's premier vineyards and is operated by his descendants today, Waldensian Heritage Wines.

The history and culture of the Waldenses are rich and varied. In 1947, as the original settlers began to pass away, a historical preservation committee was created to oversee the collection of items relative to the colonization of Valdese. The Waldensian Museum preserves this heritage of these first Waldensian settlers. The museum houses thousands of items that date to the early immigrants: clothing, quilts, tools, books, pictures, crafts, household items, a winemaking apparatus, and much more.

The museum also has historical displays that give us a glimpse into the life of the Waldensian immigrants of one hundred and thirty years ago. The Waldensian men played a lot of *boccia* ("bocce ball," *la pétanque* in French) with wooden balls they had sourced from the North Carolina forest and crafted by hand; it was their favorite pastime back home and continued to be in their new one. The women and girls danced traditional dances such as *la courente* and did beautiful embroidery. Museum curator Gretchen Costner has been a generous and informative source of information about the Waldenses of Valdese to which the author is indebted (Costner).

The Trail of Faith in Valdese also preserves the Waldensian heritage and is awe inspiring with the original buildings commemorating Waldensian history, such as Dr. Tron's home, the Refour House, a replica of the first Waldensian seminary in the Cottian Valley, the schoolhouse, and even the bocce courts. The author's favorite stop on the trail is the Community Oven. We know the French and Italians love their bread; there is hardly a village in France and Italy without a bakery, even today. The Waldensian country-style bread was also a spiritual repast for the Waldenses that connected them to their faith and their homeland. When the Waldensian women eventually opened a bakery to sell their bread and other baked goods to the local community, they were also bringing income to the community. The Community Oven was a lifeline for the Waldenses, one practical but also transcendent.

The Refour House is a rock farmhouse built in 1893 with fieldstone and evocative of the homes of the Waldensian communities in the Vaudois. The Tron House was also built in 1893. Pierre and Louise Tron lived with their children, Albert and Madeleine, in this small wood-framed home. Pierre was Charles's brother. It was a modest abode for a man of the Tron family's stature and importance to the success of the community; nevertheless, such is Waldensian humility. One can visit the inside of this one-room home and be transported to the 1890s with its rough-hewn floor, simple table and chairs, double trundle bed, bureau, handmade quilts, washbasin, fireplace, cooking area, and other original furnishings. Although a modest abode, it emanates a rustic beauty and a sense of family togetherness.

The Tron House was one of the first homes constructed and served as the prototype to prepare a settlement for the two hundred more Waldenses who were soon to follow. The most humbling station of the trail is the Church of the Cave, in the Provençal language, Gheisia d'la Tana, a replica of a cave where the European Waldenses would escape to read the Bible and worship in secret. It was a safe place hidden by rocks and trees, but the faithful had to crawl on their hands and knees to access this natural sanctuary. When visiting the Gheisia today, one has the option to do as the Waldenses did to enter the cave.

Once again, we can marvel at Waldensian determination and

The Tron House, at Valdese Trail of Faith (photograph by the author).

resilience. There are eighteen stations on the trail, and this gives the reader just a taste of them. Each year the town of Valdese stages a historical drama, *From This Day Forward*, about the history of the Waldenses and their journey to their promised land of Burke County. It is an authentic and moving spectacle.

Let us return to the question of Waldensian language. When the Rev. Soulier arrived and assessed the settlers' situation, he saw how crucial it was for the Waldenses to learn English so they could succeed in their new homeland. He understood that the colony had to assimilate as quickly as possible to survive. With the support of the Woman's Board of the Presbyterian Church, an English-language school was opened, and in 1896, it had seventy-five students, children and adults alike (Vance, 1322). On the other hand, this raised the American immigrant dilemma. The Waldenses wanted to integrate themselves into the social fabric, but also retain their native languages, customs, and culture, and they managed to do this for many generations.

The Rev. Soulier, with an eye toward assimilation, also added an English-language worship service. The children's choirs would sing songs in English and their native languages. It was a marvel to the local citizens, as reported in 1899 by the *Morganton Herald* that the children of peasants could recite and sing in three languages. The Waldenses thus brought a new multiculturalism to Burke County, and the residents were proud of capturing some of the magic of the Moravian settlers in Salem (today's Winston-Salem).

As we saw with the Huguenots, eventually, English became the dominant language of the Waldensian colony. French, Italian, and Provençal began to fade into the background. The Waldensian Church of Valdese made English its official language in 1923. From this time on, the services alternated between French in the morning and English in the evening. There was a French choir, but it too alternated between French and English. What a beautiful and harmonious French–American connection. This went on for a few generations before English replaced French as the primary language of the Waldenses of Valdese.

In 1962, there was a celebration of Waldensian Independence. The French choir presented a special program of songs, and the children gave a show of Provençal dances, ending with the most popular, *la courenta*. In 1985, many Waldenses still spoke French, and some of them their Provençal dialect (Vance, 1321). Even today, the alternating French and English hymns are still sung at Sunday worship (Costner). One of the most heart-rending that recalls the centuries of the Waldenses' suffering is "Jusqu'à la mort nous Te sera fidèles" ("Until death, we will be faithful to You").

Today, there are few older Waldenses of Valdese who speak Provençal and French, and even this population is quickly disappearing. However, in his essential study of English spoken by the people of Valdese in the 1980s, Dr. Francis Ghigo of Davidson College identified many linguistic vestiges of the Provençal language in their English speech. He is related to many of the Valdese Ghigos, particularly Filippo Ghigo, the French teacher at Valdese High School in the 1930s and '40s. Francis thus had language learning and teaching in his family ancestry. Dr. Ghigo, the foremost expert on the languages of Valdese, demonstrated in his research that part of the Waldensian lingual heritage remains in their accented English (Ghigo, *passim*).

Dr. Ghigo's work also provides a summary of other studies of the Waldensian language. What is striking about the Provençal language of the Waldenses of Valdese is that it is a southern one, and called the *langue d'oc* or *sud Occitan*. In the Middle Ages in France, northern French used the word *oïl* to say "yes" (this would become the modern word for yes in French, *oui*). The French of the south, the *Occitan*, used the word *oc* to say yes. France has been divided between the north and south linguistically, culturally, and economically since the country's early origins in the fifth century. Even today, southern French people can be identified by their accent and certain idiomatic expressions, similar to American southerners.

It is interesting to see our French North Carolina Waldenses in a language dynamic similar to that of the United States. Similarly, the north and the south of France also have had a rocky relationship at times throughout

The Waldensian Church (photograph by the author).

history. Even today, prejudices and stereotypes abound between French southerners and northerners. Let us keep in mind that the armies of François I and Louis XIV were from the north and went to punish the southern Waldenses for wanting religious independence from the dominant northern Catholic culture. Does this not echo the dynamic of the Civil War, or "the war of Northern aggression" as some call it in North Carolina? The French North Carolina Waldenses were southerners twice, in the Cottian Valley and Valdese.

Professor George B. Watts of Davidson College published *The Waldenses of Valdese* in 1965. It is the most comprehensive study on the topic to which any discussion of the North Carolina Waldenses is indebted. His catalog is extensive and required reading for the student of Valdese's history and cultural heritage. Dr. Watts meticulously documents family names, towns of origin, what the household did for a living, marriages, births, and deaths. They are too numerous to list here, but some of the more prominent of the settlers in Dr. Watts's catalog are buried in the church cemetery.

Many streets in the old part of the town have some of these same French names. Likewise, they are numerous. Some recall place names from the Cottian Valley, such as Massel, Rodoret, and Villar, others the names of the first settlers, such as Bounous, Garrou, and Jaubert, and others are simply common French names such as Bienvenue, Henri, and Louise (Vance, *passim*).

Chapter 14. Go West, Monsieur

Most striking in the cemetery are the headstones of some of the original settlers of French ancestry. Many of the inscriptions have unfortunately faded with time and are illegible. A short list as follows commemorates some of them, most of whom have numerous family members resting close by, Francis Garrou (1877–1977), Philip Louis Guigou (1882–1977), Jean-Jacques Jacumin (1847–1927), Barthélemy Pons (1832–1910), and Henri Vinay (1859–1916), among many others for readers to discover if they ever have the good fortune to visit Valdese.

The heritage of the Waldenses of Valdese is a deep and spiritual one of a resilient and unique people. Delving into their story makes one reflective and humbled by their example. The town and its people form a unique part of the landscape of western French North Carolina.

Chapter 15

Biltmore

In 1879, George Vanderbilt accompanied his father, William Vanderbilt, on a three-month tour of England and France. George was sixteen at the time and William's youngest son. In Paris, they visited the Louvre, Napoléon's tomb, and the graves of Voltaire and Rousseau in the Panthéon; they also took a day trip to Versailles. He visited Rouen and St. Ouen on this trip and wrote a journal entry (July 1879) of the latter town's "magnificent cathedral and perfect medieval architecture" (*Biltmore Estate History Archives*). George was already a discerning connoisseur of French history, art, and architecture. Thus begins George's lifelong passion for French culture. He will infuse it into the cultural history of North Carolina.

During his life, George made frequent visits to Paris, where several Vanderbilts had homes. He imported the refinement of France into the rugged mountains of western North Carolina. George loved architecture, painting, and furniture, but books were his first love. He acquired a private library over the years of more than twenty thousand volumes, over four thousand of which were in French, a language in which George was fluent. George's avid reading, and the knowledge he acquired from it, is the beginning of Biltmore.

Nestled in the mountains of Asheville, North Carolina, lies a place unique in the United States. The Biltmore Estate has enchanted its owners, guests, and visitors for over one hundred years. The estate is replete with French influence due to its owner's love for the treasures discovered during his travels in France. The grandest private residence in the United States, Biltmore was envisioned and built by George, with the help of critical collaborators.

George was the student and *littérateur* of the Vanderbilt family and primarily enjoyed reading, traveling, and studying and collecting art. Although George had grown up in a family business environment, it was not an area of interest. He was more suited for a literary career, as opposed to taking over the business ventures of his family. His father, however, still wanted to give him business experience, which led him to deed all of his property on Staten Island to George. This ownership gave George the experience that would serve him well in the planning and building of his future estate.

In the late 1880s, George first began planning Biltmore. He searched for a location that could accommodate the most elegant country mansion in America. Early designs of the estate were stylized after French châteaux that George had visited in the Loire Valley and elsewhere in France. Even the purpose of the mansion itself was infused with French ideas. George wanted Biltmore to be a working estate, modeled after the European concept, where France had been a cultural leader for centuries.

George's grand plans for a distinctive château interested the prominent New York architect Richard Morris Hunt. George and Richard toured Europe together, with an extended stay in France. They discussed and planned George's American country estate and wanted to endow it with all the character French culture had to offer. Biltmore was their American answer to the splendor that France had radiated for centuries in Europe. Biltmore would become the Versailles of the Gilded Age in America.

Hunt also had a French connection. He was the first American to study at the prestigious École des Beaux-Arts in Paris. Richard was a leading exponent of the school's architectural manner and tradition in the United States. Hunt based his style on the detail and ornamentation of the French Renaissance, and included exterior elements such as the stair tower and steeply pitched roof, modeled after the sixteenth-century French châteaux of Blois, Chenonceau, and Chambord.

We have seen that George's appreciation of French design began in his teens. He intended to display it in his future residence. Although a child of the Gilded Age, the social world did not consume George as it did many of his peers of the time. He was, instead, inclined to a quiet, studious life and spent many years nurturing and developing his ideas. When George and Richard chose the châteaux that would be the models for Biltmore, they chose elegant, bold architectural styles that suited the aesthetically inclined George.

Biltmore embodies the essence of the French Renaissance: a unique combination of Gothic structure and Italianate ornamentation. Hunt had experience commissioning buildings in this style. One prominent example is the townhouse he built in New York City for George's brother William Kissam Vanderbilt in the 1880s. Kissam's mansion (Le Petit Château) introduced the French château into the American architectural scene. The style grew in popularity in the 1890s, especially after Biltmore's completion.

When guests pass through the entrance pavilion at Biltmore, they encounter French Gothic architectural details: trefoils, quatrefoils, flowing tracery, gargoyles, and rosettes. Many of these designs imitate those of the St. Ouen cathedral George so admired. The pavilion mirrors the guardhouse at Chenonceau, but its Italianate style softens the French Gothic. The west façade is less formal in design, except for the two distinct polygonal turrets connected to the south tower by an open *loggia*. This feature bears a resemblance to the towers and bridge wing of the Chenonceau castle.

The exterior of the grand staircase features two French medieval warrior saints carved out of limestone. Placed in separate niches under elaborately carved canopies capped with pinnacles are the carvings of King Louis IX (St. Louis) and Joan of Arc, iconic figures of France's medieval heritage. St. Louis is one of France's greatest kings, and Joan of Arc's heroism marks the beginning of modern France. Hunt modeled the interior of the grand staircase after the one in the Francis I wing at Blois. The Biltmore version, however, spirals in the opposite direction from that of Blois as Hunt embeds his own design imprint.

Many of the rooms on the second floor are French period rooms in the styles of Francis I, Louis XIV, and Louis XV; here are blended the Renaissance and the neoclassical traditions. Next to the billiard room is a salon decorated with French furniture, including Louis XV–style seating pieces with their original tapestry-weave upholstery and a folding screen with petit-point pastels. The music room is in the style of the French Renaissance, featuring such period touches as polychrome painting on the boxed beams and linen-fold wall paneling.

The Louis XVI room embodies the Louis XIV neoclassical style identified by its straight lines and gilded decoration, as well as designs derived from ancient Greek and Roman art. Louis was the Sun King and wanted Versailles to radiate like the sun and his reign to rival those of the ancients. The chaise, settee, side chairs, and center table are seventeenth-century French pieces with slender, reeded legs and scroll motifs. George and Edith purchased these items on their many travels in Europe. They were discerning collectors and interior decorators and wanted Biltmore's radiance to rival that of Versailles. Much of their expertise in French design came from George's extensive reading.

Edith decorated her bedroom in the Louis XV style, which originated in France during the early 1700s and was adopted by wealthy Americans in the late 1800s. The room incorporates staples of this style, such as silk wall coverings, fancily trimmed mirrors, *Savonnerie* carpets (elegant knotted pile), and cut-velvet draperies on the windows and bed. The chairs and chaise are in the Louis XV Revival style, identified by their white frames, carved floral motifs, and curving profiles.

Before the building of Biltmore, George Vanderbilt traveled throughout Europe and collected books, canvases, tapestries, sculptures, porcelains, and historical artifacts. Thousands of the items are of French provenance.

The salon displays prints of Loire Valley châteaux at each end of the room commissioned by Cardinal Richelieu, the famed seventeenth-century French public official. The hangings are velvet and stitched with metal-thread couching depicting the cardinal's hat and armorial bearings. Richelieu used them as decoration behind the chairs of high-ranking officials at the Palais Royal in Paris to remind them of the power he held as the chief counsel for Louis XIII.

George's interest in the Napoleonic era is witnessed by the Empire walnut game table and ivory chess pieces. They had been owned and used by Napoléon Bonaparte during his exile on St. Helena. The tapestry gallery features a set of chairs and sofa from the Louis XV period, along with a sofa upholstered with a French tapestry (of Henry III, from the late sixteenth century). Also featured in the gallery is a Louis XV clock with elaborate ornamentation.

The landscapes and gardens of Biltmore are the genii of Frederick Law Olmsted in collaboration with George. The father of American landscape architecture, Olmsted teamed up with George to transform the Biltmore land into château-like scenery. The French Broad River and its fertile valley provided a setting similar to those of the châteaux of Chambord, Chenonceau, and Blois on the Loire River.

When he first encountered the topography of the Biltmore land, Olmsted found the depleted condition of the forests and fields unsuitable for the landscape George envisioned. He thus enlisted Gifford Pinchot (an American of French heritage), who had studied forestry at the École Nationale Forestière in Nancy, France, to help develop the Biltmore gardens, forests, and landscape. Pinchot was the first in the United States to demonstrate the practicality and profitability of managing forests for continuous cropping. This fits in well with George's plan for a profitable working estate.

Olmsted based the landscape plan on the gardens of the seventeenth-century French estate Vaux-le-Vicomte, imitated in part by Louis XIV in the construction of Versailles. Some elements from Vaux-le-Vicomte seen at Biltmore include the esplanade, allées, rampe douce, and vista. Olmsted borrows the early French neoclassical style seen in the formality and symmetrical dimensions of the gardens; this gives the Biltmore landscape its harmonious elegance.

When entering the estate, guests pass through wrought iron gates topped with nineteenth-century French stone sphinxes at the beginning of the approach road. The lodge gate features a peaked roof of slates, tall chimneys, and dormer windows, typical of the French Renaissance. At the end of the approach road sits the forecourt, the esplanade, which features an ascending stairway zigzagging along a rough-cut limestone wall called the rampe douce.

Two *allées*, or walkways lined with shrubs and trees, descend to the grounds leading toward the main house with a softly splashing fountain in between. Another example of the French technique used in Olmsted's design of the property was also borrowed from Vaux-le-Vicomte. A central sightline extends from the vestibule to the temple of Diana on the grassy slope, named the vista, and connects the central axis of the château with the gardens. This panorama thus provides a seamless cohesion between the residence and the gardens.

Other similarities between the two estates are the geometric flowerbeds with intricate patterns and extensive wooded areas beyond the landscaped grounds. However, Biltmore's landscape sometimes departs from the strict formality of the design at Vaux-le-Vicomte, as seen in Olmsted's shrub garden with its more casual American look. The design is less formal, with curving and sloping paths, reminiscent of his previously designed parks in New York City and Chicago. Olmsted thus left his American signature on the French-inspired landscape of Biltmore.

French culture permeates Biltmore, and George's library is its heart and soul. The estate is the American Versailles of the Gilded Age that reflects George's love and knowledge of French architecture and décor. His dream of building and living in his French château came true, and Biltmore's French legacy endures.

CHAPTER 16

Vive le Sud!

In the Revolutionary Allies chapter, we saw the French involvement in the American cause. France, the United States, and North Carolina would come together in different ways in the major wars of the nineteenth and twentieth centuries.

France's involvement in the Civil War is complex and not always a direct one. Let us remember our friend Gabriel de Choiseul who left Charleston in 1862, fearing a Union blockade. As the war wore on, and France was edging toward support of the South, Choiseul needed to return to the safety of his homeland. As with the American Revolution, France did not want to get directly involved. She rather sneakily waited in the wings, hoping for an opportunity, one that never materialized.

The French government of Emperor Napoléon III longed for a permanently divided U.S. North and South. Such a weakened nation would catalyze his colonial expansionist ambitions. The French had not forgotten about being ousted from America in the French and Indian War and still regretted the Louisiana Purchase when it sold its American real estate at a ridiculously low price. Napoléon III was poised to back Confederate independence in exchange for the South's support of his plan to rule Mexico. Yet as the tide turned toward Northern victory, Napoléon III backed off. In any case, he would have his hands full in a few years when the Franco–Prussian War broke out in 1870, a disaster for France.

Many French immigrants had been coming to the United States since the early 1800s. Between 1850 and 1860, census reports show that over one hundred thousand French immigrants arrived in North America, many in the United States (Sainlaude, 67). Numerous were those who headed straight for Louisiana, which was still very French. Some of these French Americans joined *Zoauve* units in both the Union and Confederate armies. One of the most famous was the Louisiana Tigers. Although France was not directly involved in the Civil War as a country, some French military officers served in the Confederacy, Camille Armand de Polignac and Pierre Gustave Beauregard being two of the most prominent.

They believed that the old aristocratic South was worth fighting for. How ironic since France had purged itself of such feudalism during the French Revolution.

In the Civil War, some elite regiments, Union and Confederate alike, adopted the Zouave-style military uniform. The word *Zouave* is Arabic and the name of the Berber tribe *Kabyle Zouaoua*. Its members were fierce fighters and distinguished for their dashing bravery. French colonial troops in North Africa, impressed by the tribe's fierceness, thus adopted this uniform for its premier units. Regiments in the Civil War, mostly in the North, but also in the South, adopted the Zouave style and took pride in their debonair appearance and fearless fighting abilities.

In New York, there were the Hawkins's Zouaves, and in Illinois, Ellsworth's Zouaves. North Carolina's 69th regiment, or Thomas's Legion, was also known as the Junaluska Zouaves. The regiment was made up mainly of members of the Cherokee nation, fighting primarily in the western part of North Carolina and eastern Tennessee—yes, in the former State of Franklin. The Junaluska Zouaves fired the last shot of the Civil War east of the Mississippi River. What an interesting mixture of elements, French, Arabic, and Native American.

Fort Macon in Carteret County was built between 1826 and 1834 to protect the area around Beaufort from coastal attacks. The fort was named after Nathaniel Macon, our North Carolina premier statesman of French Huguenot ancestry, whom we have met. He was pivotal in procuring federal funds to build the fort, which was named in recognition of his efforts. The U.S. Board of Fortifications had turned to France, a country with a long tradition of innovative and effective fortifications, to shore up its coastal defenses against the threat of foreign invasion. The French had been erecting castles and fortresses since the Middle Ages, based on their adaptation of Roman design, and they were masters of military construction. Fort Macon's fortified door, made of massive timber and iron spikes, resembles that of a medieval castle and reflects this French architectural s pirit.

The architect of Fort Macon was French Brigadier General Simon Bernard, who had served under Napoléon. After Napoléon's demise, Bernard was banished from France and emigrated to the United States. He ultimately became the head of the U.S. Army Board of Fortifications during the 1820s and '30s. An engineer of high reputation, he had excelled at the prestigious École Polytechnique in Paris. His assistant was Captain William Poussin, a respected topographical engineer. The Marquis de Lafayette himself recommended Bernard to the position, and the latter supervised the construction of many American forts. Fort Macon, imprinted with French heritage, was essential in protecting the North Carolina coast in the

Chapter 16. Vive le Sud!

Medieval-style entrance, Fort Macon (photograph by the author).

Carteret region. Let us remember the French origin of the name Carteret, where the French Fort Macon found its home.

Fort Macon's polygonal design, suitable to the conditions of modern warfare (i.e., cannon fire), was based on the ideas of the renowned French military engineer Marc René Marquis de Montalembert. He was yet another child of the Enlightenment and published the definitive work of military fortification at the time, *La Fortification perpendiculaire*, in 1778.

His well-reasoned design theories gained broad acceptance in the United States in the early 1800s. Fort Macon was constructed following Montalambert's concepts.

Fort Macon has symbolic import since it is where the Civil War started in North Carolina. Two days after the war broke out, North Carolina forces seized Fort Macon for the Confederacy. However, less than a year later, Union forces regained control of the fort; never again did it to fall in Confederate hands. One of the officers of Confederate garrison to surrender the fort was of French ancestry, Henry T. Guion, the family whom we have met before. Beyond its French origins, the history of Fort Macon is rich and complex; Paul Branch's definitive work on the fort is necessary reading in this regard.

James Wells Champney served in the 45th Massachusetts Regiment and produced sketches of Fort Macon during the time he was stationed there. Shortly after the end of the Civil War, Champney would travel to Europe to study art, beginning in Paris under the guidance of Edouard Frère, pursuing a lifelong career as a genre painter. Champney's sketch shows a keen eye and delicate sense of touch to capture the sparse seacoast landscape. His sketchbook is available for viewing in the North Carolina Digital Collections of the State Archives. Fort Macon today is a beautiful and serene place; along its rock jetty is a perfect fishing spot. For many years, the fort's garrison, good old southern boys, must have had some great catches there.

Now, let us meet some of our French North Carolina fallen heroes. The Faison family, whom we have met several times, were at one point the wealthiest landowners in Sampson County. Lieutenant Colonel Franklin J. Faison served in the 20th North Carolina Regiment. His headstone, located at the Faison family cemetery near Turkey, North Carolina, bears the epitaph: "He fell on the bloody field at Cold Harbor, VA. June 27th, 1862." We will soon see that Charles Choiseul was mortally wounded at this same battle. The cemetery is located off Highway 24/Turkey Highway between Curly Lane and Rowan Road, though it is not visible from nor directly accessible by a public road. As we have seen, many of our French North Carolina artifacts are hidden and take some extra effort to find.

Another Faison, Paul Fletcher Faison, served as colonel of the 56th North Carolina Regiment. The son of Herod and Gulielma Faison, Colonel Faison descended from some of the first European settlers in Northampton County. His family owned a plantation near Jackson, North Carolina (where we have visited the Faison house), though Paul was born in Raleigh in 1840. He was a cadet at West Point Military Academy before the start of the Civil War, and quickly rose through the ranks to the position of colonel by 1862. After the war, Faison became involved in the cotton trade and would later serve as an inspector of Indian affairs in the western states. He died in Shawnee, Oklahoma, in 1896, though his body would be transported back to North Carolina for internment at Raleigh's Oakwood Cemetery alongside his wife, Annie.

William Lord De Rossett, born October 27, 1832, in Wilmington to Dr. Armand J. and Eliza De Rossett, served as colonel of the 3rd North Carolina Regiment. We have met his great-grandfather, Dr. Moses John De Rossett, who immigrated to North Carolina from England with his brother Louis in 1760. Now the descendants of John and Louis defended the state that had provided them their New World home.

General Daniel H. Hill recognized William Lord De Rossett's valuable service to the Confederate effort. However, William was forced to resign his command in 1863 as the result of a severe injury sustained at the Battle of Sharpsburg, Maryland, in 1862. He then served alongside his father for several years as a blockade runner. Because of his war-incurred disability, in 1865, William joined the "Invalid Corps," resuming his position as a colonel until General Johnston's surrender at Greensboro.

Four of William's brothers, Dr. M. John De Rossett, Captain Armand L. De Rossett, Louis H. De Rossett, and Thomas C. De Rossett, all served for the Confederacy in various capacities during the Civil War. Their parents also took up the banner of the South during the war, his father as a member of Wilmington's Committee of Safety and his mother as president of the Soldier's Aid Society of Wilmington.

After the war, William Lord De Rossett became a successful businessman heavily involved in veterans' affairs. He served as president of the Cape Fear Agricultural Society and Chamber of Commerce, and also on the Diocese of the Episcopal Church of eastern North Carolina. He died in Wilmington in 1910 at the age of seventy-eight and is buried in Oakdale Cemetery.

Catherine Ann Devereux Edmondston, married to Patrick Edmondston, lived on the Looking Glass and Hascosea plantations in Halifax County, inherited from her father, Thomas P. Devereux (yes, the very man who escorted Lafayette in Raleigh). She was a successful and respected member of the planter aristocracy. She actively supported the South's cause, lamenting what she saw as the loss of southern culture and its way of life (yes, unfortunately, the rule of slavery). Her diaries beginning in 1860 offer a staunch Confederate perspective on the events of the Civil War. In 1872, Catherine published anonymously "The Morte d'Arthur Pamphlet" (borrowing the name of the medieval French tale). In it, she recounts the "Chivalry of the South" in a scathing critique of Northern values and an elevation of the Southern knightly ideals of chivalry, honor, and sacrifice, referencing numerous legendary figures, both French and British. She was an educated woman and had learned French along the way, and this informed her writing. Unfortunately, her worldview was not a humane one, and she was on the wrong side of history.

Catherine's diaries provide valuable firsthand information on the Civil War in North Carolina. She is our French North Carolina author. Let us add her to the company of the French North Carolina women who fought for the cause, Emeline Pigott and Susan Piver Longest, whom we met in the French North Carolina chapter. Catherine's sister, Mary Bayard Devereux, was a poet and novelist, married to William John Clarke, colonel of the 24th North Carolina Regiment. Husband and wife are buried in New Bern's Cedar Grove Cemetery. The name Bayard comes from the Old French *baiard*, meaning "magnificent but reckless." It was the nickname given to Renaud, the favorite horse of the great French king of the 800s, Charlemagne. The French bloodline thus runs on both sides of Mary's lineage, the second of our French North Carolina women authors. True to her roots, Mary was also well versed in French. In the 1870s, she translated a collection of Victor Hugo poems that was well received, especially in England and France.

George Henry Faribault, born circa 1830, was a planter in Wake County before the Civil War and would continue farming there after the war. His ancestors migrated from France to the United States and Québec in the 1700s, and he is their descendant. George served as colonel of the 47th North Carolina Regiment and was wounded at Gettysburg. He and his wife, Rosa Alston, moved to San Antonio, Texas, in 1885, where he is buried. Wallace Bruce Colbert served as colonel of the 40th Mississippi Infantry Regiment. He was taken prisoner of war at the Battle of Vicksburg and later killed in action at the Battle of Bentonville in 1865. He is buried in Raleigh's Oakwood Cemetery.

The Frenchman Pierre Gustave Toutant Beauregard, a Louisiana native, served as one of the first generals in the army of the Confederate States. Although he spent little time on the battlefield in North Carolina, he led North Carolina troops at the second battle of Petersburg, Virginia, in June 1864. He ended his fighting at the Battle of Bentonville, North Carolina, in 1865, one of the last of the Civil War. Our Frenchman with the elegant name served the cause from start to finish and ended his fighting in our state.

The Battle of Bentonville, like many other battles, saw the use of the twelve-pound, or "Napoleon," cannon, nicknamed as such due to its popularity in the Napoleonic wars. The Napoleon cannon acted as a massive shotgun, extremely effective within a three-hundred-yard range. The Union Army had twice as many Napoleon cannons as the Confederate Army. Still, the latter managed to confiscate numerous cannons on Southern

Chapter 16. Vive le Sud! 223

battlefields and at plundered U.S. Army arsenals in Southern states; they used these French cannons to combat their northern enemy. One of the Napoleon cannons is on display at the Bentonville historical site.

The visitor's center at Bentonville features letters from Private John Curtis, addressing *ma chère soeur* ("my dear sister") and his mother, sharing details of life among the ranks with occasional French phrases interspersed in his native English writing. His letters are a charming addition to our French North Carolina archive.

We have one final French North Carolina hero of the Civil War in Lieutenant Colonel Charles de Choiseul of the Confederate Army, whom we have briefly met. In 1850, Charles moved from Flat Rock to New Orleans, where he worked as an attorney and served in the French Creole militia. Since he spoke French, he was a principal officer in the regiment who could communicate with the French-speaking troops. During the war, Charles served in the 7th Louisiana Regiment, as did many French immigrants and French Creole soldiers.

In 1861, Charles, passionate about the Confederate cause, wrote in a letter to a friend, "I have made up my mind to leave my bones on the *sacré* soil of Virginia" (Coddington, 2). His native French slips into his writing. The word *sacré* (sacred), a powerful concept in French, signals Charles's religious devotion to the Confederate cause. His French royal blood would spill onto southern soil in the war because Charles's premonition came true. In 1862, he was shot through the lungs at the Battle of Cold Harbor, Virginia. The losses of his French and Creole comrades were numerous. It was a horrible end for Charles; he suffered terribly and died of his wounds a week later.

As his coffin was being transported home, one of the doctors commented, "[i]n that box lies the body of a young man whose family antedates the Bourbons of France. He was the last Count de Choiseul, and he has died for the South" (Coddington, 4). Charles, fallen French North Carolina warrior of the South, rests near his mother and sisters in the cemetery of the St. John in the Wilderness Episcopal Church in Flat Rock. Today, a French flag, the gift of France in his memory, is still displayed in the church. French North Carolina was meaningfully involved in the Civil War, and, thank you for your patience, *Vive le Sud!* means "Long live the South!"

And what of Emancipation in North Carolina? It is a vast topic worthy of book-length discussion. In brief, let us remember Lafayette's efforts to abolish slavery. He would have been pleased to see the first haven for fugitive slaves in North Carolina and even delighted by its French name, the encampment called the Hotel De'Afrique on Hatteras Island. One can visit the location today and contemplate the less savory side of American history, yet also the joy of Emancipation. *Vive la Liberté!* A color lithograph of the hotel is housed in the Digital Collections of East Carolina University for viewing.

In the twentieth century, there would be more French–American military interaction with essential French North Carolina components. During World War I, North Carolina sent more than eighty-six thousand soldiers overseas to combat the German occupation of France. Over six hundred died, and over three thousand were wounded. Most of these casualties took place on the front lines in eastern France. The iconic belltower at N.C. State University honors its alumni, who died as a result of military service in World War I. In 2019, the North Carolina Museum of History presented an immersive exhibit, "North Carolina in the Great War." It is a war that has been forgotten by many, so it is good to see its memory revived.

On a personal note, the author has taken groups of N.C. State students to France over the years. The host school is in the northeastern France city of Lille, on the Belgian border. The students attend field trips to Ypres and the World War I Museum and visit Flanders Fields with its tens of thousands of graves of World War I combatants. The students are visibly moved during these visits and learn some essential history about Europe and the United States. Most of these students are North Carolina natives, and to have them study and travel in France for a month in the summer, learning about World War I along the way, is a special educational French–North Carolina connection.

The State Archives house quite a rich selection of French North Carolina materials from World War I. The first of note is a fifty-one-page manuscript of an address delivered by Jean Jules Jusserand, French ambassador to the United States, at the annual meeting of the State Literary and Historical Association in Raleigh on November 21, 1913. Jusserand's paper provides an overview of General Jean Baptiste, Comte de Rochambeau, leader of the French expeditionary force sent in 1780 to aid in the American Revolution.

Jusserand describes the voyage of the French army and navy to America and participation in the war. He reminds his audience of the money, ships, supplies, horses, and men "belonging to the best known French families" that France provided for the American cause (State Archives of North Carolina, PC 659, MARS ID: 1169). Jusserand's writing is eloquent (for a Frenchman, his English is excellent), detailed, and entertaining with anecdotal asides. One wonders if France had a premonition about the possibility of an impending war and that Jusserand was making sure to garner American support in advance by reminding us of our historical debt to France.

Joseph Mackay, John B. Exum, Earlie Smith, Leonidas Polk Denmark, and James Alston, all North Carolina natives, served in France during World War I and left behind fascinating collections of French North Carolina materials. The Joseph J. Mackay, Jr., Papers contain transcripts of original letters written by Joseph Jenkins Mackay Jr., of Raleigh, to his parents and other relatives during Joseph's service in France and Germany during World War I. He was a postal regulating officer with the U.S. Army Infantry, serving mostly in France during the war.

Joseph's letters are primarily written to his mother, Katherine, and detail life in the military camps and French towns. Joseph spent most of his time stationed in the cities of Tours, Paris, and Nancy, which are all beautiful cities. As an officer, he was well educated and knew how to type, had a personal orderly, and spent a good deal of time living in a country manor outside of Tours. Joseph tells us of the excellent French meals and wine provided by the manor's hostess at low prices. He lived well in France, mostly away from the fighting.

One of Joseph's most entertaining letters tells about his efforts to learn French and how the fishing is in France. Joseph recounts, "I am learning French a great deal easier than I thought I could and can now carry on quite a little conversation. Have been to Paris and enjoyed the trip through the country. 'La Belle France' is a pretty true expression, but 'La Belle Amerique' is truer and more reasonable. Please tell Father that he should move to this country for one thing—To fish. The French people remind me of him every day. They fish incessantly" (World War I 18, MARS ID: 5923). Fishing, dear to the hearts of many North Carolinians, connects Mackay with France, but true to his roots, he prefers his Carolina home.

The papers of John B. Exum, Jr., are a fascinating collection of letters, military service documents, handwritten service history, French souvenir postcards, newspaper articles, a souvenir military silk handkerchief, and miscellaneous items. John served in the motor battalion as a driver, so he traveled around quite a bit, and saw a good deal of France as his copious postcard collection shows. John writes almost exclusively to his mother about where he is stationed in France, and what the conditions are like where he is at the time. His letters offer a poignant view of the war, and John often struggles to find the words to share his war experiences with his mother. On a lighter note, John had the opportunity to see some of Italy and spend a week in the sunny resort town on the French Riviera, Nice. He also went on leave in the French Alps to the city of Grenoble. What unique experiences for this brave son of Wayne County.

In several letters, John mentions by name several soldiers from Wayne County he encountered on the front lines in France at various military camps. One of the highlights of the Exum collection is a photo of John in the driver's seat of a convertible with an army friend and two young, well-dressed, and attractive French women. It was taken at a souvenir kiosk while he was on leave in Paris. The look of pride and contentment on John's face and in his pose is that of someone who is feeling like a million bucks at the moment. This North Carolina country boy, helping save France five thousand miles from home, is enjoying himself along the way.

Earlie Wright Smith, of the Black River Township in Harnett County, served in a field artillery unit and was stationed on the front lines in northeastern France; he reached the rank of corporal and excelled in his assignment. The Earlie W. Smith Collection contains handwritten correspondence, a war diary, military field notebook, collectible postcards, military camp newspapers, French and American souvenir postcards, souvenir military camp booklets, and miscellaneous items that document his time in France. This treasure chest of twenty folders in three boxes gives us a detailed eyewitness account of the frontline experience of the American soldier.

A particularly interesting item in the collection is a field pocket notebook of Smith's handwritten artillery notes that provide information about the training Smith received on military tactics, artillery measurements, signals for firing, the identification and drawings of various types of electrical power lines, the differences between French and American circuit boxes, and notes on the movements of his field artillery unit. As a humorous aside, yes, French and Americans are indeed wired differently, metaphorically, and as seen literally in Earlie's sketches.

Earlie was a very smart person; he could have gone to N.C. State and become an electrical engineer, but duty and then family called. He came home safely from the war, settled in Harnett County, married Adna Byrd, and lived out his life as a farmer. In his later years, he moved to Fuquay-Varina, our French North Carolina town; what a coincidence, and the author wonders if Earlie knew the story of William Fuqua as we do.

Leonidas Polk Denmark of Raleigh (1892–1964) was the grandson of Colonel Leonidas Lafayette Polk (1837–92); yes, there is some Frenchness in the family name. Colonel Polk was a moving force behind the establishment of the North Carolina College of Agriculture and Mechanic Arts (1887) that became N.C. State University and a Baptist women's college, Meredith College (1889). He was a great and forward-thinking man who helped Raleigh's civic recovery and social progress after the Civil War. The collection of Leonidas Polk Denmark contains over two thousand items (he was a prodigious collector). Leonidas worked as a flight instructor at the Aviation Instruction Center in Tours, the same beautiful town (it is the gateway to the magnificent castles of the Loire Valley) in which Joseph Mackay was stationed.

Leonidas preserved seventy letters from his family and friends in addition to extensive memorabilia of his tours of duty, such as menus, opera and concert programs, ticket stubs, museum catalogs, brochures, his embarkation card, an insignia (including wings), signal flags, dog tags,

Chapter 16. Vive le Sud! 227

manuals, sixty pictures (postcards, photographs, snapshots, and aerial photographs), newspaper clippings, and French money. His letters chronicle the daily life a soldier in France, but also, in the letters Leonidas received, how World War I was affecting everyday life in Raleigh. It is a valuable collection of World War I memorabilia that anyone can browse through, as with many other of the documents I have referenced, for no charge at the State Archives on Jones Street in downtown Raleigh.

Leonidas returned to Raleigh after the war and held numerous professional jobs. He worked at one point as the Alumni Secretary for State College (he had received his degree as a civil engineer from State in 1915). His grandfather would have been pleased. When Leonidas retired, he worked on genealogical research at the State Archives and assembled his collection. He died in 1964 and is buried in Oakwood Cemetery. Leonidas is our French North Carolina archivist. And yes, one more aside. To connect some French North Carolina dots, before being deployed to France, Leonidas trained at Camp Sevier in Greenville, South Carolina. Let us remember John Sevier, our hero of western North Carolina, and the Choiseul sisters who lived for many years in Greenville, South Carolina.

James William Alston of Wake County was African American. He attended St. Augustine's School in Raleigh during the 1920s. When the war started, he was forty years old and sent to the first Black officer training school in the United States at Fort Dodge, Iowa. James earned the rank of first lieutenant and served in France from March 1918 through January 1919 under French command in the Meuse-Argonne sector. In a letter of October 6, 1918, he mentions that he was lying in a hospital bed in France with "a machine gun bullet through my right shoulder" (State Archives of North Carolina, World War I 15, 3B). He was wounded one more time later that month by a German machine gun. After the war, he returned to Raleigh, reunited with his wife and daughter, and worked as a clerk for the North Carolina Department of Buildings and Grounds. He died in 1940 and is buried in the Raleigh National Cemetery.

The James W. Alston Papers contain letters, a training manual, and a map, all created by or used by James during his service in France. The training manual, *Supplement to Instructions for the Offensive Combat of Small Units,* is the personal copy owned and used by Alston. The manual was adapted from a French-language version for the American Expeditionary Forces stationed in France. James's collection is a small one, but we learn much about his experience in France. Several letters detail the time he spent at training school there and what it was like for the Black enlisted men; unfortunately, there was segregation and racism in the U.S. military of the time. James survived his wounds, how painful they must have been. What would Le Marquis de Lafayette have thought about the descendants of American slaves fighting to save his country? James is an original French North Carolina hero.

There are North Carolinians of French descent who served in World War I some of them in France: Edgar Bain, Edgar Blanchard, Albert Cayer, Duncan Devane, James Dubois, and the following from our French Carteret County: James Fodrie, Kenneth and Thomas Noe, Clarence and Lionel Pelletier, James Leroy Pigott, and Joshua Piver (Stanford). The French North Carolina transatlantic circle revolves. When General John Pershing landed the American Expeditionary Forces in France, he exclaimed, "Lafayette, we are here!" The Americans now repay France for their efforts on our behalf during the Revolutionary War, and French North Carolina is part of this history.

During the Second World War, we again see the French North Carolina dynamic at work. Over three hundred and sixty North Carolinians, of whom sixty-nine thousand were Black and seven thousand were women, served in World War II, and more than eight thousand five hundred died. Dozens of North Carolinians lost their lives in the 1944 D-Day Invasion

La Comtesse de Feis à Raleigh (courtesy the Raleigh *News and Observer*).

and are buried at the American Cemetery at Colleville-sur-Mer in Normandy, France, the land of many of our French North Carolina ancestors. It is another example of French North Carolina transatlantic reciprocity.

The Lost Souls Genealogy Project lists hundreds of other men and women from North Carolina who were deployed to France, some of French descent. The names are by now familiar to us since we have seen them elsewhere: Deviney, Dufour, Fonville, Fuqua, Lanier, Lenoir, Pelletier, Purefoy, Rochelle, and Venters are some of them.

The collection of the State Archives, in contrast with its World War I collection, has much less material regarding North Carolina and France during World War II. Nevertheless, there are a couple of interesting items. The first is a photograph of Gaston Henry-Haye, French politician and diplomat, who spent time in Raleigh at the Sir Walter Hotel in 1941. He had been invited by Bill Howard and Kedar Bryan of the city's International Relations Club to talk about the dire situation in German-occupied France. Henry-Haye was the French ambassador for the puppet government installed by the Germans in Vichy, France, after they took over the country. He had come to the United States seeking support and was glad to spread the word wherever he could.

By the end of the war, over two million soldiers had been trained in North Carolina at more than one hundred military training camps. Monsieur Henry-Haye had come to the right place, and he must have been a convincing speaker. The second gem is that of Private First Class Charles M. Johnson Jr., of Raleigh, who served in the 79th Division of the U.S. Army. He is pictured in a photograph celebrating Christmas 1944 with an army companion looking out from their tent about a mile from the French and German border near Strasbourg, France. *Joyeux Noël, Charles*!

The final piece of French North Carolina and World War II is the extraordinary story of Lucien "Lou" Feldman, who passed away in Raleigh in 2018. Lucien was born in Paris, France, in 1929 to Jewish parents and managed to escape the Holocaust. As a boy, when it became evident that France would fall to Germany, his parents moved to the small town of Paulhaguet in the isolated province of Auvergne. They lived there until the local police warned them that they were going to be arrested and deported because they were foreign Jews.

To hide Lucien, the town doctor pulled some strings to admit Lucien and his sister Gisèle to the Preventorium of Chavaniac-Lafayette, a rest home and school for sick and frail underprivileged French children. The Preventorium was on the grounds of the castle and estate of none other than the Marquis de Lafayette. How pleased would the Marquis have been to know his former estate was being used for such a just cause.

Lucien spent the remaining years of World War II hiding out at the

Preventorium. French was his first language, but he was also taught English. After the war, he emigrated to the United States and had a distinguished Air Force career, which included receiving the bronze star for service in Vietnam. He also adopted the Anglicized nickname, Lou, and served with distinction the country that had saved him from the Nazis. Lucien Feldman passed away in 2018 and was mourned and honored by his family and friends; he rests in Raleigh Memorial Park Cemetery. His obituary photograph shows a man with a demeanor that is both proud and humble.

On February 3, 1949, over two hundred thousand New Yorkers gathered along Broadway in Manhattan. Three boxcars filled with French goods traveled up the avenue, painted with the insignia of the forty French regions and a tricolor band with the words *Train de la Reconnaissance Française* ("French Gratitude Train"). France sent Gratitude Trains to all forty-nine U.S. states in appreciation for securing the Allied Victory over Nazi Germany and for the liberation of France from occupation.

The American "Friendship Train" inspired this generous gift. In 1947, an American effort was launched to support the reconstruction of Europe; the United States sent seven hundred boxcars filled with food, clothing, medicine, and fuel. Six million tons of goods worth forty million dollars were distributed across France to help the war-torn country get back on its feet. This generosity inspired a French railway worker and a war veteran, André Picard, to establish a national committee to organize a gift to the United States.

The French response was overwhelming. In the name of French–American friendship, Prime Minister Robert Schumann encouraged his fellow citizens to contribute everyday French objects and souvenirs. The French went into action; more than fifty-two thousand cultural artifacts were collected from six million people, including glassware, crystal items, porcelain, art objects, French provincial headwear and costumes, stained glass, bells, and much more. President Vincent Auriol donated forty-nine Sèvres porcelain vases, and the city of Lyon, a textile center (as we have learned), contributed twelve silk dresses. A descendant of the Marquis de Lafayette added one of his ancestor's walking canes. Parisian dressmakers offered forty-nine plaster dolls representing the evolution of French fashion since the early 1700s.

An oil painting, *Spring in Brittany*, was added to the collection along with hand-painted toy soldiers of a boy from Marseille; other gifts included books, tableware, lingerie, a silver cutlery set, a plaster replica of the *Winged Victory of Samothrace* sculpture that stands in the Louvre, a coach belonging to King Louis XV, a motorized tricycle, several medals of the Legion of Honor, a bugle from the World War I Battle of Verdun, and a fragment from a cannonball fired during Napoléon's Battle of Valmy in 1792. This is an incredible collection of items that delve deep into the history, heart, and soul of France. The train was given the nickname "Merci Train" (*merci*, "thank you"), and it continues to fascinate historians, Francophiles, and railway admirers alike.

The boxcar itself is perhaps the most interesting artifact. These were French military boxcars built between 1872 and 1885. The boxcars had been used in both world wars to transport troops and horses. The French called them *Hommes 40/Chevaux 8* since they were designed to carry either forty men or eight horses. Many of the boxcars of other states have suffered decay and vandalism over the years and are no longer with us, but North Carolina's boxcar is intact and on display. One can visit the North Carolina Merci Train today at the Museum of Transportation in Spencer. It was brought there in 1981 after being repaired and restored in Wilson by the North Carolina chapter of the "Forty-and-Eight Society." The author recently gained permission to photograph the inside of the boxcar and was eerily carried back to World War I when peering inside.

North Carolina's Merci Train came to downtown Raleigh on February 8, 1949. It was quite an event. Governor W. Kerr Scott welcomed the contingent of French dignitaries who had accompanied the train. Among them was the Comtesse de Feis, chair of the Paris Committee that oversaw the implementation of the French Gratitude Train initiative. A parade with music provided by bands from Camp Lejeune and Fort Bragg marched through downtown. In his welcoming remarks at the ceremony held in Memorial Auditorium, Jonathan Daniels, editor of the Raleigh *News and Observer*, recalled that the Marquis de Lafayette had ridden in a similar parade up Fayetteville Street in an open carriage in 1825. He expressed his and the people of North Carolina's gratitude to the French for their friendship and generosity.

The French boxcar was filled floor to ceiling with wooden crates. In the Hall of History, a precursor to today's North Carolina Museum of History, the containers were unpacked. The gifts included handmade lace, dolls dressed in traditional French costumes, ceramic plates, porcelain demitasse sets, vases, historical artifacts, handmade scarves, baby clothes, paintings, historical postcards, and much more.

Some of the items were donated to museums, libraries, and schools around the state, but most of the gifts were kept and ultimately housed in the North Carolina Museum of History. They are not on display but are accessible to researchers by appointment. One of the most original offerings is a fabric knot woven from the combed fibers of the U.S. and French flags that had flown from the Eiffel Tower on the day Germany surrendered, May 8, 1945. In the following months, a trailer was equipped with an exhibit of the gifts, and it traveled around the state from school to school, France for all North Carolinians.

Unpacking the Merci Train (courtesy the Raleigh *News and Observer*).

The State Archives house precious photographs of the Merci Train's arrival in Raleigh. It is fascinating to see the well-dressed women of Raleigh unpacking the crates and admiring the items while schoolchildren look on. One of the most interesting photographs is that of a Boy Scout troop studying one of the gifts, a map of France. For the author, some of the most noteworthy of the North Carolina Merci Train's gifts are a French peasant style gown, a leather-bound book with gold lettering, *French Without Toil*

Chapter 16. Vive le Sud!

(anyone who has ever studied French would want this book!), a watercolor painting of the French *Savoie* countryside, from where our Waldensians hailed, and finally, a textile patch from the city of Le Havre, Normandy, the town from where Captain Conflans and Giovanni da Verrazzano sailed to discover the North Carolina coast over four hundred years ago. That is quite a transatlantic French North Carolina coincidence.

The patch displays the royal symbol of François I, a salamander with a crown. This fabled animal was reputed in French legends of the Middle Ages to be able to survive on water and land

Le Havre, Once Again (courtesy North Carolina Museum of History).

and withstand fire. It was an apt symbol for François, who saw himself as a resourceful and invincible king to his people. Let us remember that he funded Verrazzano's voyage, which began the history of French North Carolina. Many of our French ancestors have been as resilient as François I's salamander in making their way in life.

Finally, as a cultural aside, let us note that in one of the photos of the unpacking of the train, the workers are Black (except for the white foreman). What would Lafayette have thought of Black Americans unloading treasures from France in the very city he once visited? And one hundred and twenty-five years after his visit to Raleigh, how would he have felt about the fact that there was still a long way to go toward social equality for all Americans?

The Vietnam War took place in the area that the French referred to in their nineteenth-century colonial expansion as *L'Indochine française* (French Indochina). The French eventually established a monopoly in the markets of opium, salt, and rice alcohol; the French colonization of Indochina was lucrative for France. At the turn of the twentieth century, the French established rubber plantations to produce tires for the Michelin Company as part of the burgeoning automobile industry in the early 1900s.

After World War II, Vietnam had started to throw off the yoke of the French and finally expulsed them in 1954 at the grueling battle of Dien Bien Phu. It was a catastrophic disaster for the French military that showed poor planning and ineffectual leadership. The battle also ushered in the imminent collapse of France's colonial empire.

In the aftermath of World War II, France was an American ally, and the United States gradually became involved in Vietnam in the 1950s. If French Indochina collapsed, the United States was fearful of the expansion of communism in Asia. After the French withdrew in 1954, the United States started gradually moving in; the Vietnam War broke out in the early 1960s and lasted over a decade. The United States inherited this conflict of the dying French colonial empire from its former ally, and we know the rest.

Ironically, the Viet Minh were fighting for exactly what the French and Americans had two centuries earlier: self-determination and freedom from foreign intervention. Before he became the Viet Minh leader, Ho Chi Min, starting in 1911, worked three years as a cook on a French steam liner and got to see quite a bit of the world. He then spent six years in Paris as a gardener, sweeper, waiter, taking whatever jobs that would keep him afloat. While in Paris, however, Ho also encountered members of the French intelligentsia, met working-class leaders, read widely, and educated himself about the history and ideology behind the cherished values of the French motto, *liberté, égalité, fraternité* ("liberty, equality, brotherhood"). Ultimately, Ho turned France onto itself and eventually ended the French occupation of his country. Ho's ideas were fueled by the concepts fostered by the French *philosophes* of the Enlightenment, yet he gave these ideas a communist bent, something unacceptable to the United States.

Over two hundred and sixteen thousand servicemen and women from North Carolina served in the Vietnam War, with over sixteen hundred casualties. They are commemorated on the Vietnam Memorial in Washington, DC, and there are some of French descent among them. In 2019, the author had the pleasure of meeting with a Vietnam veteran, Mr. Phil Fonville of Apex, North Carolina; he is a direct descendant of our very own Jean Fonvielle. French North Carolina roots, as we have seen, run deep. Phil was generous with his time in discussing the Fonville family ancestry as well as the French North Carolina families of Onslow County. Many thanks for his assistance and especially his service to our country.

Today, the United States and France collaborate in strategic military venues, most notably in combating terrorism, in joint efforts to stem the proliferation of weapons of mass destruction, and on regional problems in Africa, the Middle East, the Balkans, and Central Asia. As one of the leaders of the European Union, France was a significant contributor to the coalition toward the defeat of ISIS. In the Israeli-Palestinian conflict, France supports U.S. engagement in the peace process.

There have been political tensions though between the United States and France since the end of World War II. Charles de Gaulle was not pleased when the French were told by the Americans and British to bring up the rear of the 1945 victory parade down the Champs Elysées, and he never forgot it. In 1961, President John F. Kennedy and de Gaulle met in Paris, and they did not see eye to eye on many things. As a result of this icy meeting between de Gaulle and Kennedy, France and the United States have tried to stay out of each other's way for the last fifty years. On a lighter note, President de Gaulle got along quite well with Jacqueline Bouvier Kennedy, who was charming and beautiful, spoke fluent French, and was knowledgeable about French history and literature. De Gaulle was impressed and somewhat captivated by her. Yes, once again, those Frenchmen, but de Gaulle's infatuation with Jackie did not lead to improved French–American relations for decades to come.

Phil Fonville in Vietnam, 1965 (courtesy Phil Fonville).

There is little American military presence in France today, and the United States treats France like a second-rate power. France's refusal to support the U.S. invasion of Iraq in 2002 created a backlash of anti-French sentiment in many Americans. There were immediate symbolic reactions in North Carolina: country clubs in High Point and Winston-Salem stopped serving French wine. Cubbie's restaurant in Beaufort changed its menu to read "Freedom Fries" instead of "French Fries." Walter B. Jones, of the U.S. House of Representatives for North Carolina, declared that all references to "French Fries" and "French Toast" be removed from the House snack bar menu. Closer to home, the mother of a potential student for my study abroad program to France said that her daughter would not be permitted to go "until the French apologize to us."

On the other side of the coin, there has been a constant streak of anti-Americanism in France since the end of World War II. France was one of the world superpowers for centuries. Taking a political back seat to the United States and being inundated with American commercialist culture has been tough on the French psyche. Nevertheless, trade and investment between the United States and France are strong. Over one billion dollars in commercial transactions between the two countries take place, on average, every day. In 2020, there is the usual uneasy political alliance between the two countries, but we stick together on the crucial points. Educational, commercial, and cultural ties remain substantial, so let us look next at the contemporary French–North Carolina connection.

CHAPTER 17

French North Carolina Today

A photograph from the Raleigh *News and Observer* collection in the State Archives depicts a scene on the steps of the N.C. State Memorial Belltower from 1949. The photograph's title is "French Book Given to North Carolina State College, 1949." The book given to members of the college's administration by a French dignitary is in a large format and appears to be an image book. The onlookers seem fascinated by it. After extensive inquiry, the author has not managed to identify the individuals in the photo definitively, nor locate the book in N.C. State's libraries or the State Archives. It is another French North Carolina mystery. This event, nevertheless, has significance for us.

Belltower book dedication, 1949 (courtesy the Raleigh *News and Observer*).

The year of 1949 is the year the belltower was inaugurated as a World War I memorial. The names of the fallen alumni are engraved inside the belltower; many lost their lives in France. The dedication of the book was a display of France's gratitude for their sacrifice. We know that 1949 is the same year that the Merci Train came to Raleigh. Both events mark the start of French–American relations in North Carolina since the end of World War II.

The names of the thirty-four heroes inscribed in the belltower are symbolic of the French–North Carolina connection. Twenty-one of them died in France, most in battle, some of pneumonia on the ocean voyage over, and one in a flying exhibition for General Pershing a few months after the war had ended. The latter misfortune is a French North Carolina tragedy for sure. Two of N.C. State's alumni received the prestigious French military medal, *La Croix de Guerre*. The French book given to State for the dedication ceremony of the belltower and the Merci Train of North Carolina thus honor North Carolina's efforts in supporting the French in times of war, and ties together the state's connection to France in the two world wars.

Also filed in the photo archive of the Raleigh *News and Observer* is a 1951 photograph of Madame Yvonne Tourte, a French exchange teacher at Broughton High School in Raleigh. She taught French language, culture, history, literature, and geography. Madame Tourte had the equivalent of a French MA degree, and it was quite a treat for the students studying French at Broughton to have such a cultured teacher who could share with them her native knowledge of France and the French language.

An April 1952 edition of the campus newspaper the *Daily Tar Heel*, of UNC-Chapel Hill, contains a short publicity article on a gathering of the school's French Society for an upcoming presentation to be given by Madame Tourte. She, like the Merci Train and the French book given to State, ushers in a postwar educational era in which the study of French was to increase dramatically in North Carolina's schools, colleges, and universities. There were other French exchange teachers in the state like Yvonne Tourte. The French language, its culture, and ideas are an essential component in the formation of the cultivated world citizen. North Carolina educational administrators have understood this and promoted the study of French in the state, increasingly so since the 1950s.

French education in North Carolina has thrived over the last seventy years; there are twenty-one colleges and universities that offer French programs and study abroad options to France or Francophone countries. Most people are not aware, for example, that foreign language instruction has been part of N.C. State's curriculum almost since the university opened in 1887. The first foreign language instructor was Captain John C. Gresham, hired in 1896

Chapter 17. French North Carolina Today

Madame Yvonne Tourte (courtesy the Raleigh *News and Observer*).

to teach elective courses in foreign languages: Latin for first-year students, German for sophomores, and French for juniors and seniors. French has been a central component in the humanities curriculum ever since. Initially an agriculture and mechanical arts school, N.C. State has always been progressive in its educational outlook and values the practical side of education, yet one that is also historically and culturally informed; the study of French has been an integral part of this educational philosophy.

Some noteworthy university French programs in the state with national rankings are Duke University (third in the country), UNC-Greensboro (twentieth), UNC-Charlotte (thirty-ninth), and UNC-Wilmington (fifty-seventh). Davidson College, Elon University, Campbell University, Wake Forest University, Appalachian State University, and UNC-Chapel Hill all have active and successful programs.

The study of French at UNC-Chapel Hill dates back to the early years of the university. Founded in 1789, foreign languages, including French, have played an essential role in the education of its students since the early 1800s. Nicolas Marcellus Hentz was the first professor at UNC to teach French regularly. His time in North Carolina had its ups and downs, as have many of our French North Carolina stories. Hentz held the title of professor of modern languages from 1826 to 1830. He was born in Versailles, France; his father, Charles Arnould Hentz, was an active Republican and participant in the French Revolution.

In 1815, with the restoration of the monarchy in France, Charles Hentz was banished from the country and immigrated with his family to the United States. Marcellus Hentz earned his living teaching French and miniature painting, at which he was very adept. He was also the foremost entomologist in the United States at the time and was offered an honorary degree by UNC in 1829. However, his Catholic religion and suspected French revolutionary liberalism went against the grain of the conservative and Presbyterian university community. He resigned from UNC in 1833, and the administration dropped French from the curriculum for some time; it was not to return until the late 1800s. The study of French at UNC has thrived ever since. The story of Marcellus Hentz reminds us of the two sides of the French North Carolina coin.

Similar to the other universities in the state, UNC offers major and minor courses of study and sponsors a top-notch study abroad program in Montpellier, France. UNC also offers an MA and a PhD in French. The French program can boast of some outstanding scholars over the years, such as the nineteenth-century specialist Dr. Alfred Engstrom and one of the foremost specialists of twentieth-century French Literature, Dr. Edouard Morot-Sire. The latter was Kenan Professor of French Civilization during the 1970s, a prestigious appointment.

Duke University has strong French-language programs at the undergraduate and graduate levels; we have learned of Duke's architectural French pedigree in the work of Julian Abele, and Duke's French program has been one of the strongest in the country for decades. The first mention of French courses at Duke is in the course catalog of 1852, and French has thrived at Duke ever since. Anne-Marie Després Bryan, from Burgundy, France, put Duke's French program on the map in the 1960s as it was emerging from a regional southern college to a university of national prominence.

Anne-Marie immigrated to the United States after World War II, taught French language and culture for thirty years at Duke, and put French studies on a path to success. She was a pioneer in her teaching, introducing courses in French law and business, as well as the first on feminist writing. She served tirelessly to internationalize student life at Duke and launched an experimental "French Corridor" language immersion initiative where students lived, worked, dined, and socialized together exclusively in French. A Chair of French and Francophone Studies was established in Dr. Després Bryan's honor in 1998 (Solterer).

In the decades that followed Anne-Marie's distinguished service to French studies at Duke, outstanding French faculty included Marcel Tetel, Alice Kaplan, Linda Orr, Philip Stewart, among others, and, more recently, Anne Garréta and Deborah Reisinger. The author had the good fortune to work with Dr. Tetel in the 1990s on the life and work of the renowned sixteenth-century writer Michel de Montaigne, the inventor of the modern essay. Dr. Tetel was one of the foremost scholars in the world on Montaigne's life and writings. Marcel had a brilliant mind and was a generous mentor of young scholars.

Dr. Garréta is one of the top French scholars in the United States today and has also published half a dozen acclaimed novels. Dr. Reisinger is one

Chapter 17. French North Carolina Today 241

of the most innovative instructors in foreign language education today, teaching courses in "French for Specific Purposes," including global health, business, and advertising. She also researches Central African refugee resettlement, a topic to which we will return shortly. In 2000, Duke established a center for French and Francophone Studies in collaboration with the French Cultural Services offices in New York and Atlanta. The center is active in sponsoring film series, bilingual lunches, as well as student and faculty exchanges with universities in the French-speaking world.

Duke has several active French student organizations and sponsors undergraduate study abroad programs to Paris, Aix-en-Provence, and Montréal. Graduate students have the option to study for a semester at the prestigious École normale surpérieure (ENS) in Paris. French graduate exchange students come to Duke from the ENS to conduct research and teach French courses. This truly enriches Duke's French curriculum.

Duke also houses an important French book archive, the Gustave Lanson Collection. The Lanson Collection was acquired by Duke in 1927, for one hundred and twenty-five thousand francs, the equivalent of three hundred and twenty-five thousand dollars at the time. Today the collection is priceless. Thousands of books were sent to Duke from Paris over several years. This acquisition made it possible for Duke to establish its graduate programs in French.

The collection totals eleven thousand books, each bound uniformly in the French style with the imprint of a *fleur-de-lys* (the stylized lily that is the symbol of France) and Professor Lanson's name engraved on the back cover. These were his specific conditions before selling this valuable collection to Duke. Dr. Lanson (1857–1934) was the premier French historian and literary scholar of his time and a significant force in the modernization of the French university system in the early twentieth century. The Lanson Collection, comprised of rare editions of masterpieces of French literature, history, philosophy, linguistics, and much more, is one of the top compilations of French books in the United States; Duke's French legacy is a pronounced one.

An amusing anecdote is as follows. In the 1960s, the renowned French professor Dr. Wallace Fowlie exchanged correspondence with Jim Morrison, the lead singer of the American rock band the Doors. The latter had avidly read Fowlie's translations of the work of Arthur Rimbaud, the infamous bad boy poet of the late 1800s. Rimbaud's writings, as translated by Fowlie in the academic heart of North Carolina, were a significant inspiration for Morrison's artistic vision. Dr. Fowlie was an old school professor who knew nothing of the Doors and their music. He was flattered, though, when Morrison reached out to him and was pleasantly bemused at the thought that a nineteenth-century French poet was relevant to American youth in the 1960s. When Dr. Fowlie passed away in 1998, his papers were donated to the Duke University Library; among them is his correspondence with Jim Morrison.

Wake Forest University provides a unique French language program. It shares common similarities with other universities in the state, such as the French major, minor, study abroad opportunities, and student organizations. Wake Forest, however, offers the only program of its kind in the state, a French business major. Its French study abroad programs in Paris and Dijon require a family homestay residence for students, thus immersing them in daily life and everyday use of French.

French is taught in many community colleges, high schools, some middle schools, and even a few elementary schools throughout the state. The French Festival of Wake County is held each year in downtown Raleigh for French middle and high school students and their teachers. There are competitions in recitation, spelling, original skits, music, cultural presentations, and more. The North Carolina Association of Teachers of French (NC-AATF), whose membership is comprised of university faculty and secondary school teachers, organizes an annual conference for the exchange of effective teaching methods and innovative pedagogy. It supports the efforts of the professors and teachers who teach French throughout the state.

In a more experiential type of education, the Tournées Film Festival is hosted each year by N.C. State's arts program. The Cultural Services of the French Embassy sponsors the festival to bring French cinema to American college and university campuses. The festival reflects the diversity and the richness of French cinema through various genres. Students studying French have the opportunity to complete some of their course work by viewing the films, writing reviews of them, and presenting their findings in class. This is engaged learning at its best.

L'Ecole is a private French-language school in Raleigh established in 2009 by local parents, composed of Francophones, Americans, and French nationals, led by the honorary French consul at the time, Marie-Claire Ribeill. The focus of the school is to teach children written and spoken French in an immersion environment. The school offers preschool, afterschool for K–12, and summer camps. The French government recognized these programs in 2011 through a grant from Français Langue Maternelle (FLAM). This grant is designed for French children (bi-nationals) whose parents are settled in non–Francophone countries.

These French children are enrolled in local schools yet attend L'Ecole to practice the French language and to stay in contact with French culture and current events through afterschool programs.

L'Ecole is supported by the French Consulate in Atlanta, Georgia.

There are numerous French university faculty and private enterprise professionals in the Triangle who benefit from the program and whose children will be prepared to reintegrate into French society should they ever move back to France. L'Ecole is a unique school that enriches the French North Carolina educational landscape.

C'est si Bon is also not a typical school; it is a French culinary school based in Chapel Hill that has had a following in the Triangle since 1997. The school rests on three acres with seasonal herb and vegetable gardens and a wood-fired oven. There are many culinary experiences offered by C'est si Bon: cooking classes for children, teens, families, couples, and individuals. The school provides a "teen chef week" course of study during the summer months where students work and stay on a local farm, take cooking classes, and visit the kitchens of area restaurants. The students learn to produce recipes from locally sourced agricultural products. Since 2004, C'est si Bon has offered food-related travel; its culinary tours take participants to southern France where there is no better place for fresh, rustic, and delicious French cuisine. Teens are welcome on these programs.

The French have always understood that culinary skills enrich, nourish, and empower individuals in one of life's most important connections to the environment, the food we prepare and consume. This is an important lesson for young people that the French have always respected and promoted in the development of their youth as productive citizens and useful human beings. French cooking is more than tasteful and artfully designed food; it is steeped in history, tradition, and the land and connects us with one of the deepest levels of human culture. This is undoubtedly a worthy lesson for young people today.

The three principal art museums in the state—the North Carolina Museum of Art in Raleigh, the Ackland Museum at UNC-Chapel Hill, and the Nasher Museum at Duke University—all house masterpieces of French art. One is transported to a foggy morning on a river in Normandy while gazing at Claude Monet's visionary impressionism in the North Carolina Museum's "The Seine at Giverny." The color and drama of the great French romantic painter Eugène Delacroix jump out at the viewer in the painting "Cleopatra and the Peasant" at the Ackland. And what could be more appropriate than a panel of colorful medieval stained glass from France at the Nasher? It is a stunning depiction of "God and the Tree of Knowledge" created around the year 1250. The panel is similar to what Julian Abele would have observed and sketched while studying in Paris.

Finally, the North Carolina Museum of Art has dozens of works of French art, both painting and sculpture. The Auguste Rodin statues in the museum's foyer and gardens provide a dramatic entrance into the world of French art that one can view in Raleigh. The Rodin collection features

French, *God and the Tree of Knowledge*, c. 1250. Stained glass and lead, 26 x 17 ⅞ x ¼ in. (66 x 45.4 x 0.6 cm) (courtesy collection of the Nasher Museum of Art at Duke University, Gift of Mrs. Ella Brummer in memory of her husband, Ernest Brummer, 1978.20.9 photograph by Peter Pay Geoffrion).

Chapter 17. French North Carolina Today

thirty sculptures that were compiled and donated to the museum by the Iris and B. Gerald Cantor Foundation in 2009. It is the most extensive Rodin collection between Philadelphia and the West Coast. One of the most original and graceful pieces is "The Cathedral," which shows two hands depicting the arch of a Gothic cathedral, the fingers reaching toward heaven. An artistic aside is that Rodin and Camille Claudel (let us remember Robert Mihaly's hooded figure atop the Castle Mont Rouge) were creative collaborators and lovers for many years; now, they are reunited in French North Carolina.

We have seen how the production and culture of North Carolina wine began with the efforts of Dr. Sidney Weller. Let us take a closer look at the French–North Carolina wine connection. In the last few decades, with the decline of the tobacco industry, grape growing and winemaking have increased significantly. There are currently over one hundred and thirty wineries in the state, and some of them have produced award-winning wines. The grape varieties include *Vitis labrusca*, *Vitis vinifera*, and French American hybrids such as *Chambourcin* and *Vidal blanc*.

In 1960, William Cecil, George Vanderbilt's grandson, assumed management of the Biltmore Estate. While pondering ways to improve the enterprise, he decided that it would be appropriate for a French-inspired château to have vineyards and a winery to match. In 1971, the first vintage was bottled at the estate. In 1977, Cecil hired the sixth-generation French wine master Philippe Jourdain to help establish the Biltmore vineyard and winery. The Jourdain family has a long history of winemaking and vineyard ownership from the Loire Valley to Provence.

Many of the grapes cultivated at Biltmore are French American hybrids. The Biltmore winery has been a great success and has produced excellent wines over the years; it is one of the most visited wineries in the United States. Biltmore's chenin blanc won the Tasters Guild Gold Award in 2013. True to their French roots (yes, a pun), the Biltmore vineyards appropriately overlook the French Broad River, not far from the former French trading post of East Laport.

Today, there are other vineyards and wineries in North Carolina that are associated with French wine culture. The first curiously enough is the Château Jourdain in the Yadkin River valley, named after Biltmore's wine master. It grows *Vitis vinifera* grapes that have produced outstanding wines for centuries in France. The Yadkin River valley has numerous other vineyards, and while looking at a map of North Carolina, one can see that the area is in John Sevier's State of Franklin. Many of the best wineries in North Carolina are in the western part of North Carolina. The organization that oversees the viticulture there has a French name, the French Broad Vignerons of WNC (French, *vigneron*, "winemaker" from *vigne*—"vine").

Some other western North Carolina wineries of note with French provenance are as follows. Shelton Vineyards in Traphill uses French varieties of grapes and turns them into pleasing boutique wines. In 2012, Shelton won two awards for its white wines. Its sauvignon blanc is made from a light-skinned grape from the Bordeaux region of France called the "wild white." It is a zesty wine with aromas of various fruits that is refreshing and has a clean, crisp finish. Jones von Dreher Vineyards in Thurmond advertises itself as an "Old World Classical French-Style Winery," and produces dry varietals and some elegant reds. In 2012, Dreher won a national award for its petit verdot, a full-bodied red wine that originates in the Bordeaux region.

Roaring River Vineyards, also in Traphill, promotes itself as a French-inspired vineyard and even has a French restaurant, Chez Joséphine. Walking through the vineyard's front gate transports one into southern France, so strikingly similar are the landscape and design of Roaring River. Overmountain Vineyards in Sandy Hills (where John Sevier gathered his militia) makes handcrafted and distinctive French-style wines. One of its finest is the petit manseng, an elegant aromatic white originally from southwest France, mostly in the Jurançon region, which has been making wine since the fourteenth century.

Finally, the Junius Lindsay Vineyard in Lexington produces a red Syrah wine that captures the essence of southeastern France. It is crafted with handpicked grapes from wines descended from the Rhône Valley's celebrated Château de Beaucastel vineyards. This Syrah Reserve Redux is a savory wine with notes of dark fruits that has a smoky depth, qualities that define a fine Syrah.

French wine has a renowned reputation throughout the world. North Carolina's wine industry has more than a hint of France in it. Many of the state's western vineyards, starting with those in Valdese, resemble southern France in topography, design, and climate. Let us once again remember the Pangaea effect. The French vines find their home away from home in French North Carolina. One could trace French-inspired wines in most of the state's wineries, and this was just a sampling of some of the most noteworthy.

French commerce in North Carolina is well established. The French-American Chamber of Commerce-Carolinas (FACC-Carolinas) is an independent, non-profit, member-driven organization headquartered in Raleigh. It is part of CCI France International (Chambre de Commerce et d'Industrie Françaises à l'International). This French government chamber seeks to connect different parts of the world to France in over one hundred and twenty countries. The FACC-Carolinas creates opportunities for its members to network, connect, and collaborate. FACC-Carolinas also

Chapter 17. French North Carolina Today

provides a range of trade services to its members and French companies seeking to develop an enterprise in the Carolinas.

A sampling of the significant French North Carolina companies, some located in the Triangle area, are Michelin, Biomerieux, Areva, Dassault Systemes, Safran Electrical and Power, Sonepar *North* America, and Zodiac Nautic Americas, to name a few. These companies participate in N.C. State's annual career fair. FACC-Carolinas hosts frequent presentations and receptions where French and American business professionals, students, and faculty can intermingle. Finally, to facilitate the growth of French–North Carolina commerce, FACC-Carolinas also offers international internships and webinars on market research and business development.

N.C. State hosts a French business school on its Centennial Campus, SKEMA, one of the top business schools in France. The program hosts eight hundred French students a year, the largest concentration of French students in the United States. The SKEMA program integrates them into the N.C. State community; they participate in various cultural, community service, and academic activities. This provides numerous opportunities for N.C. State students, especially the many hundreds who study French, to develop meaningful language and intercultural exchanges with the French cohort of SKEMA.

The Charlotte French Festival has been celebrated around or on July 14, Bastille Day, for the past several years. It is recognized as an important festival by several organizations, including the FACC-Carolinas, the Carolina Pétanque Club, and the French Ministry for European and Foreign Affairs. The most notable of the festival's activities are displays and samplings of French wine and cuisine, a French market, a World War II reenactment, and a *pétanque* tournament. Many French North Carolina restaurants, bakeries, vendors, and cultural organizations attend the event, and let us turn to them now.

The French culinary scene in North Carolina is significant. Most of the major cities, and some of the lesser ones, can boast of French restaurants and bakeries. The Triangle area, which has become cosmopolitan over the past few decades, has the highest concentration in the state.

There are at least a dozen French bakeries in the Triangle; the most well known are the Layered Croissanterie, French Corner Bakery, La Farm, Amitié Macaron, Lucettegrace, Tous Les Jours, and Loaf. Besides, what grocery store in the state does not have some type of baguette and a selection of French cheese and wine? Specialty grocery stores provide a wider variety of French baked goods (baguettes but also croissants and patisseries) and cheeses along with other culinary delights, such as chocolate truffles, dried sausage, paté, and jams; the list goes on.

La Farm is an authentic French bakery in the heart of the Triangle. It has been an iconic French North Carolina enterprise of Lionel Vatinet and his wife, Missy, since 1999. Monsieur Vatinet learned his craft in France's prestigious artisan guild *Les Compagnons du Devoir* ("Comrades of Duty"). The mission of the guild is to promote centuries-old baking traditions and techniques while honoring the traditional French bakery (*boulangerie*) that still flourishes in cities and towns throughout France.

At La Farm, Lionel produces fifteen different styles of bread along with twenty seasonal loaves, using a European-style hearth oven that was handcrafted and assembled by a team of French artisans. All La Farm breads use unbleached, unbromated flours, and are handcrafted daily, blending an Old World artisanal approach with New World tastes. La Farm has a bread truck that circulates to various events in the Triangle; Lionel also offers baking classes. We are fortunate to have in the state wheat farmers and millers dedicated to producing high-quality flours for Lionel's bread. La Farm is a French North Carolina success story and a delicious one.

The newest of the Triangle's French bakeries is the Layered Croissanterie, and it also deserves special mention. The bakery emulates a sleek contemporary Parisian shop; its pastries and croissants are neatly layered on museum pedestals, in praise of culinary art. The Layered Croissanterie specializes in croissants, and as the bakery describes itself, it is a croissant bakery that also meticulously crafts traditional French pastries with a modern flair. And that description is an appropriate one considering some of its current specialized croissants, such as the "Margarita Pinwheel," "S'mores," and "Popeye." For a traditional croissant lover, though, the bakery crafts the typical *croissant* and the *pain au chocolat*.

The Layered Croissanterie even makes the exotic *Kouign-amman*, a buttery multilayered cake from Brittany in northwestern France. The layers of dough, butter, and sugar are carefully assembled and slowly baked until the butter puffs up the dough. The result is a muffin-shaped, caramelized croissant, crispy on the outside and densely moist inside. The *Kouign-amman* originated at the westernmost tip of the maritime town in Brittany, Finistère, and is considered one of France's most exceptional baking accomplishments. Let us remember that French ships sailed from Brittany to North Carolina over the centuries; now, a little bit of this French region has found its way back to North Carolina.

There are some authentic French restaurants in the state. Noteworthy are Saint-Jacques, Coquette, and Royale in Raleigh, Vin Rouge in Durham, Provence in Carrboro, La Residence in Chapel Hill, Brasserie du Soleil in Wilmington, and the Bank Bistro and Bar in Washington. The latter has been cited as representing the gold standard for dining in the town. Let us recall the French heritage of Washington, as discussed in the Revolutionary Allies chapter. Charlotte has the French bakeries Renaissance Patisserie

Chapter 17. French North Carolina Today   249

and Amelie's, and restaurants Café Monte, La Belle Helene, and Crepe Bistro. Wilmington also has a French bakery, Far from France, which offers a variety of French edibles such as *bonbons* (chocolate candies), pastries, *gâteaux* ("cakes"), macaroons, mustards, vinegars, and even soaps from Marseille. One could search elsewhere in the state and find other French bakeries, restaurants, and specialty shops. *Bon Appetit!*

The Triangle's Alliance Française dates back as we know to 1915 and the efforts of Marie Besson Linehan. Below is the cover of the initial alliance

Alliance Française of Raleigh, 1915 (courtesy State Archives of North Carolina).

roster handwritten by Marie herself. The Charlotte Alliance Française has been in place since 1949, inspired by the arrival of North Carolina's French Gratitude Train. Let us recall that the mission of the Alliance Française is to promote the French language and Francophone cultures and to foster exchanges and friendships among Francophiles from around the world.

The Triangle's Alliance Française maintains a center that serves as a resource for individuals, universities, corporations, and cultural groups to learn more about French-speaking countries and their people. The organization offers many services; the most notable are weekly conversation lessons, the national French exam Test de Connaissance du Français (TCF), a variety of cultural events, readings, tutoring, and an online library. The organization also sponsors French book, cinema, and choir clubs, annual celebrations of Bastille Day, the *Fête des Rois* (a feast to mark the Epiphany), a French Haiku contest, and English lessons for French speakers.

The Charlotte chapter of the alliance is similar in design to that of the Triangle but distinguishes itself with an annual Méchoui Festival. This is a form of barbecue with a Francophone twist prevalent in North Africa. Some argue that the best *méchoui* is prepared in the former French colony of Morocco, where the goat or lamb is slowly roasted in an earthen oven underground, then served with cumin and salt to taste on a decorative ceramic dish. The festival also holds a *pétanque* tournament. The Charlotte Alliance Française, moreover, offers a virtual French school certified by the National Centre for Distance Education while collaborating with the Mecklenburg County School System. There are levels from K-12, with different levels of immersion. The French North Carolina chapters of the Alliance Française are strong ones. *Vive la FraNCe!*

Another significant contemporary French–North Carolina connection are the state's following French sister cities: Asheville (Saumur), Beaufort (Beaufort-en-Vallée), Cary (Le Touquet), Charlotte (Limoges), Greensboro (Montbéliard), Matthews (Sainte Maxime), and Raleigh (Compiègne). The sister cities initiative seeks to promote friendship and understanding. Its goal is to enable the citizens of North Carolina and the residents of its sister cities in the sharing of ideas and experiences in the areas of education, culture, sports, the arts, business, and economic development, and to promote exchanges between the cities and their citizens.

The author's family had the good fortune some years ago to host a student from Compiègne and, in turn, visited the student's family in that town. It is one of the most beautiful in France, dating back to the Middle Ages, and showcasing the Château de Compiègne, a royal residence built for Louis XV and restored by Napoléon. In Raleigh, just across the street from N.C. State on Chamberlain Street, is the small but quaint Compiegne Park.

French retail stores and boutiques abound in North Carolina. We have

Chapter 17. French North Carolina Today

Compiegne Park, Raleigh (photograph by the author).

visited La Petite Boutique on Frenchman's Creek in Kinston. French Connections in Pittsboro stocks an eclectic array of fabrics, antiques, table linens, art, and crafts from France, Francophone Africa, and elsewhere. There are many other shops in the state with French names and products. Let us remember the French-inspired Lafayette Village in Raleigh and the Bordeaux Shopping Center in Fayetteville.

The French Heritage Showroom in High Point, an exclusive venue, is replete with French furniture and household accessories from the antique to contemporary. French Heritage is known for recreating classic styles of the past with the flair and colors of today. It designs and manufactures side tables, desks, dining room sets, antique chests with a modern twist, accent pieces, and fashionable upholstery. The contrast of textures, design, finishes, colors, and patterns in the showroom are uniquely French and reminiscent of its neoclassical heritage.

French Heritage is *très spécial*, and in visiting the showroom, one is captivated by the French *joie de vivre* ("joy of life") and love of home comfort that emanates from its beautiful array of furnishings. French Heritage was founded by Jacques and Hennesey Wayser; the former grew up in a Parisian home filled with French antiques, and the latter became an American-born fashion model who grew up loving travel and architecture. The enterprise is thus an excellent French–American collaboration, blending Jacque's expertise in French furniture with Hennesey's flair and creativity, skillfully combining fashion and craftsmanship. French Heritage is known worldwide and is a French North Carolina jewel in the state's heartland.

French Interiors in High Point offers a unique window into high French culture and dovetails nicely with its neighbor French Heritage. The shop has hundreds of chairs, mirrors, and other decorative items all hand-built in the French Italianate style. The trumeau mirrors of French Interiors form the centerpiece of its offerings. The trumeau is a mirror set into an elegant wooden frame with a panel of painted or carved sculptural decoration at the top. This style was prevalent in France during the glamorous age of Louis XVI and Marie Antoinette.

Master craftsman William Thorpe builds, and paints his trumeau mirrors by hand to recreate traditional French artistry. He uses the least amount of technological advances as possible in his work and constructs trumeau mirrors by traditional seventeenth-century methods, using wood plaster, gesso paint, and ornament gilt, with a patina style hundreds of years old. Trained under an Italian master carver, as were many of France's artisans in the seventeenth and eighteenth centuries, Thorpe's work takes us back to the elegance and joyful spirit of the French golden age that glorified the monarchy and aristocracy.

William also restores furniture of all kinds, but his passion is creation and decoration in the French Italianate style. The author has had the pleasure of meeting and conversing with him in his High Point shop. He is a talented artisan who has much knowledge to share about traditional methods of Italian and French Old World craftsmanship. French Interiors is a marvel to behold with its hundreds of mirrors, chairs, William's original sketches, and fabrics linings its walls and covering its floor.

A cultural aside is to note how the French–North Carolina connection has intersected with Italy on more than one occasion. A pivotal moment was the French ship, *La Dauphine*, and its famous Italian explorer Giovanni da Verrazzano who discovered North Carolina. Moreover, let us remember what, in effect, was the French and Italian ethnic and cultural blend of the Waldensians. William Thorpe's training by an Italian master carver (Dominic Pannisi) to design his French furniture and trumeau mirrors harks back to the Italian apprenticeship of French artists and artisans over the centuries. The popularity of the Italian style in France was started by François I, the patron of Verrazzano's voyage. Williams's designs, in an unexpected way, connect us to the founding of French North Carolina itself.

Des Livres et Délices in Raleigh's Five Points neighborhood is a Francophile's delight. On the *délices* ("delicious goodies") side of this specialty shop are imported French culinary goods, from bottles of Bordeaux and

Chapter 17. French North Carolina Today

A trumeau mirror (courtesy William Thorpe, French Interiors).

Burgundy wine to Camembert and Roquefort cheeses, mustards, honeys, macaroons, and more. On the *livres* ("books") side is a well-stocked bookstore with a variety of genres, reference and travel books, and current French magazines and bestsellers. The storefront itself is reminiscent of a provincial French village, and the shop transports one to France.

The majority of the books in the *librarie* ("bookstore") are French, and those written in English sport a tiny American flag bookmark. It is a delightful place owned by a French couple, Laurence and Philippe, from Dijon, France, in the Burgundy region known for its centuries-old culinary traditions. The shop also hosts events such as a cider tasting with *Galette des Rois* (a French puff pastry cake with a prize in it) to celebrate the Epiphany, wine and cheese tastings, and a book club for varying levels of French speakers. The shop is unique to the area and provides a French immersion experience for the local community. Des Livres et Délices has quickly become a home-away-from-home to the French and Francophones in the area.

As we near the end of our French North Carolina story, there are two short anecdotes, both personal to the author, and one that bears a broader significance to the social climate at the writing of this final chapter.

The first concerns N.C. State basketball player Ilian Evtimov and his father, Illia Evtimov. They are French of Bulgarian descent. Illia was a legendary basketball player in the French professional leagues during the 1980s. He stood at 6'10" and had two sons, Ilian and Vassal, who followed his example and became professional basketball players. Ilian played for N.C. State from 2001 to 2006. During the 2004–05 season at State, Ilian injured his knee and had to undergo surgery. His father was very concerned and flew overnight from France to Raleigh to see Ilian and consult with the orthopedic surgeon who repaired Ilian's knee. The author received a phone call from the Athletic Office the day before Mr. Evtimov's arrival requesting if I knew of anyone who could translate for him; I replied yes, and that person was me. I was directed to meet him in the lobby of the surgery center and translate for him as he spoke to Illian's surgeon. I asked how I would recognize him, and the staff member replied, "Oh, you'll know."

Sure enough, when this giant of a man entered the lobby, I went over to him and introduced myself. My hand was swallowed up in his. Illian's surgeon reported the excellent news that the surgery had gone well and that Illian would be able to play basketball again. I recounted this to Illia, who was relieved; I spent some time with him that day, making sure his accommodations and visit were up to his satisfaction. He was so appreciative of my attention that he graciously invited me to his home in Vienne, a beautiful old Roman town outside of Lyon, the next time I visited France. He repeated the sincere offer, and I was touched. That evening I received a phone call from Ilian himself thanking me for helping out, as he put it, "mon père." After Illian graduated from State, he went on to have a successful professional basketball career in Spain and France. As we know, the French–North Carolina connection always has its surprise stories, and this is a happy one.

The second anecdote has particular relevance today. The Democratic Republic of the Congo (formerly Zaire) was a Belgian colony for many years and today is the largest Francophone country in the world of over eighty-four million citizens. Since 1996, regrettably, it has been in the throes of civil unrest and bloody wars between rival political and ideological factions. Numerous Congolese that had the means to do so sought refuge as asylees in other countries. Many came to the United States, and some have settled in the greater Raleigh area. The Triangle's Congolese

Chapter 17. French North Carolina Today 255

community comprises hundreds of families and is a mostly unknown, yet praiseworthy group of Francophone immigrants to North Carolina.

Many of the Congolese adults have advanced degrees and were forced to leave professions in business, education, and the health industry. The Congo has endured decades of violent civil strife; these Congolese of North Carolina suffered hardship, lost much of what they had, yet like the Huguenots and Waldensians before them, are resilient, hardworking, and ambitious to improve the lives of their families. They are eager to pursue American opportunities and succeed in a new world. The author has had the good fortune to meet and work with some Congolese families in a volunteer capacity for Lutheran Family Services. The individuals the author has worked with have overcome the language barrier by learning English and have taken employment in areas far below their education and professional training.

Some of the North Carolina Congolese with the means to do so have enrolled at colleges and universities to become certified in the areas in which they worked back home. At N.C. State, the author has served as a translator for Congolese employees just getting their feet under them, helping them navigate their employee benefits, and even mentoring some who enrolled in university classes. The Congolese community is a close-knit one, and in 2010, under the leadership of the Rev. Dr. Jean-Pierre Kamuabo, opened the Alliance Community Church, the first Congolese church in the state. The Congolese of Raleigh is a North Carolina Francophone success story. They are warm, family-oriented people who are worthy in every way of our inclusion and support.

The question of race in France is more important than ever today. Let us remember the many West African and Caribbean slaves in North Carolina, Blackbeard's French slave ship, the teacher Pierre Henri of Beaufort, Lafayette's experience of North Carolina slavery, the Hotel De'Afrique, and now the Congolese of Raleigh. The Black Lives Matter movement has recently taken hold in France. Centuries of the same oppression and inequality are not new to French Africans (and Muslims). France, as many do not know, is not a homogenous Caucasian society. Over 20 percent of its population hails from Africa and North Africa. Today, there are profound social tensions between the far right political party, Le Front National, and its immigrant communities. Many of the latter have been in the country for decades and are French citizens; it is time they are accepted as such.

There is one final fascinating piece of the Black French-North Carolina connection. Anna Julia Cooper (1858–1964) was a Black educator, writer, and liberation activist born into slavery in Raleigh in 1858. She was educated at St. Augustine's College, receiving classical training, and went on to earn a world-class education. In 1924, Anna Julia was awarded the

Ph.D. in history at one of the most prestigious universities in the world, the Sorbonne in Paris. She was only the fourth Black woman at the time to have earned a doctoral degree. Anna Julia spent her career promoting racial justice and the progress of the African American community in the United States. Her educational experience in France informed her social agenda significantly. The reader is encouraged to read more about her extraordinary life. Anna Julia died at the age of one hundred and five years and rests in the heart of Raleigh at the City Cemetery, Raleigh's oldest and most revered. She is a unique member of our French-North Carolina family.

Let us remember France's illustrious historical culture, yet also heed today's protests against her racial injustice. The French made fortunes over the centuries at the expense of the lives of their African slaves. Let us remember the discussion of the French Atlantic Triangle in previous chapters. Moreover, the citizens of France's former colonial empire living in France today have suffered prejudice and humiliation over the years. Now, the people gathered in protest in front of the country's hallowed cultural icons such as the Eiffel Tower, and one the oldest buildings in Paris, the Palais de Justice (the main tribunal and prison for centuries) to change that. Let us remember Lafayette and his enlightened thinking; it is now finally arrived at its logical outcome, liberty, equality, and mutual respect for all French citizens. There is still a long way to go. In 2017, French President Emmanuel Macron apologized for the unsavory side of France's colonial past and asked for a *partenariat d'égal à égal* (an equal partnership) with its former colonies. Let us remain hopeful of more such progress and that the protests will spawn greater inclusiveness and fairness for French society as a whole.

France is a multicultural mosaic, and the colonization and oppression of people, with slavery a part of it at different points in time, are ingrained in the collective cultural psyche. In today's French social arena, many people are imbued with fossilized stereotypes and hushed racism (sometimes overt) inherent in a postcolonial society. Nevertheless, it must also be said that many of France's African immigrants have done quite well socially and economically. However, many of them suffer some of the same social, economic, and political woes of American Black people. The Congolese of Raleigh form a bridge between France, Africa, and North Carolina and point to the collective and reciprocal decency needed that could alleviate our torn social fabric and fractured civil society.

There has been a noticeable decline in France's world influence since 1945; many French feel a particular social, economic, and political malaise. The future, in fact, for the French language and culture may be in its former French colonies that comprise today over three hundred and fifty million speakers of French, many of them in African countries such as the Congo,

Chapter 17. French North Carolina Today   257

Mali, La Côte d'Ivoire, Cameroon, and others. These are the very countries from where innumerous slaves were brought to North Carolina over the centuries. The number of Francophones in the United States today is well over a million. There are many from the above countries residing in North Carolina today as well as from French Caribbean islands such as Haiti and Martinique, the North African countries Algeria, Morocco, and elsewhere. The multicultural richness of Francophone North Carolina is a topic worthy of future study.

France has always had a flair that attracts Americans, and North Carolina has its fair share of things French. How and why French culture is so prevalent in the United States is explained in the essential work of Joan DeJean, *The Essence of Style: How the French Invented High Fashion, Fine Food, Chic Cafés, Style, Sophistication, and Glamour*. Yet, even today, this enthusiasm for things French is tempered by the perennial ambivalence Americans have toward the French, as discussed in the entertaining *Sixty Million Frenchmen Can't Be Wrong (Why We Like France but Not the French)* by Jean Benoît Nadeau and Julie Barlow. As the French say, *plus ça change c'est la même chose* ("the more things change, the more they stay the same"). This French American ambiguity is what makes the relationship so interesting.

Today, there are direct flights from Raleigh and Charlotte to Paris and thousands of French students, faculty, and professionals living in the state. North Carolina could market itself to French tourists and encourage them to visit French North Carolina. A map with the French North Carolina places we have visited can be their guide. Let them visit Beaufort and see the beautiful Crystal Coast of Carteret County, spend a few days in the Triangle to enjoy its French cosmopolitan offerings, and then head to the mountains to marvel at our forests, waterfalls, and especially the locales of French heritage in western North Carolina such as Chanteloup, the State of Franklin and its French-named towns, Michaux's historical markers, Valdese, the French Broad River, the Biltmore Estate, and elsewhere. In doing so, the French would have a greater appreciation of North Carolina and the United States in general as they learn that it is more than a country of highways and Walmarts, one with a rich multicultural heritage of which France is a part.

North Carolina has a captivating natural beauty, unique history, and rich cultural heritage. The French were a small part of the historical evolution of the state, but they have always been here. North Carolina is not the popular urban venue of major American cities that the French are most familiar with; it is instead an area the French would call *l'Amérique profonde*, loosely translated as the "authentic America," more typical of where most people live in the United States. This is what makes North Carolina such a special place; it has it all from the seashores to the mountains, from its small towns to major cities, from its rural schools to excellent universities, from its down-to-earth people to its urbane citizens. North Carolina has a bit of everything, and the French–North Carolina connection has always been a part of it.

Epilogue

How to end? *The French Heritage of North Carolina* has taken ten years to research and write. Paraphrasing a favorite saying of an N.C. State colleague, one never really finishes a research project, but finally has to let it go. I know there are stones left unturned. More genealogical research needs to be undertaken, both in North Carolina and in the Huguenot libraries in Paris and London. There are undoubtedly more documents to be uncovered in libraries and archives throughout the state, other researchers whom I have not met with relevant material, and people with stories to tell about their family ancestry. So many folks I have met in North Carolina while working on this project had French North Carolina anecdotes to share. I am sure there are others, and I hope to know them someday.

Other books are waiting to be written about the diverse immigration to the state, beyond our English founders. I refer many times to the Welsh, Scottish, Irish, Swiss, Germans, Italians, and Francophone groups from Canada, the Caribbean, Africa, and elsewhere. It is a vibrant and multifaceted topic waiting to be brought to light by interested researchers. Thank you for reading this book. I hope my efforts were worthy of your interest.

Appendix 1
Family Names

Mr. Dennis Jones is a retired educator (MA, Geography, 1972, UNC) with a background in the historical geography of settlement patterns in eastern North Carolina. He has presented lectures and discussion sessions on French settlers and ancestry in the state. Much of his work stems from the earlier research of the late Dr. W. Keats Sparrow, professor emeritus of East Carolina University. The ECU Library has most of the known Huguenot scholarship and documentation in the state. Dr. Roger Kammerer's *A History of the Huguenot Society of North Carolina* (2013) is a tribute to Dr. Sparrow's work. Mr. Jones has also drawn on the valuable work of the late Onslow County local historian and genealogist, Mr. Tucker Littleton.

Mr. Jones's knowledge of Huguenot migrations in North Carolina, as informed by the work of these scholars, is a sound one. We met by chance while I was working in the archive room of the Museum of Onslow County. We had been working on the same material for years and had much information to share and compare. It was a fortunate encounter, and our separate research has complemented that of the other. Mr. Jones's work is far more important to mine than mine to his, and he filled in some important missing links for me. What follows is a summary of the family names Mr. Jones has compiled.

Numerous French ancestral families still call eastern North Carolina home. Mr. Jones's direct ancestor Pierre Ferrier (Farrior) of Manakin Town, Virginia, came to the Trent River settlement about 1707, along with other French settlers. The following names are some of the French families (with Anglicized derivatives) who settled in eastern North Carolina in the early 1700s: Averit (Averette), Bachelier (Bachelor), Ballard, Barber, Bergeron, Berry, Blanchard, Boyer (Boyette), Broc, Chesson, Debruhl, de la Hunte (Dillahunt), Dieppe (Deppe/Depp), Dubose, Dulaney (Delaney), Dupré (Dupree), Durand (Durant), Duval (Duvall), Fayson (Faison), Ferrand, Fontaine (Fountain), Fonvielle (Fonville), Fortescue (Foscue), Foushee, Foye (Foy), Gaines, Gaspar, Gaston, Gauthier, Gilbert, Giles, Gillet (Gillette), Guion (Gwynn), Haskins, Haye (Hay), Jarrett, Jourdain (Jordan), Lanier, LaPierre, LaRue, Laroque, LeNoble (Noble), Lenoir, Magny (Manney), Mahieu (Mayhew), Marot (Merritt), Martin, Maurice (Morris), Maury, Monette (Money), Montfort, Moriset, Moulin (Mullen), Pasteur, Pelletier, Perrie (Perry), Powell, Prévot (Provo), Privet (Privette), Purefoy, Richebourg, Rochelle, Rousseau, Rouse, Roussel (Russell), Simon (Simmons), Vause, and Venter (Venters).

Appendix 1

Names that appear on both the Manakin Town roster and on Mr. Jones's list are as follows: Jacob Amonet, Jacques Ballenger, Jacques Brousse, Daniel de la Hunte, Peter Depp, Claude de Richebourg, Mareen Duvall, Christophe Du Breuil, Henry Fayson, Jean Fonvielle, Bernard Gaines, William Gaston, Pierre Gilbert, Jonathan Gillette, Louis Guion, Simon Hay, James Jarrett, William Jourdain, John Lanier, Hester Mahieu, Jacques Magny, Jean Marot, George Martin, Isaac Monnette, Nicolas Maurice, Michel Paquinet, Jean Pasteur, Gutielmus Provost, Thomas Purefoy, Hilliaire Rousseau, Benjamin Simon, and Jean Vause.

Of the thirteen original American colonies, North Carolina had fewer French settlers than did Massachusetts, New York, South Carolina, and Virginia, but it ranks fifth behind them. French North Carolina lives on today in this array of family names.

Appendix 2
Names in Phone Directories

New Bern, Havelock, Morehead City, and Newport
Aguion, Barbour, Barteau, Beauchamp, Beaudrey, Beaulieu, Beaumont, Beliveau, Bellefleur, Beregeay, Bernard (Dionne), Berteaux, Bilodeaux, Bissotte, Blanchard, Bonapartian, Bordeaux, Boucher, Boudreau, Boulanger, Bouler, Boulier, Brouillard, Carriere, Chamblin, Chauvin, Chevalier, Cloutier, Colbert, Collier, Connour, Crovell, Dampier, Davant, Delacour, DeMolet, DeNeau, Deroulin, Descheves, DeSeau, Dionne, Dubeau, Dubois, Dupree, Duprey, Durand, Falardeau, Fontaine, Fonville, Fougere, Fournier, Francoeur, Fremont, Gagnon, Gastineau, Gaudette, Gaulin, Gault, Gauthreaux, Gautier, Gavignan, Gereaux, Gilette, Godette, Grasier, Grignan, Guirgues, Guiselle, Hachet, Jacques, Jaques Labonte, Laboeuf, LaBrie, Lachance, LaCroix, La Ferte, Lafond, Lafreniere, Lagrande, LaLonde, Lanier, Lapier, La Pointe, La Prairie, La Rouge Tete, La Tour, Lavigne, Le Blanc, Lecompte, Leduc, Leverette, Maille, Maisonet, Marquardt, Michaud, Midyette, Monnier, Montague, Moulton, Padgette, Paradis, Perrault, Pierre, Poulson, Prioleau, Rabideau, Revelle, Revette, Tetrault, Vermillion, Vernsier, Youraine.

Crystal Coast: Atlantic Beach, Beaufort, Cape Carteret, and Emerald Isle
Affourtit, Aguion, Arnoult, Arthaud, Baptiste, Baquer, Barbeau, Bastien, Batiste, Beaujean, Beaulieu, Beaumont, Belandres, Belanger, Bercegeay, Bernard, Berrier, Bessette, Bille, Billett, Billodeau, Bissette, Blanchard, Bonnette, Bouchard, Boucher, Bouchillon, Boudreau, Bougie, Boulanger, Bouquet, Bourbeau, Bourdeau, Bourgeois, Bourquin, Boutigue, Boutilier, Brisson, Brouillard, Broussard, Burchette, Burdette, Cardier, Cartier, Chanter, Chantiles, Charboneau, Charbonneau, Charette, Charlery, Chevalier, Clairmont, Cloutier, Cordes, Dauchet, Davant, Davignon, Delacourt, Delorier, Delorme, DeMichelle, Demonet, Demoranville, Denault, Deneau, Derovin, Deschamps, Desrochers, Deveau, Devereaux, Devore, Donavant, Doucette, Dubois, Dubuisson, Dufour, Dulac, Dupree, Duprey, Dupuis, Duran, Faison, Faucette, Fayson, Fernau, Fontaine, Fonville, Forelle, Fournier, Gareau, Gardinier, Gasque, Gaucher, Gauthreaux, Genereux, Gillette, Goulette, Grenier, Griset, Grisette, Grissett, Guyant, Guyer, Harmande, Hubert, Jacques, Jarquin, Jean-Baptiste, Jeanette, Labare, Labranche, Labrecque, Labrie, Lachance, Lacroix, Laferte, Lamoreaux, Lanier, Lapointe, Laroque, Larue, Lebeau, Leblanc, Lebleu, Leboeuf, Lebron, Lechene, Leclair, Lecompte, Leconte, Lefebvre, Lefevre,

Lemere, Lemieux, Lepere, Letendre, Leverette, LeVesque, Marcoux, Marquardt, Mullineaux, Noe, Paschall, Paschien, Pelletier, Perdue, Petit, Picard, Preneveau, Prevette, Prioleau, Privette, Quebedeaux, Rabideau, Rabidon, Rabidou, Robinett, Robinette, Rochefort, Rochelle, Rochon, Sable, Sabourin, Simoneaux, Simonette, Soule, Soulet, Tessier, Theriault, Tourigny, Toussaint, Trottier, Truaux, Vasseur, Vermillon, Vigneaux, Villeneuve, Youraine.

Onslow County: Maysville, Pollocksville, Swansboro, and Jacksonville

Adriance, Andre, Arsenault, Arthaud, Avant, Babineaux, Bardon, Batchelder, Beauchamp, Beauchemin, Beaufort, Beaujean, Beaulieu, Beauregard, Bellanger, Belluche, Belville, Benoit, Bequette, Bercegeay, Berger, Bernard, Bernier, Bissette, Blanchard, Blanque, Bonaparte, Boneau, Bonnette, Bordeaux, Bouchard, Boucher, Boudreau, Bourgeois, Bosquet, Boutiller, Boulanger, Brissette, Brodeur, Broussard, Brosseau, Cadet, Carteaux, Cavalier, Cerveny, Cetoute, Charbonneau, Chasserot, Chavous, Colette, Collier, Comeau, Comeaux, Corpier, Courchaire, Crozier, Daigneault, Dareneau, Dauchert, Davignon, Davoren, Deleplancque, Derosier, Detreux, Deupree, Douville, Doucotte, Dubois, DuFresne, Dupree, Dupuis, Duval, Fabre, Faison, Fonville, Formyduval, Foscue, Fournier, Fuqua, Fuquay, Fuquea, Gagnon, Gautier, Genereux, Gregoire, Grenier, Guy, Hebert, Hubert, Isabelle, Jacqueline, Jacques, Jean-Charles, Jeansonne, Jennette, Jerome, Labonte, Labrecque, LaDebue, Ladue, Lafayette, Lafleur, Lagasse, Lamontague, Lamont, Lamotte, Landeau, Langille, Langois, LaPoint, L'argent, LaRocque, Larue, Latourrette, Lavache, Lavigne, Leblanc, Leblond, Leclair, Leconte, Lechotte, LeDoux, Le Duc, LeFebvre, LeGrand, Le Maire, Le Mere, Lemieux, Lenier, Lepere, LePley, Leroux, Levasseur, LeWellyn, Lien, L'oignon, Louis, Mallette, Malpass, Maupin, Michaud, Michel, Moniot, Monique, Monerrate, Montaque, Montcreiff, Montenguide, Nadeau, Napier, Paschall, Peletier, Pelletier, Pelligren, Peltier, Pierre, Pointe, Ponthiaux, Prevatte, Privett, Privott, Puette, Rabidau, Rabideau, Rabidou, Renaud, Roche, Rochefort, Rochelle, Rochon, Rousseau, Roussel, Sartain, Sartin, Sylvain, Tessier, Therency, Theriault, Therrien, Thibault, Tourigny, Toussaint, Traubert, Valentin.

This is only a small sampling of French names. More work could be undertaken to assemble a complete directory of French family names in North Carolina. It is estimated that there are several hundred thousand.

Appendix 3
French North Carolina Place Names

Alamance County (Neighborhoods/Settlements):
  Bellemont
  Piedmont Heights

Alleghany County (Neighborhoods/Settlements):
  Amelia
  Ennice

Ashe County (Neighborhoods/Settlements):
  Transou

Avery County (Neighborhoods/Settlements):
  Altamont

Beaufort County (Town/Municipality/City):
  Aurora
  Belhaven

Bertie County (Neighborhoods/Settlements):
  Sans Souci

Brunswick County (Neighborhoods/Settlements):
  Clairmont

Caldwell County (Towns/Cities/Municipalities):
  Lenoir

Caldwell County (Neighborhoods/Settlements):
  Baton
  Olivette

Camden County (Neighborhoods/Settlements):
  Bogue Shores

Chatham County (Towns/Cities/Municipalities):
  Moncure

Craven County (Neighborhoods/Settlements):
  Bellair
  Jasper

Cumberland County (Neighborhoods/Settlements):
  Ardennes
  Bastogne Gables
  Belair
  Bonair Place
  Bordeaux
  Bougainville
  Cherbourg
  Montclair

Dare County (Neighborhoods/Settlements):
  Saltaire

Franklin County (Neighborhoods/Settlements):
  Moulton

Gaston County (Towns/Cities/Municipalities):
  Belmont

Gaston County (Neighborhoods/Settlements):
  Nims
  Vantine

Gates County (Neighborhoods/Settlements):
  Dort

Graham County (Neighborhoods/Settlements):
  Dentons

Henderson County (Neighborhoods/Settlements):
  Beaumont
  Claremont
  Jeter Mountain Terrace

Hertford County (Neighborhoods/Settlements):
  Tunis

Iredell County (Neighborhoods/Settlements):
  Belmont

Lenoir County (Towns/Cities/Municipalities):
  La Grange

Lenoir County (Neighborhoods/Settlements):
  Dupreeville
  Lenoir Pines

Lincoln County (Neighborhoods/Settlements):
  Orleans

Mecklenburg County (Neighborhoods/Settlements):
  Belmont
  Chantilly
  Chateau Woods
  Montclaire

Pamlico County (Towns/Cities/Municipalities):
  Alliance

Appendix 3

Pender County (Neighborhoods/Settlements):
    Montague
Richmond County (Neighborhoods/Settlements):
    Cognac
Robeson County (Towns/Cities/Municipalities):
    Rennert
    Rowland
Surry County (Neighborhoods/Settlements):
    Albion
Transylvania County (Neighborhoods/Settlements):
    Quebec
Wake County (Neighborhoods/Settlements):
    Bellevue Terrace
    Clairmont
    Damont Hills
Wayne County (Neighborhoods/Settlements):
    Lafayette Park
Wilson County (Neighborhoods/Settlements):
    Bel-Air Forest
    Montclair

Appendix 4
Names of French Origin:
The N.C. Gazetteer

Amour (Columbus County)
Beaumont (Chatham County)
Beautancus (Duplin County)
Beaux (Wilkes County)
Belhaven (Beaufort County)
Bellamy (Robeson County)
Bellamy's Lake (Alamance County)
Bell Island (Currituck County)
Peregrine Bertie, Lord Willoughby de Eresby (Roanoke Voyage of 1585)
Bellvue Mountain (Avery County)
Belmont (Gaston County) (Nash County)
Belvidere/Belvidere Township (Perquimans County)
Belville (Currituck County)
Belvoir Township (Pitt County)
Belvoir Township (Sampson County)
Bonaparte Landing (Brunswick County)
Boyette (Wilson County)
Nathan Boyette (1897)
Buie (Robeson County)
Buies (Robeson County)
Calvert (Transylvania County)
French Broad River
Cantrell Creek (Transylvania County)
Carteret County (Beaufort)
Ca-Vel (Person County)
Cefare (Wilson County)

Cefare Bissett
Cognac (Richmond County)
Coleville (Stokes County)
Colett Camp Branch (Caldwell County)
Colettesville (Caldwell County)
James H. Collet
Colvard Creek (Cherokee County)
Cottrell Hill (Caldwell County)
William Cottrell
Cromartie (Robeson County)
Crozier Branch (Mecklenburg County)
Delmar (Halifax County)
Del Mar Beach (Pender County)
Delmont (Henderson County)
DeRosett Creek (Pender County)
DeRosett family
Devereux's Ferry (Bridgers Island)
Dimmette (Wilkes County)
Dosier (Forsyth County)
East Fayetteville (Cumberland County)
East Laport (Jackson County)
Ennetts Point (Carteret County)
Faison (Duplin County)
Faisons Old Tavern (North Hampton County)
Faucette Township (Alamance County)
Fayette County
Fayetteville (Cumberland County)
Le Marquis de LaFayette
Fortiscue (Hyde County)

Appendix 4

French Branch (Jones County)
French Broad River (Transylvania County)
French Creek (Onslow County)
Alexander Nicola (1744)
Gallant Point (Carteret County)
Gallants Channel (Carteret County)
John Galland
Hugo (Lenoir County; in honor of Victor Hugo)
Jean Guite Creek (Dare County)
La Grange (Lenoir County)
Lamont (Guilford County)
Luneville (Polkton)
Medoc (Halifax County)
Medoc Mountain
Médoc, France
Mon Beau (East Monbo)
Moncure (Chatham County)
Thomas Jefferson Moncure
Mon Swamp (Tyrrell County)
Montague (Pender County)
Montpelier (Wagram)
Montrose (Chowan County)
Montvale (Transylvania County)
Mount Collier (Orange County)
North Belmont (Gaston County)
Olivet (Caldwell County)
Olivette (Buncombe County)
Otaré (Mountain Region)
Paris (Anson County)
Peletier (Carteret County)
Peletier Creek (Carteret County)
Jerome Pelletier
Quebec (Transylvania County)
Rendezvous Mountain (Wilkes County)
Sardis (Mecklenburg County)
Sevier (McDowell County)
Shallotte (Brunswick County)
Shallowbag Bay (Dare County)
"Chalon-Bas" (1800s)
South Belmont (Gaston County)
Viands (Wilkes County)

Appendix 5
Cemetery Records

Counties of Beaufort, Carteret, Craven, Onslow, and Pasquotank
Amyette, Aubert, Ballamy, Ballance, Ballard, Beaubien, Beaufort, Beaulieu, Bergerson, Blanchard, Boise, Bourgeois, Boutilier, Bovard, Brouillard, Chesson, Dosier, Dechaux, De Garsie, Delamar, Delisle, Delon, Denoyer, Deppe, Divour (Strasbourg, France), Domec, Dosier, Dubois, Duboise, Dumont, Faison, Ficquett, Fontain, Fonvielle, Fonville, Foscue, Foy, Foye, Fuquay, Geoffroy, Gillet, Gillette, Gilotte, Godette, Goquen, Guion, Guyon, Jaquett, La Boyteaux, La Foustain, LaMotte (Bordeaux, France), Lanier, Laroque, La Rue, Loiselle, Midgette, Midyette, Missillier, Montfort, Noe, Pasteur, Pelletier, Pellitier, Pettit, Pigott, Piver, Prevost, Roche, Rochelle, Savoie, Tebault, Vergon.

This is a small sample of French North Carolina cemetery markers. A more complete listing by county is available at https://go.ncsu.edu/af290fq.

Bibliography

Abenon, Lucien-René, and John A. Dickinson. *Les Français en Amérique*. Lyon, France: Presses Universitiares de Lyon, 1993.
Almond, Jay, ed. *Badin North Carolina: The First 100 Years*. Badin, NC: Badin Historic Museum, Inc., 2015.
Ashe, Samuel A., and Stephen B. Weeks. *History of North Carolina*. Greensboro, NC: C.L. Van Noppen, 1908.
Baird, Charles. *History of the Huguenot Emigration to America*. New York: Dodd, Mead, and Company Publishers, 1885.
Baker, Thomas E. *Another Such Victory: The Story of the American Defeat at Guilford Courthouse*. Fort Washington, PA: Eastern National, 2013.
———. *The Moores Creek Bridge Campaign, 1776*. Raleigh, NC: NC Division of Archives and History, 1986.
Beaufort County Deed Book (1696–1729). Washington, NC: Beaufort County Register of Deeds.
Biltmore Estate History Archives. https://www.biltmore.com/blog: 14–15.
Bisher, Catherine. *North Carolina Architecture*. Chapel Hill: University of North Carolina Press, 2003.
Bledsoe, Jerry. *North Carolina Curiosities*. Guilford, CT: The Globe Pequot Press, 1984.
Blythe, John. "Crusoe Island and the French Revolution." *North Carolina Miscellany* (blog), The North Carolina Collection at the University of North Carolina at Chapel Hill, July 14, 2011. https://blogs.lib.unc.edu/ncm/2011/07/14/crusoe-island-and-the-french-revolution/.
Boyd, James. *Drums*. New York: C. Scribner's, 1928.
Boyette, Charles Martin. Email correspondence with author. 2014.
Bradley, Stephen E. *New Bern District: North Carolina Loose Estate Papers*. Morehead City, NC: Carteret County Historical Society, 1973.
Branch, Paul. *Fort Macon: A History*. Charleston, SC: The Nautical & Aviation Publishing Company of America, 1999.
Bugg, James L. "The French Huguenot Frontier Settlement of Manakin Town." *Virginia Magazine of History and Biography* 61, no. 4 (October 1953): 359–92.
Cain, Barbara. "A Whole Cargo of French Folks." Private Papers, 1983.
Carley, Rachel D., and Rosemary G. Rennicke. *A Guide to Biltmore Estate*. Asheville, NC: The Biltmore Company, 1997.
Cecil, William A. V. *Biltmore: The Vision and Reality of George W. Vanderbilt, Richard Morris Hunt, and Frederick Law Olmsted*. Asheville, NC: The Biltmore Company, 1975.
———. *The Biltmore Estate: A Pictorial Guide*. Asheville, NC: The Biltmore Company, 1985.
Chiorazzi, Michael G. "François Xavier-Martin: Printer, Lawyer, Jurist." *Duke Law Magazine* no. 4 (1989): 6–13.
Clément, Thierry. "The Merci Train, a Locomotive Built on French-American Goodwill." *France-Amérique*, June 28, 2018. https://france-amerique.com/en/the-merci-train-a-locomotive-built-on-french-american-goodwill.
Coddington, Ronald. "LTC Charles de Choiseul." *Find a Grave Memorial*. https://www.findagrave.com/memorial/6862394/charles-de_choiseul.

Coon, Charles. *North Carolina Schools and Academies: 1790-1840*. Raleigh, NC: Edwards & Broughton, 1915.
Costner, Gretchen. Telephone interview with author. March 7, 2020.
Covington, Howard E., Jr. *Lady on the Hill: How Biltmore Estate Became an American Icon*. Hoboken, NJ: John Wiley & Sons, Inc., 2006.
Cranford, Fred. "Valdese, NC: A History." *Tar Heel Junior Historian* (Spring 2006). https://www.ncpedia.org/geography/valdese.
Cuthbert, Robert B. *Flat Rock of the Old Time: Letters from the Mountains to the Low Country, 1837-1939*. Columbia: University of South Carolina Press, 2016.
Davies, Horton, and Marie-Hélène Davies. *French Huguenots in English-Speaking Lands*. New York: Peter Lang, 2000.
Day, Jean. *The Revolutionary War in Coastal North Carolina*. Morehead City, NC: Carteret County Historical Society, 2005.
DeJean, Joan. *The Essence of Style: How the French Invented High Fashion, Fine Food, Chic Cafés, Style, Sophistication, and Glamour*. New York: Free Press, 2005.
Deleuze, J. P. F. *Notice Historique sur André Michaux*. Translated by Carl D. E. Köenig and John Sims. London: Annals of Botany, 1805.
Dill, Alonzo. "Eighteenth Century New Bern: A History of the Town and Craven County, 1700-1800." *The North Carolina Historical Review* 22, no. 6 (1943): 483-524.
Dubois, Laurent, and John D. Garrigus. *Slave Revolutions in the Caribbean, 1789-1804*. Boston: Bedford-St. Martin's, 2017.
Dudley, Jack. *Swansboro: A Pictorial History*. Coastal Heritage Series. Jack Dudley, 1998.
Dunn, Susan. *Sister Revolutions: French Lightning, American Light*. New York: Faber & Faber, 1999.
Edmunds, Pocahontas Wight. *Tales of the North Carolina Coast*. Raleigh, NC: Edwards & Broughton Company, 1986.
Fisher, Primrose Watson. *Early Records of North Carolina: Wills, 1663-1722*. Morehead City, NC: Carteret County Historical Society, 1975.
———. *One Dozen Pre-Revolutionary War Families of Eastern North Carolina and Some of Their Descendants*. New Bern, NC: New Bern Historical Society, 1958.
Forbes, Esther. *Paul Revere and the World He Lived In*. Boston: Houghton Mifflin, 1999.
Foreman, Nicolas. "The History of the United States' First Refugee Crisis." *Smithsonian Magazine*, January 5, 2016. https://www.smithsonianmag.com/history/history-united-states-first.
Freedman, Russell. *Lafayette and the American Revolution*. New York: Holiday House, 2010.
Gallay, Alan. *The Indian Slave Trade: The Rise of the English Empire in the American South*. New Haven: Yale University Press, 2003.
Gannt, Amy Lavonne. "The Sociolinguistic Significance of Peripheral Communities: The Case of Crusoe Island, North Carolina." Master's thesis, NC State University, 2000.
Gerard, Philip. "The Strange Case of the Life and Afterlife of Michel Ney." *River Teeth Ashland* 13 (Fall 2011): 39-58.
Ghigo, Francis. *The Provençal Speech of the Waldensian Colonists of Valdese, North Carolina*. Valdese, NC: Historical Valdese Foundation, 1980.
Hakluyt, Richard. *Divers Voyages*. London: Thomas Woodcocke, 1582.
Hathaway, J. R. B. *North Carolina Historical and Genealogical Record*. Edenton, NC: 1900.
Haun, Weynette Parks. *Perquimans County North Carolina: Record of Deeds*. Durham, NC: Weynette Parks Haun, 1983.
Hawks, Francis L. *History of North Carolina*. Fayetteville, NC: E. J. Hale, 1858.
Haywood, Richard B. "Lafayette Visits Raleigh." Private Papers, 1880.
Helsley, Alexia Jones. *A History of North Carolina Wine: From Scuppernong to Syrah*. Mount Pleasant, SC: Arcadia Publishing, 2010.
Higginbotham, Don, ed. *The Papers of James Iredell*. Raleigh, NC: Department of Archives and History, 1976.
Hoyt, William Henry. Collected Papers. North Carolina Digital Collections: P.C. 48.1-2.
Inscoe, John C. "André Michaux." *NCpedia*, 1991. https://www.ncpedia.org/biography/michaux-andre.

Bibliography 273

Jones, H. G. "François Xavier-Martin." *Ncpedia*, 1991. https://www.ncpedia.org/biography/martin-fran%C3%A7ois-xavier.
Jones, William. "Rekindling the Spark of Libert: Lafayette's Visit to the United States, 1824–1825." *The American Patriot* (November 2007): 54–63.
Kammerer, Roger. *A History of the Huguenot Society of North Carolina*. Raleigh, NC: Huguenot Society of NC, 2013.
Lambert, David E. *Protestant International and the Huguenot Migration to Virginia*. New York: Peter Lang Publishing, 2009.
Lawson, John. *A New Voyage to Carolina*. Chapel Hill: University of North Carolina Press, 1967.
Le Bris, Melani. *La Cuisine des flibustiers*. Paris: Editions Phébus, 2002.
Levasseur, Auguste. *Lafayette in America, in 1824 and 1825: Journal of a Voyage to the United States*. Manchester, NH: Lafayette Press, 2006.
Lewis, Taylor, and Joanna Young. "The Palmer-Marsh House." https://historicsites.nc.gov/all-sites/historic-bath/history/palmer-marsh-house.
Littleton, Tucker. *The Tucker Littleton Notes*. Raleigh, NC: Coastal Genealogical Society, 1998.
Lucas, Jill Warren. "Merci, From France to North Carolina." *Our State Magazine* (February 2016): 33–35.
Mace, James. *Courage Marshal Ney: The Last Stand of the Brave of the Brave*. Meridian, ID: Legionary Books, 2014.
MacNeill, Ben Dixon. "Crusoe Island: French-Haitian Settlement in the Green Swamp of North Carolina." *New York Herald Tribune*, November 1, 1931, 1–7.
McClain, Molly. "A Letter from Carolina, 1688: French Huguenots in the New World." *The William and Mary Quarterly* 64, no. 2 (April 2007): 377–94.
McLivenna, Noeleen. *A Very Mutinous People: The Struggle for North Carolina, 1660–1713*. Chapel Hill: University of North Carolina Press, 2009.
Mennear, Catherine. "French Language in the Carolinas—Its History and Vitality." *The Researcher* (Carteret County Historical Society) (Fall/Spring 2010): 17–21.
Messer, Pamela Lynn. *Frederick Law Olmsted's Landscape Masterpiece*. Alexander, NC: World Community Press Inc., 1993.
Mihaly, Robert. Email correspondence with author. December 2, 2019.
Miller, Daniel L. *The French Atlantic Triangle: Literature and Culture of the Slave Trade*. Durham, NC: Duke University Press, 2008.
Mitchell, Patricia B. *French Cooking in Early America*. Chatham, VA: Patricia B. Mitchell, 1991.
Morison, Samuel Eliot. *The European Discovery of America*. New York: Oxford University Press, 1971.
Murphy, Henry C. *Early History of Maritime Discovery in America*. Freeport, NY: Books for Libraries Press, 1970.
Murray, Elizabeth Davis Reid. "Ellen Mordecai." *Ncpedia*, 1991. https://www.ncpedia.org/biography/mordecai-mrs-ellen.
Nadeau, Jean Benoît, and Julie Barlow. *Sixty Million Frenchmen Can't Be Wrong (Why We Like France but Not the French)*. London: Pavilion Books, 2014.
Paschal, Herbert R., Jr. *A History of Colonial Bath*. Raleigh, NC: Edwards & Broughton, 1955.
Patton, Charles E. *Crousilleau: The Formy-Duval Family Saga*. Scotts Valley, CA: CreateSpace Publishing, 2010.
Pelletier-Harman, Lisa. Personal interview with author. Morehead City, NC, August 14, 2014.
Perdue, Theda, and Christopher Arris Oakley. *Native Carolinians: The Indians of North Carolina*. Raleigh, NC: North Carolina Division of Archives and History, 2010.
Perquimans County Deed Book. Hertford, NC: Perquimans County Register of Deeds.
Pezzoni, Daniel. *The History & Architecture of Lee County, North Carolina*. Sanford, NC: The Railroad Historical Association, NC, 1995.
Powell, William S. *North Carolina: A Bicentennial History*. New York: W. W. Norton, 1977.
Quynn, Dorothy Mackay. "La Liquidation d'une légende: la survivance de Ney en Amérique." *Revue de l'Insitut Napoléon* no. 125 (1972): 154–70.
Rankin, Hugh F. *The North Carolina Continentals*. Chapel Hill: University of North Carolina Press, 1971.

———. *North Carolina in the American Revolution*. Raleigh, NC: NC Division of Archives and History, 1959.
Ready, Milton. *The Tar Heel State: A History of North Carolina*. Columbia, SC: University of South Carolina Press, 2005.
Sainlaude, Stève. *France and the American Civil War*. Translated by Jessica Edwards. Chapel Hill: University of North Carolina Press, 2019.
Simpson, William C., Jr. *The Huguenot Trail: The Life and Descendants of the Reverend Claude Philippe de Richebourg and Ann Chastain*. William Simpson Jr., 1999.
Smith, Roch C. Email correspondence with author. September 5, 2006.
Solterer, Helen. Telephone interview with author. July 1, 2020.
Sparrow, W. Keats. John LaPierre Manuscript Collection. East Carolina University.
Stanford, Herbert W. III. *In Our Country's Service: The Men and Women from Carteret County, North Carolina Who Served During World War I*. Morehead City, NC: Carteret County Historical Society, Inc., 2018.
Thornton, Julia Forbes. "North Carolina's Own Huguenot Families." *The Huguenot* no. 12 (1945): 113–16.
Traxler, George. "James Cole Mountflorence." *NCpedia*, 1991. https://www.ncpedia.org/biography/mountflorence-james-cole.
Vance, Christine W. "Héritage Vaudois en Caroline du Nord." *The French Review* 80, no. 6 (May 2007): 1319–35.
Vass, L. C. *History of the Presbyterian Church in New Bern, NC*. Richmond, VA: Whittet & Stephenson, 1886.
Volk, Victoria Loucia. *The Biltmore Estate and Its Creators: Richard Morris Hunt and Frederick Law Olmsted*. PhD diss., Emory University, 1984.
Watson, Alan D. *A History of New Bern and Craven County*. New Bern, NC: Tryon Palace Commission, 1987.
———. *Society in Colonial North Carolina*. Raleigh, NC: Division of Archives and History, 1996.
Watts, George B. *The Waldenses of Valdese*. Charlotte, NC: Heritage Printers, Inc., 1965.
Weeks, Stephen B., ed. *Colonial and State Records of North Carolina*. Charlotte, NC: The Observer Printing House, 1912.
Wilson, Mamré. "The French Connection." Unpublished manuscript, 2012.
Xavier-Martin, François. *The History of North Carolina from the Earliest Period*. New Orleans, LA: A. T. Penniman, 1829.

Index

Africa 99, 156, 234, 251, 255, 256, 259
African 96, 97, 99, 100, 104, 156, 160, 241, 255, 256
African American 131, 153, 183, 184, 227, 256
agriculture 12, 14, 30, 32, 45, 47, 48, 63, 68, 104, 112, 172, 226, 239
Albemarle 4, 12, 14, 29, 30- 37, 39, 40, 41, 44, 45, 111, 119, 123
Alliance Française 10, 19, 181, 182, 249, 250
American colonies 14, 15, 27, 46, 77, 106, 123, 125-128, 133, 151, 169, 262
American Revolution 11, 15, 17, 83, 125, 126, 127, 132, 133, 142-144, 161, 166, 217, 224, 272, 274
André the Giant 189
Atlantic Ocean 12, 13, 22, 26, 30, 38, 47, 70, 74, 100

Badin 18, 189, 190, 191, 192, 193, 271
Badin, Adrien 18, 189, 191-193
Barbe Noire 99, 100
Barker, Penelope 126, 132
Bath 14, 32, 34, 40, 44, 46-52, 56, 63, 83, 85, 85, 91, 99, 100, 127, 273
Beaufort (North Carolina) 3, 11, 12, 15, 16, 17, 22, 35, 36, 44, 48, 52, 57, 85-89, 91-103, 105-107, 111, 112, 132, 218, 235, 250, 255, 257, 263, 268, 271
Beaufort (South Carolina) 85
Beaufort-en-Vallée 101, 250
Bellair Plantation 73-74
Besson family 179-182, 249
Biltmore Estate 18, 19, 212, 245, 257, 271, 272, 274
Black 18, 97, 98, 183, 184, 187, 190, 227, 228, 233, 255, 256
Blackbeard 17, 51, 52, 91, 98, 99, 100, 255
Blount, John Gray 130, 131, 140
Bordeaux 18, 36, 42, 127, 130, 151, 169, 172, 175, 246, 252, 270
Brittany 21, 97, 111, 119, 129, 230, 248
brownstone 184-187
Brunswick Town 66, 67, 68, 154, 178

Cabarrus, Stephen 17, 128, 129
Cape Lookout 16, 124, 134, 135

Carteret County 3, 15, 22, 26, 36, 86, 88, 89, 92, 94, 102, 104, 218, 268, 271-274
Castle Mont Rouge 184, 185, 245
castles 18, 72, 90, 184, 198, 214, 218, 226, 229
cemeteries 4, 60, 67, 72, 74, 106, 108, 112, 119, 135, 148, 150, 151, 169, 171, 181, 183, 187, 199, 210, 211, 220, 221-223, 227, 229, 230, 256, 270
Chanteloup 17, 197-199, 200, 257
Charles IX 13, 14
Château de la Grange 152
children 32, 38, 40, 43, 64-67, 72, 73, 82, 87, 89, 97, 98, 106, 110, 111, 116, 117, 119-121, 144, 176, 180-183, 198, 201, 203, 204, 206, 207- 209, 229, 232, 242, 243
Choiseul, de family 17, 197-199, 217, 220, 223, 227, 271
Civil War 11, 88, 92, 118, 152, 177, 178, 180, 182, 199, 217, 218, 220-223, 226, 274
Colonie perdue 51, 53, 72, 109, 115
Conflans, Antoine de 22, 233
Continental Army 15, 16, 17, 111, 125, 127, 134, 135, 151, 182
cooking 19, 32, 51, 64, 100, 108, 146, 207, 243, 273
Craven County 15, 34, 35, 53- 55, 59-68, 70, 71, 74, 76, 77, 84, 90, 116, 118, 266, 272, 274
Crusoe Island 17, 68, 104, 157-162, 187, 271-273

Edenton 15, 17, 40, 46, 47, 99, 125, 126-133, 135, 138, 139, 181, 183, 272
Edict of Fontainebleau 27, 45, 80, 89
Edict of Nantes 14, 27
education 1, 16, 19, 46, 65, 66, 86, 96, 98, 117, 126, 129, 133, 139, 140, 166, 176, 177, 178, 180, 181, 183, 224, 236, 238, 239, 241-243, 250, 255, 256
elegance 77, 78, 114, 117, 173, 182, 186, 190, 215, 252
Elizabeth City 4, 30, 39
England 4, 14, 15, 16, 27, 28, 29, 32, 36, 37, 41, 47, 49, 53, 54, 59, 68, 71, 78, 81, 85, 92, 94, 102, 119, 125, 132, 144, 154, 183, 195, 197, 212, 221, 222

275

Index

Faison 11, 17, 61, 102, 111–112, 117, 122, 133, 144, 178, 220, 261, 263, 264, 268, 270
farms 32, 56, 57, 116, 196, 203
fashion 80, 114, 127, 129, 231, 251, 252, 257, 272
Fayetteville 11, 16, 148–151, 153, 167, 175, 176, 251, 268, 272
Fayetteville Street 180, 181
Fonvielle family, 49, 58, 61, 65, 67, 71–77, 122, 133, 139, 156, 234, 261, 262, 270
Fonville family 58, 59, 65, 72–75, 81, 82, 84, 114, 116, 117, 178, 229, 234, 235, 261, 263, 264, 270
food 32, 38, 50, 64, 88, 92, 99, 100, 136, 146, 174, 189, 197, 203, 230, 243, 257, 272
Formy-Duval, Jerome Prosper 156–158, 160, 162
Fort Hancock 124, 134, 135
Fort Macon 218, 219, 220, 271
France 1, 2, 4, 7, 11, 12–15, 17–19, 21, 22, 24, 25, 27, 28, 31–33, 36, 38, 40, 41, 42, 44, 45, 47, 49, 50, 54, 55, 59, 62, 63, 65, 68, 70, 72, 74, 76, 78- 92, 94, 97, 99, 101, 102, 106, 108, 110–114, 116, 118–121, 123, 125–129, 131–133, 136, 138–143, 146, 147, 148, 150–157, 160, 162–168, 170–184, 189, 190, 195–202, 205, 207, 209, 212–214, 217, 218, 222, 223, 224–236, 238–241, 243, 245–257, 269, 270, 271, 273, 274
Francis I 214
François I 12, 21, 22, 24, 210, 233, 252
Franklin, Benjamin 125, 146, 194
freedom 28–30, 131, 146, 150, 151, 153, 154, 234
Freedom Fries 12, 235
French and Indian War 12, 15, 21, 83, 120, 125, 217
French Atlantic Triangle 99, 256, 273
French colonies 33, 45, 256
French Gratitude Train 230, 231
Fuquay-Varina 17, 182, 226

gardens 18, 63, 76, 80, 81, 168, 178, 190, 199, 215, 216, 243
Gaston, William 121, 262
geography 4, 13, 61, 115, 139, 169, 176, 238, 261, 272
gold 38, 50, 86, 88, 89, 98–100
Gonella, Frenchy 186, 187, 188
Graffenried, Baron von 36, 56–58, 70, 79
Great Dismal Swamp 14, 29, 30, 37, 127

Haiti 13, 17, 51, 68, 83, 100, 102–104, 126, 155, 156, 158, 257
Halifax 39, 144, 145, 146, 151, 167, 172, 182, 183
Halifax County 18, 72, 146, 221, 268, 269
Halifax Street 147
Henri, Pierre 96
homes 4, 7, 16–18, 32, 38, 58, 64, 94, 101, 112, 116, 117, 127, 144–146, 159, 166, 190, 203, 205, 207, 212, 242
Huguenots 4, 11, 13–15, 17, 24, 25, 27–39, 44–46, 48–69, 80, 83–86, 89, 91, 111, 114, 116, 117–119, 123, 127, 131, 154, 176, 200, 203, 206, 209, 255, 272, 273

immigrants 11, 13, 15, 20, 26, 28, 38, 45, 48, 53, 55, 56, 70, 86, 92, 94, 122, 131, 156, 201, 206, 207, 217, 223, 255, 256
Iredell, James 132

La Grange (France) 111, 152
La Grange (North Carolina) 11, 102, 111, 152, 266, 269
Lafayette, Le Marquis de 11, 16, 17, 72, 111, 112, 114, 131, 133, 142–153, 162, 169, 176, 177, 182, 218, 221, 223, 227–229, 230, 231, 233, 255, 256, 268, 272, 273
Lake Waccamaw 17, 158
land deeds 2, 15, 28, 39, 40, 61, 63, 74, 75, 94, 108, 109, 117, 153, 155, 160, 161, 178, 179, 196
language 1, 14, 16, 36, 38, 55, 63, 64, 65, 70, 72, 80, 98, 106, 139, 142, 150, 154, 156, 161, 176, 177, 181, 202, 203, 205–209, 212, 227, 236, 238, 239, 240–242, 247, 250, 255, 256, 273
LaPierre, John 45, 65–68, 74, 75, 110, 113, 123, 154, 261, 274
Lawson, John 35, 37, 56, 57, 58, 70, 273
Lenoir County 17, 61, 102, 110, 111, 266, 269
Lenoir family 111
letters 3, 15, 16, 28, 54, 55, 74, 78, 88, 95, 120, 130, 132, 134, 150, 172, 179, 223, 225, 226, 227, 272
liberty 16, 29, 46, 125, 137, 144, 150, 152, 167, 172, 234, 256
Little Switzerland 196, 197, 202
London 37, 38, 40, 43, 55, 65, 67, 71, 74, 86, 119, 133, 259
Lords Proprietors 14, 28, 29, 31–33, 36, 37, 53–57
lost colony 15, 53, 59, 63, 68, 69
Louis XIV 14, 27, 44, 79, 80, 89, 201, 210, 214, 215
luxury goods 15, 87

Macon, Nathaniel 121, 142, 148, 218
Manakin Town 34, 36, 37, 43, 55–57, 61, 62, 65, 68, 71, 72, 74, 86, 87, 115, 116, 118, 261, 262, 271
maps 4, 12, 13, 15, 16, 22, 24–26, 33, 43, 52, 57, 58, 71, 73, 76, 78, 80, 127, 150, 227, 232, 240, 246, 257
Marseille 85, 127, 128, 163, 230, 249
Medoc Mountain 18, 172–174, 269
Merci Train 231, 232, 238, 271
Michaux, André 17, 163, 166–168, 194, 272
migration 3, 4, 12, 14, 18, 20, 22, 25, 27, 28, 30, 31, 42, 45, 53, 56, 61, 65, 68, 80, 83, 92, 110, 115, 123, 168, 261, 273
militia 15, 16, 54, 62, 72, 84, 87, 89, 120, 121, 125, 133, 136, 137, 139, 143, 148, 153, 166, 223, 246
Mountflorence, James Cole 16, 131, 139–142

Index

Napoleon Bonaparte 17, 152, 155, 168–171, 212, 215, 219, 230, 250
Napoleon Cannon 222, 223
Napoleon III 217
New Bern 2, 7, 8, 15, 16, 35, 44–46, 53, 55, 57, 61, 65, 66, 67, 70–75, 77, 79, 80, 82, 85, 92, 94, 116, 118, 121, 125, 127, 137, 139, 140–142, 163–165, 176, 186, 222, 263, 271, 272, 274
Ney, Peter 17, 163, 170–172
Normandy 31, 33, 36, 38, 42, 50, 81, 90, 92, 97, 102, 118, 119, 147, 154, 160, 229, 233, 243
North Africa 127, 218, 250, 255, 257

Old Burying Ground 92, 94, 96
Onslow County 4, 41, 82, 89, 108, 109, 110, 114–117, 119, 234, 261, 264, 269

Pacific Ocean 21, 24, 25
Pangaea 12, 36, 173, 246
Paquinet, Michel 86–88, 91, 99, 262
Paquinet family 16, 61, 86–88, 91, 94
Paris (France) 16, 39, 42, 80, 86, 88, 111, 125, 130, 131, 133, 139, 146, 152, 153, 168, 169, 178, 179, 181, 183, 189, 190, 192, 196, 212, 213, 215, 218, 220, 225, 229, 230, 231, 234, 235, 241–243, 251, 256, 257, 259, 273
Paris (North Carolina) 269
Paris Trail 16
Pelletier 17, 81, 102, 103, 106, 107, 269
Pelletier, Jerome 3, 102, 105, 269
Pelletier-Harmon, Lisa 3, 102, 105, 106, 107, 114, 273
Piedmont 11, 176, 184, 201
Pigott, Emeline 92–94, 222
Pigott family 92, 94, 228, 270
Piver family 16, 86, 88, 92, 94, 155, 222, 228, 270
Protestants 13, 15, 27, 28, 32, 42, 154, 201

Quakers 29, 30, 46
Québec (Canada) 11, 13, 25, 50, 84, 184, 195, 196, 222, 269
Quebec (North Carolina) 267

Ralegh, Sir Walter 14
Raleigh 3, 4, 14, 16, 19, 25, 99, 102, 144, 147–149, 172, 178–183, 186, 220–222, 224–233, 237, 238, 242, 243, 246, 248–252, 254–257, 271–274
religion 27, 32, 36, 50, 67, 80, 239
religious freedom 14, 27, 28, 34, 46, 201
religious persecution 13, 27, 28, 30, 40, 46, 54, 55, 71, 74, 88, 91, 92, 102, 111, 112, 118, 119, 136, 201
Ribault, Jean 13, 14
Riccoboni, Marie-Jeanne de 164, 165
Richebourg, Philippe de 14, 35, 44, 55, 56, 62, 65, 71, 261, 262, 274
rivers 4, 13–15, 17, 18, 29, 30, 32, 34, 35, 37, 39, 40, 43, 44, 47, 49, 53, 55–57, 59, 63–65, 67–69, 70, 73, 80, 83, 86, 89, 103–105, 107, 108, 110, 112, 116, 118, 120, 123, 127, 144, 146, 157–159, 189, 190, 194, 195, 215, 218, 226, 243, 245, 246, 257, 261, 268, 269, 272
rum 50, 51, 87, 98, 99, 100, 127

Sailly, Charles de 14, 55, 56, 62, 109
salt 64, 108, 127, 132, 233, 250
Sanford 184–186, 187, 189, 273
Sauthier, Claude 52, 76, 80, 127
Sevier, John 131, 136, 194–196, 227, 245, 246
shipping 37, 87, 88, 94, 99, 120, 125, 128, 130, 131, 133, 157, 163
slavery 25, 56, 148, 152, 221, 223, 255, 256
slaves 51, 74, 87, 96–100, 104, 120, 126, 153, 155, 156, 160, 161, 164, 177, 223, 228, 255, 256, 257
South Carolina 11, 13, 14, 29, 36, 44, 45, 52, 56, 65, 85, 117, 136, 137, 154, 156, 166, 169, 171, 173, 197, 199, 227, 262, 272, 274
Southport 17, 125, 130, 155, 156, 157
sugar 32, 50, 51, 87, 96, 99, 102, 127, 157, 162, 249
Swansboro 81, 103, 106–110, 116, 264, 272, 274
Switzerland 27, 58, 70, 79, 119, 197, 201, 202, 203

Tennessee 2, 11, 136, 193–195, 218
timber 15, 63, 86, 125, 218
tobacco 15, 30, 47, 50, 92, 121, 127, 129, 245
transatlantic 18, 24, 32, 79, 86, 131, 151, 153, 168, 169, 180, 228, 229, 233
Trent River 14, 15, 34, 35, 53, 55–57, 59, 63–65, 68–70, 80, 86, 110, 112, 116, 123, 261
Tron, Charles Albert 203, 205, 207
trumeau mirror 252, 253
Tryon, Margaret 7, 8, 66, 78
Tryon, William 7, 66, 76–78, 125
Tryon Palace 3, 7, 8, 15, 58, 77–80, 166, 274
turpentine 15, 39, 49, 50, 51, 87, 99, 104, 108, 125, 127
Tuscarora tribe 21, 49, 56, 59, 61
Tuscarora War 44, 59, 62, 70, 75

United States 11, 102, 140, 142, 143, 150, 155, 163, 165, 166, 167, 171, 173, 174, 177, 180, 181, 183, 184, 185, 190, 191, 194, 195, 197, 201, 202, 205, 209, 212, 213, 215, 217, 218, 222, 224, 227, 229, 230, 234–236, 239–241, 245, 247, 254, 257, 272, 273

Valdese 17, 200–211, 246, 257, 272–274
Vanderbilt, George 18, 212–215, 245, 271
Verrazzano, Giovanni da 13, 21–27, 172, 233, 252
Verrazzano, Girolamo da 22, 24–26
Versailles 18, 73, 79, 80, 166, 212–216, 239
Vietnam War 233, 234
Virginia 11, 14, 29, 30, 32, 34–7, 39, 43, 44, 47, 52, 53, 55, 62, 63, 89, 92, 111, 112, 119, 121,

127, 136, 166, 169, 180, 182, 187, 222, 223, 261, 262, 272, 273

Waccamaw River 157, 158, 159
Waldenses 200–211, 274
Washington, George 78, 132, 136, 143, 148, 150, 166
Weller, Sidney 18, 163, 172–175, 245
wills 15, 28, 38, 39, 43, 60, 111, 120, 272
Wilmington 15, 44–46, 56, 65, 66, 68, 99, 112, 119, 120, 121, 125, 130, 133, 155, 156, 157, 167, 174
Wilson, Mamré 3, 86, 101, 274
wine 12, 15, 18, 19, 35, 37, 50, 51, 56, 63, 64, 78, 127, 128, 146, 166, 171, 172–175, 177, 206, 225, 235, 245–247, 253, 272
wineries 18, 173, 245, 246
women 13, 64, 80, 91, 95, 98, 120, 126, 127, 132, 164, 165, 176, 180–182, 201, 203, 207, 222, 225, 226, 228, 229, 232, 234, 274
World War I 182, 187, 191, 224, 225, 227, 229, 230, 231, 274
World War II 19, 151, 157, 228, 229, 234–236, 240, 247

Xavier-Martin, François 57, 85, 121, 142, 163–166, 175, 271, 273, 274

www.ingramcontent.com/pod-product-compliance
Lightning Source LLC
Chambersburg PA
CBHW032033300426
44117CB00009B/1047